IS FOR HEALING

HL SCHAEFFER

H IS FOR HEALING

INSIDE THE LIFE OF A PSYCHIC HEALER AND 9/11 SURVIVOR

BY HL SCHAEFFER

iUniverse, Inc.
Bloomington

H is for Healing

Copyright © 2011 by HL Schaeffer

iUniverse books may be ordered through booksellers or by contacting:

iUniverse
1663 Liberty Drive
Bloomington, IN 47403
www.iuniverse.com
1-800-Authors (1-800-288-4677)

ISBN: 978-1-4620-5864-8 (sc)
ISBN: 978-1-4620-5866-2 (hc)
ISBN: 978-1-4620-5865-5 (e)

Library of Congress Control Number: 2011917964

Front and back cover, title page and bio photos by Dalila Kriheli

Photos on page 61: black checked top, and hat shot by MarkAlhonote; with glove, and sparkle shirt by Zianni

Printed in the United States of America

iUniverse rev. date: 11/21/2011

DEDICATIONS

For Grandma: You were my guardian angel in life and now you are one of my guardian angels in Spirit. Thank you so much for teaching me that is okay for me to just be me. You helped pull me back, when I needed to be pulled back. Words cannot express how blessed I am for you to have been my grandmother. I love and miss you my beautiful angel. I love you Grandma.

For Mom: I could not have asked for a better, blessed soul to be mother. You have always been and continue to be a beacon of pure love and unquestionable strength. You are the epitome of a class act. You have always loved me, even when I would try to push the world away. You truly are the absolute elegant model of what a beautiful, loving mother and soul should be. You are just phenomenal. Words cannot express how blessed I am to have you as my mother. I love you Mom.

For Dad: When looking up strength and integrity in the dictionary, your picture should be there. You have faced every challenge life has presented you head on. You have never backed away from anything. Always with that monumental inner and outer strength of yours out there for everybody to see. You are one of the most genuinely loving and giving souls this world has ever seen. Words cannot express how blessed I am to have you as my father. I love you Dad.

For Michael: I could write a thousand books on how your love has made my life feel complete. I have always believed in true love. But the whispers in the back of my psyche always put enormous doubts that it would ever happen. I never imagined how I could ever find a loving relationship where my gift would not be considered a curse. You have shown me how I am capable and worthy of giving and receiving love unconditional in all levels of my being and the core of my soul.

You are the most truthful, nurturing and extraordinary loving soulmate, I am so blessed to share my life with.

Many times I wonder what I did right, to have someone as incredible as you with me. Your down to earth grounding has helped rein me in, especially when I need to be. There is no way I would have ever finished this book if it was not for your persisting support.

I knew within two minutes of our meeting, I had found my soulmate husband. You are the most loving, supremely special soul I am blessed to spend my life path with. You are so passionate about everything life has to offer.

I know being married to an intuitive is definitely not a walk through the park. I know you have taken on a lot more than you bargained for. (Anybody who is in a relationship with someone of the intuitive medium neighborhood will agree. We can be extremely intense people and many times you will truly not be sure who or how many beings are here with, around, through and inside of us.) Yet you have never flinched for an instant. I cannot imagine my life without you by my side. Words cannot express how blessed I am to have you as my soulmate. I love you, my beautiful husband.

For Precious: My gorgeous, furry, little daughter. You have opened up a place in my heart that will always be yours. I have always known you are an enlightened soul who blessed our lives. So much love exudes from your small little stature. Every parent thinks their child is the most intelligent. I don't have to think. I know that to be true. One of the sweetest souls our lives have ever known. I love you my beautiful, furry baby.

THANK YOU

Marie Fountaine: You have been essential in bringing my book to reality. I brought you what were piles of an unorganized chaotic mess and you turned it into an edited cohesive masterpiece, without taking away my true voice. Your fantastic editing and constant pushing kicked my procrastination to the curb to allow "H IS FOR HEALING" to be a published book ready to assist the world. You are just one fierce dynamo and friend in my life, who is secretly from Wonder Woman's Paradise Island.

Ellen Swandiak: Your editorial and graphic design expertise for my book has been nothing short of masterful. From the moment we met, you have been one delicious diva, who has also been very instrumental in helping me be the person and healer who I am today. Your friendship helped me to cultivate my playful flair for the fabulous, but also helped me not to take the whole fabulousness too seriously.

Robert and Meryle: Thank you for always being my loving brother and sister.

My Timbers Family: I could not have asked for a better second family to be a part of.

Dalila Kriheli: My fantastic, personal photographer, whose pictures are works of art. See for yourself at rockstarpix.com.

Bliss Chadwick: What would I do without your astrological and planetary energetic advice. Your copy edit helped start me off on the right foot.

Max, Victoria, Gabby and Michelle: Thank you for your lifelong friendships and support throughout this whole thing.

Thank You iUniverse's Amy and Krista for all your assistance with the detailed publishing production aspects for this book.

Thank You to everyone who I have not mentioned due to space constraints.

TABLE OF CONTENTS

Prologue 11
Introduction 12

SECTION 1 – WHERE IT ALL BEGAN

Hello Early Childhood 16
Elementary to Junior Hell to High School 17
Grandma – My Hero 30
Angelic Visitations 38
9/11 And Caroline Myss 43

SECTION 2 – MY HEALING PATH: TRANSFORMATIONAL STEPS FROM SELF-HELL TO SELF-HEALING

Panic Attacks. 58
My Stammering Stutter and How I Overcame It. 62
Pain in the Neck 67
Dr. Quack. 70
Dr. Deva—at Last 73
Lille O'Brien: Awakening My Healer Roots. 76

SECTION 3 – SESSION SECRETS

Psychic 101 82
What Goes On in One of My Sessions 84
Lilith. 86
Alice: Through the Looking Glass 89
Janet: The Control Factor 95

SECTION 4 – THE CORPORATE INTUITIVE CONSULTANT

How I Got Started 102
The Model Agency 103
The Record Company. 106
Wall Street Fortune 500 Company 109
The Hip Hostess Nyc 111
The Nightclub Owner 114
The Book Tour 116
The Hill: The Investigation. 117

SECTION 5 – TRAVELING BACK TO THE PAST
Greece. 130
Egypt 135

SECTION 6 – FROM HEALER TO A HEALER'S HEALER
Agela and Sylvaine 146
Sylvaine: My Teacher, My Friend and Healing Teammate 149
The Three Monkeys: My Healing Trio and Our Post-9/11 Work 155

SECTION 7 – MORE SESSION SECRETS
Delta Dawn, What's That Flower You Have On 176
Mr. S and Bobo. 180
Ms. Mona and Mr.Bruno 183
9/11: Another View from Beyond 186

SECTION 8 – TIME TO THINK OUTSIDE THE BOX
Religious Nonsense. 194
Death 198
The Famous Who Have Inspired Me 200
Soulmates 208
Psychic Hotlines – UUUGGGHHH!. 216
Ouija Warnings. 217

SECTION 9 – MINDFUL MEDITATIONS
The New Seminary of New York Exorcism Ritual. 232
Stroll Through My Meditation Garden. 238

SECTION 10 – WRAPPING IT UP
Some Last Thoughts 258
Epilogue 261
Bio 263

PHOTO ALBUM
PART ONE: Through the Ages 50
PART TWO: The Healer's Realm 164
PART THREE: The Family 220

PROLOGUE

It was a Wednesday morning. I hadn't had much sleep the night before. I awoke to learn that I had a client waiting for me in the other room. I was a little startled because I hadn't been expecting anybody that day, needless to say, certainly not that early. I proceeded to make myself a cup of coffee and I greeted my client, whom we shall call Bill. Bill was very upset. He had experienced a horrific accident. Bill had been trapped in a burning building and had become traumatized and paralyzed by fear. He apparently had lost his way, both figuratively and literally.

Bill, like all my clients, would become familiar with my slightly unorthodox rules.

Please do not drop by when I am sleeping.
Please do not drop by when I have company.
In the mornings, please wait in an orderly fashion, until I am awake and have had my coffee.
When I politely ask you to leave, please do so promptly.

Strange rules, you may be thinking to yourself. Oh—wait a second—I forgot to mention something very important about Bill. You see Bill was on the 104th floor when the planes hit the Twin Towers. He also perished when the World Trade Center was assassinated.

INTRODUCTION

Let me introduce myself to those of you who are not familiar with me. My name is HL Schaeffer, but everyone affectionately calls me H or HL. There are many names and labels that have been placed upon me. I am known in some circles as a talented intuitive consultant, an ordained interfaith minister, and a hypnotherapist. To some, I am known as a gifted spiritual healer and a reikimaster. To others, I am an empathic medium, a psychic and an exorcist. And then there are those who just plain and simple call me a nut. I personally don't subscribe to the name/label game. I never have and never will. My attitude has always been the same. Call me what ever you'd like, as long as you get the letter right.

I consider myself to be a human telephone pole between our world and the Divine. I am able to communicate and assist in helping to heal the living and, at times, just as easily to heal the dead and communicate with the spirit world. I have been able to see and feel spirits for as long as I can remember being conscious.

I hope to serve as a motivator for you. Someone who has been able to reach the infinite levels of our spiritual world, but whom you can also find very approachable.

I would like to be open and upfront about myself and set some things straight. I am a regular person just like everybody else, except I just happen to also be psychic. In my personal life, I too, will drink, eat meat, be loud, sometimes show a Brooklyn potty mouth, am politically incorrect, and love to wear my furs. I don't put on airs. Plus, once I get going, I have a very infectious laugh. I am not perfect, I am just me. And like all of us, I am also a work in progress. I am very encouraged to see other colleagues in this field who also share my same down-to-earth attitude about things.

The purpose of writing this book is to shed light onto some of the mysteries of life. Throughout the book, you will see a combination of challenges I have personally gone through, along with how-to strategies developed from the lessons and knowledge gained along the way. Also, included are some extremely helpful meditations I have created to assist you in optimal healing.

I hope sharing my experiences will open a door to new infinite possibilities for you and Spirit to work together. I share with you my vulnerabilities and how I overcame many of them. Follow my lead and you, too, will be able to manage to overcome many of your own problems. That is, only if you will allow yourself to look outside of the proverbial box. Remember, fear is nothing but a big stop sign, which blocks you from truly living your life. We all have fears and phobias that hinder our ability to be all that we can be. In part, that is what we are here for. To learn how you can transform those dark spots to the higher lights. Allow yourself to move past your own limitations and challenges, to a life of bliss and abundance.

My life and my practice have completely changed since that fateful day

9/11/01, which I have annotated by the initials BC (before Christ) and AD (anno domini, in the year of the lord). For most Washington DC-ites, Virginians, Pennsylvanians and New Yorkers, myself included, time is now measured in terms of before and after 9/11. It was that biblically traumatic for anyone who lived through it. Let me open a window into the inner workings of my psyche and give you a glimpse of how I was impacted by that apocalyptic event.

I had just come out of the train station on Broadway and John Street, exactly one block from the World Trade Center. It was less than two minutes after the first plane had violently crashed into Tower Two. I looked up to see a gaping hole in one of my beautiful towers, gushing flames and thick, black smoke. Just like everyone else, I stood there stunned for a few minutes. Then I continued down the block thinking that some crazy stunt plane had messed up again. I heard a loud noise and looked up in time to see the second plane, like a soaring piranha in the sky, crash directly into the other tower. Both towers were now engulfed in flames and smoke. New York City was now obviously under terrorist attack. I ran into the Chase Bank, just in time to avoid an avalanche of glass windows shattering onto a defenseless passerby. Just inches away from me, I witnessed this poor woman's face get very badly sliced. Blood was gushing everywhere. In my darkest, grimmest nightmares, I never could have imagined such horror. Nor could I imagine that within two hours, I would never see my elegantly-towering twins ever again.

WHERE IT ALL BEGAN

HELLO EARLY CHILDHOOD

I am asked all the time, "When did you first realize that you had the gift?" I always explain—it's not about realizing that I could talk to spirits, see auras, and get intuitive messages. The news to me was that others didn't. Deep down, I believe we all have these abilities. It's part of our very make-up as energy beings. Think of it as a muscle. The more you work and exercise this muscle, the stronger it gets. There are some, like myself, whose muscle or antenna is stronger than others. That's all.

As with many psychics and sensitives, childhood was a baffling time and not always pleasant. I remember when I was a little child going to a funeral, not understanding why everyone was crying and upset.

I turned to my mom and asked her, "Why is everyone crying?"

Mom explained that this person had passed away, and had gone up to heaven to be with God.

I responded to her very matter-of-factly, "But Mommy, she's not dead. She's right here, sitting next to me."

Mom was suddenly very perplexed. She first looked towards the casket and then she looked back at me. She tried explaining to me that this was not possible.

"But Mom," I exclaimed, "she's talking to me right now!"

I proceeded to tell Mom extremely personal details about the woman's life. I barely even knew the woman. I think I had met her only once, so it was impossible for me to have known anything about her.

I don't know what was scarier for Mom. The fact that I told her I was talking to the dead or that what I had just told her was absolutely, one hundred percent on-the-money. A bewildered, perplexed look glazed over her face. It was a look with which I would become very familiar with throughout my life. As you might expect, Mom quickly whispered that I should just keep that kind of talk to myself or people were going to think that I was crazy as a loon.

Sorry, I love you Mom, but you know that I could never keep my mouth shut! Life would present me with countless experiences that many would call paranormal or psychic. I'm sure you have had your own experiences as well.

ELEMENTARY TO JUNIOR HELL TO HIGH SCHOOL

When I was a child, I was always the sensitive one who never really seemed to get the hang of being just a kid. I didn't relate to other children very well. My grades in school were never an issue. I was always in the top class. But my social skills were awkward at best. I could talk volumes with adults, especially the elderly. I could easily relate to the memories they shared with me about their younger years. I just felt that adults didn't judge me so much. They always told my mom that I was an old soul.

Almost nobody had any idea that I was a psychic with a very strong, sensitive connection to the spirit world. When I sometimes appeared to be staring into space, they could never have guessed that I was an empathetic sponge, intuitively communicating with the spirit world. I was very comfortable when I was engulfed in that world. In the spirit world, I had many encouraging Spirit guides and felt none of the pressures or anxieties associated with the conscious, physical world. I felt limitless and had no difficulty recognizing and accepting unconditional love in the highest form. Back in my body, in our physical world, I was often overwhelmed. I could hardly recognize unconditional love if it smacked me in the face.

My parents repeatedly tried to break through to me about love. Everyday my mother would affectionately ask me, "Who loves you?" My whole family tried their best, but it was Grandma who always had the ability to reach me. From the beginning, Grandma and I always had a super-strong, intuitive bond. This bond enabled her to connect with me even when nobody else could get anywhere near me. She could always read what my heart and soul were trying to say. With just one look and a warm embrace, she was able to energetically convey to me what words never could. My parents gave their absolute best to reach out to me. I always knew they loved me, but sometimes love was hard for me to understand. Especially since I didn't always love myself back then.

The childhood and grade school years can be a very difficult period for so many of us growing up. There are so many added pressures in the developmental school years, where children are faced with the obstacles of learning social, cognitive, psychological, emotional, educational, and motor skills. We all have had some issues with some of these skill sets. For an overly sensitive, intuitive psychic child, the obstacles are magnified.

In elementary school, I was awkwardly shy and timid. At times, I had major difficulty functioning socially. My intuitive abilities put an invisible barrier around me that made it difficult for many people to get close to me. Yes, there were times when the gift would get the best of me. I would sometimes walk into a room and almost be knocked down by the thoughts and vibration of the other children. My knee-jerk reaction was to retreat into my private world and nobody was the wiser. I was usually labeled as strange or weird. When the occasional bully would tease me, I was defenseless. I wore my vulnerabilities on my sleeve, which made me an easy target. When confronted by bullies, my anxieties would escalate and send me into a panic attack.

I am sure that anybody who knew me while I was growing up would be a bit shocked by how challenging my childhood was. At a very early age, I had learned to conceal my pain from others. Even when I was feeling absolutely miserable inside, I tried not to show it outwardly. As the years passed, I learned how to mask my torment and bury it deeper inside. Even when taunted, I managed with all my might to conceal the hurt. Most of the time, I just stood there and took it. The occasional taunters may have thought it was nothing but harmless fun. They had no clue how their comments wounded me internally.

Children can be absolutely darling. But innocently, they can also verbally repeat the most vicious of things they have heard spoken by others, since they haven't developed a verbal edit switch yet. Not surprisingly, some quite nasty comments can come out of the mouths of babes. Since I never felt comfortable with myself, I naturally became one of the quintessential favorites for the bullies to pick on. They would approach me like a pack of wolves, detecting my painfully obvious vulnerability. They tormented me like there was no tomorrow. As if I wasn't enough of an oddball already, I was also walking around with the birth name HARVEY LEWIS SCHAEFFER. This old fashioned name fueled the fire and put the proverbial icing on the cake.

I dreaded mornings when the teacher called attendance. That was the absolute worst. The teacher had an accent and every morning would pronounce my name in a tone of voice that caused everyone to laugh. During this time, episodes of the classic TV show The Honeymooners were constantly rerun on all the local TV stations. In one of the all-time classic episodes, Ralph Kramden, and his pal Ed Norton go to the local pool hall to shoot a couple of games. When they get there, no tables are empty except for one, which is occupied by this puny, nerdy, weakling. Ralph pushes him aside and begins his game. The nerd says in this pipsqueak, high-pitched twang that Ralph had better leave the table before his friend Harvey comes. Ralph, the typical loudmouth, for the rest of the show makes humiliating fun out of the name Harrrrr-vey. To this day, when someone hears my birth name, I still get joked about it. Thanks to the ever-popular Honeymooners re-runs which never seem to go off the air ... oh yeah!

I tell parents all the time, be very careful when naming your baby. Remember, you may love the name Angus, but you are not the one who has to walk around with it. Often I came home from school in tears after being relentlessly teased because of my name. I absolutely hated that name HARVEY. I would argue with my parents all the time.

"How could you hate me so much, to give me such a horrible name?" My folks just never understood and I can't blame them. They were never raised like that and couldn't understand others being so cruel just because of an uncommon name. We had the same argument all the time. They questioned me, "You mean to tell me that the children in school pick on you, just because of your name? I find that hard to believe."

Trust me on this one. Someone might use any excuse to make someone else's life miserable, just so they will fit in. Nobody wants to be the person picked on. With the peer pressure scenario, if they teased you, then others wouldn't tease them. I totally understand it now. Boy, do I wish I knew then what I know now. But, I do understand that I had to go through these torments in order to learn how to be the compassionate person I am today. It, in turn, has allowed me to be even more open and sensitive to my clients and to the struggles many people endure in this lifetime.

All of my teachers noticed my painfully obvious social awkwardness. Neither my brother nor my sister ever had this issue. They were both popular and were able to make friends easily. I was as different from them as possible. Though I would sometimes see spirits or things around people, I never said a word. I couldn't even entertain the idea of talking to others in school about what I psychically was seeing and empathically feeling. Even if I had wanted to talk about it, I honestly just didn't know how.

Luckily for me, my sister and brother became my saviors. They were older, braver, stronger, more confident, and popular. I love, love my sister and brother. They both used to take me places with their friends, long after the time it was obligatory for them. My brother was graduating when I was entering school, but my sister was only three years ahead of me. Thankfully, I had her to defend me during my first few years. She was not afraid of anybody and was my fiercest protector against anyone who bothered her baby brother. It was a sad day when she graduated from my elementary school. To this day, my brother and sister will still defend my honor, anytime and anywhere. Like all siblings, we may not always see eye to eye on some things, but we love each other like crazy. And though I have come a long way since those painful days, I will always be their baby brother.

Once my sister graduated, it forced me to develop friendships with my classmates. My love of TV quickly taught me to put other people, as well as myself at ease by showing my humorous side. By being funny, I was able to talk to my schoolmates and not be as self-conscious or feel like an outcast. Little did they know I was hiding behind my sense of humor. Nobody had even the slightest clue that I was psychic and regularly saw the spirits of the deceased following them around. My intuitive abilities were active, but they weren't completely overpowering, as they would become for me later.

As time went on, I was able to lower my guard enough to become friends with several of my classmates. By the time I was ready to graduate from elementary school, I had made several friends and I was actually beginning to feel good about myself. After graduation, however, that all drastically changed.

THE SUMMER MOVE: THE BEGINNINGS OF JR. HELL

The summer after my graduation from elementary school, my family moved away from my childhood home and into a new neighborhood. I was completely unprepared for this. We left the only home I had ever known. The safety of my childhood home had helped to shelter me from the effects of my psychic, mediumistic abilities. It had taken me awhile, but I had actually cultivated real, true friendships in the latter part of elementary school. The familiarity of going to school with the same kids all the way from kindergarten through sixth grade had eventually given me a sense of belonging. I always knew what to expect and from whom. When I graduated, everything changed.

When we moved, everything drastically changed. Everything and everyone that was familiar to me was completely gone. I had gotten used to the energy of my home and my neighborhood. It was my cocoon. My new neighborhood, though beautiful, felt like it had an extremely different and dark vibe. I was aware that, before homes had been built there, the area had been used as a dumping ground for human carcasses. My psychic senses shifted into overdrive. My intuition intensified. It was almost as if Spirit had turned up the knob to maximum on my psychic levels. In my new neighborhood absolutely nothing was familiar and nothing felt safe.

I was not prepared for the astronomical increase in my intuition. It completely threw me off balance in ways I never could have expected. Now I was seeing and hearing spirits all time. It was so constant that it started to become difficult for me to separate the spirits of the dead from those of the living.

My emotional anxieties skyrocketed. I started experiencing panic attacks constantly. It felt like I had left my safe home and gone out into a heavy thunderstorm with no coat or umbrella. My shyness, in addition to the heightened levels of the gift, made it a bit of a challenge to open myself up and create new friendships.

Being in a new neighborhood home and new home, as well as the anticipation of going to a new school, all became overwhelmingly unbearable. I just couldn't handle all these drastic changes at once and found myself starting to fragment. I literally felt like a part of my own spirit had splintered from me. Whatever confidence, self-love, and social skills I had cultivated in elementary school had just disintegrated. Whatever protection I felt I had in the physical world absolutely disappeared. I now regularly got intuitive messages. I could hear and feel what people were thinking and see the spirits of the deceased. I was having serious difficulty separating my feelings from other people's feelings because the gift was now so strong.

I was born on the astrological cusp of Gemini and Cancer. This also had something to add to the mix. For Cancers, the home is a sanctuary. (Not to mention, Cancers generally don't take all that well to change in general.) Leaving the home where I was born was just devastating for an extra-sensitive Cancer child like myself. Add in my newly emerging adolescence to all the other factors and you will understand that life was not exactly a bowl of cherries for me at the time. On top of everything, now I had to start a new school without knowing a single soul.

The little self-confidence I had developed in elementary school was decimated. Not only did I feel alienated in my new school, but I also I felt alienated from society and the world in general. I wanted to escape to the spirit world where I felt safe and protected.

JUNIOR HIGH SCHOOL

I can say without a shadow of a doubt, junior high school was the most challenging part of my childhood. The majority of the time I spent there was exhausting. Back then making friends was a hard enough task to begin with. To start over was horrifying. Yes, junior high school was indisputably the most difficult period of my childhood.

My new school went from sixth through eighth grade. I entered in the beginning of the seventh grade. Many of my new classmates had known each other since elementary school. Many others had started in sixth grade. So I was the strange new kid in the seventh grade. Just great. Not only was my home life completely different, so was my school. Like I really needed another drastic change in my life.

When I started my new junior high school, the protective layer I normally had around myself was virtually non-existent. So from my very first steps into the school, the experiences that I felt intuitively were almost indescribable. I empathetically sensed the thoughts and emotions from what felt like hundred of adults and students coming at me all at once.

I was not prepared for the sudden intensification of my psychic sensibilities. As I walked down the school's hallways, I increasingly heard the thoughts of many people entering my head. The strong energy patterns that I sensed were throwing me off balance and making me nauseous. I could perceive many of the darker energies such as depression, pain and suicidal thoughts brewing in the air. Right before I would enter a classroom, I would experience what felt like somebody punching me extremely hard in my stomach. I had no clue what was happening. I had never experienced anything like this ever before.

Many times as I walked down the hallways of school, I would see the spirits of deceased students and teachers who had attended the school years earlier. My body would intuitively take on whatever illnesses that were associated with their spirits. I could feel the deep waves of suicidal depression some of their souls were still attached to. Some would poke me. Some touched me and would do whatever they could to get my attention. I tried blocking out these visions the best I could. But there were some spirits who were very persistent in making their presence known to me in a variety of intensive ways. I could feel the drowning feeling of suffering from pneumonia. I could feel painful effects how cancer had ravished a body. I could feel anxiety fueled self-mutilation and cutting throughout my arms, legs and stomach. Imagine standing at the beach in the center of a tidal wave. That would accurately describe the magnitude of what I was experiencing.

I remember from the very first moment I was introduced to the class, Harvey was ostracized. Right off the bat, the teacher pronounced my birth name with enough of an inflection that the whole class laughed immediately. Just great! Your first day in a new school is never easy to begin with. But to be the butt of a never-ending array of jokes from day one was not an easy pill to swallow. Kids at that age are all trying to fit in and to be cool. I was extremely vulnerable. There were some obnoxious brats who sensed a target and quickly zeroed in on me. It was as if I had a bull's-eye on my body from the minute I entered the classroom.

It was horrible. I was able to intuitively feel many of their cruel thoughts about the "strange new kid." It felt like a chorus of mean-spirited laughing waves pointed directly at me. My mind, body and psyche were totally overwhelmed in every which way. I didn't have the thick skin that I have today. Many times, I still send Harvey the love to endure.

Several of my attempts to make friends were quickly scoffed at by many of the popular classmates. It's not like I was treated like a total leper, where nobody ever said a single word to me. There were some very nice classmates who actually did talk with me. But there were the unspoken words amongst some of those in the popular cliques. It was understood that I was absolutely not one of the cool kids. Well far from it. I was some kind of defenseless weirdo quite different from the norm. They just really never understood me and certainly weren't going out of their way to try to. I look back now and can understand the xenophobia that comes along with someone like myself with the gift. Fortunately for my very sanity, I did make some acquaintances with some of my classmates, which eventually did develop into very nice friendships. Still, I was afraid to open up to them completely because of all that was happening internally, as a result of the psychic overload I was experiencing. If I didn't understand what was going on with myself, how could I possibly expect anybody else to understand me?

Eventually some of the kids in the popular cliques made occasional attempts to be friendly. I could hear what was going on inside their minds. What they were really thinking about me. I knew they were really trying to make me look like a complete fool. These occasional condescending attempts would feel like daggers aimed straight at my core. I didn't have my sister to fight my battles for me anymore. I was defenseless. I didn't know the first thing about how to control the gift. During this period of time, it felt more like a curse than a gift.

Just imagine that somebody is talking to you. They are being all nice and friendly. But at the same time, you can actually hear their real thoughts. Not only those nice things they are saying. You can hear their cruel comments about you. I was insecure to begin with. The last thing I needed to hear was how strange some of these kids thought I really was. I knew they thought I was weird, strange, brain damaged and just about every other nasty thing you could think of.

Lunchtime in the cafeteria was something was like something straight out of a movie. I usually tried to keep to myself. When someone would come talk to me, the odds were 50/50. Some genuinely wanted to talk with me. Then there were those brats, who just wanted to make fun of me. The whole thing just made me feel even more insecure and confused than I already was.

Those same brats also made gym class a nightmare for me. I remember at the beginning of the year, when we were all given combination locks for the gym lockers. I had never used one before and didn't know how to operate it. I nervously asked one of the gym teachers to help me. He looked at me with pathetic disgust. His eyes went right through me. I was not the most coordinated of kids. He wanted as little to do with me as possible. He purposely called over one of the pranksters of the class for his own amusement. I could intuitively hear him laughing to himself. He knew this kid was going to mess with me. This joker showed me how to open the combination lock and then broadcast the combination out loud to the entire boys locker room. A few days later, my gym locker was opened and vandalized. The contents were ruined.

I had a James Bond book I was reading at the time. Over the course of the next several months, I would find torn pages of my stolen book scattered all over the school. Each time I would find a page, it would instantly and energetically bring me back to that humiliating experience. Each time I brought the incident to the gym teacher's attention. He could not have cared less. Once he even told me, "If you would just act normal like everybody else, then you would not be having these problems."

My family encouraged me to talk to the staff about the bullying. My complaints to the teachers fell completely on deaf ears. They did absolutely nothing. I heard their thoughts too and some of them were even more negative than the class bullies. I could hear them say to themselves in their heads that there was something about me that scared them. They couldn't figure me out and it just made many of them very uncomfortable. I actually heard one teacher think to herself, "I wish he wasn't in my class, but his grades are too good. So they won't transfer him out."

I can very clearly remember the most excruciating moment from junior high and my adolescence. The highlight (or I should say abyss) of junior high school occurred in my seventh grade English class. I was able to sense my English teacher was uncomfortable with me. I knew that when she was a child, she had been one of those snotty, vicious girls. She decided that the lesson of the day would be: Why do people pick on Harvey?

I thought I was just hearing things. But when she viciously repeated herself, I was immediately overcome by terror and panic. How could this really be happening to me? It should have been a Twilight Zone or Alfred Hitchcock Presents episode, not my seventh grade English class.

During the class, she had everybody write an essay directed toward me. Afterward, my teacher went around the room having everybody read their essays out loud, as I sat there painfully cowering in my seat. I just wanted to crawl into a corner and die right then and there.

This was first time I had any suicidal thoughts. I cried all the way home. I tried to tell my parents what had happened. But like most reasonable people, of course they found it was hard to believe. There was no way they could have imagined that something like this could happen in one of the top junior high schools around. As I look back now, I don't blame my parents whatsoever for not believing me. They had always been told that I had a very vivid imagination. This was years before they understood me and whole-heartedly accepted my psychic gift.

My mother couldn't understand any reason why anyone would pick on me like that. How could or would any teacher ever be allowed to do something like that? Nonetheless, my wonderfully loving Mom came up to school to complain of this horrendous, bullying treatment. All the administration told her was I needed to man up.

Well, unfortunately it all was true. By the next day, the whole school knew about what had happened in English class. Thankfully, one of my other caring teachers felt I was despondent and I was sent to the guidance counselor.

The guidance counselor Mrs. W was truly my savior. She could sense that I was fragile and fractured. Most important of all, she was able to recognize that I was a gifted psychic/clairvoyant. She was vaguely familiar with the field and didn't think I was some space alien. At last! Finally, someone in this school actually believed me and didn't want to send me to a padded cell. I felt very safe in Mrs. W's office. I frequently spent many lunch hours of the school year having lunch in her office.

She realized I was not comfortable living in my body. I was much happier and freer when I communicated with the spirit world. I spent as much time out of my body, as I did in it. Mrs. W recognized this. She saw the suicidal tendencies in me and she actively helped me to begin the difficult process of integrating my human and spiritual self.

She spoke to the teachers in my defense. I can tell you this, that English teacher never taught that kind of lesson at my expense ever again. However, this didn't stop her from taking the opportunity to embarrass me in class as often as possible. Mrs. W helped me to block out some of the constant laughter and taunting that I received. It was my first step in learning to control the gift by means of an inner dimming switch.

Thanks to Mrs. W, I was then able to start slowly adjusting. I still loathed every second I spent in this school. I was being teased, but at least now I had a refuge when I needed it. Thank You Mrs. W for making a safe space for me, in the middle of that nightmare. She truly helped me more than I can express in words.

When eighth grade came, I was no longer the new kid in class. I was able to make friends with some of my classmates, as well as some of the new kids who had transferred into the school that year. Fortunately, I now had some friends who I could hang out with outside of school. But as the gift intensified, it created more problems for me. I started having difficulty connecting my thoughts and my speech together as one. Unconsciously, my past life energies were starting to come back to me. I remember one day I was sitting in my eighth grade history class. History naturally was my favorite subject. I was trying to answer a question when all of a sudden I couldn't get the words out of my mouth. I felt like there was a vice grip around my throat. It was at that moment that my stutter first reared its ugly head.

As the difficulty in expressing my thoughts increased, my nerves kicked in and my stutter quickly worsened. As if I didn't already have it hard enough, now my stutter gave the world even more ammunition with which to intimidate me. My self-esteem was at an all time low. The stuttering devastated me, distancing me further from the physical world. Increasingly, I was afraid to participate in class, which further cemented my place on the list of targets to be ridiculed. If the world had ended then, I couldn't have been happier.

There were a number of children like myself, who couldn't be put into a nice, neat, little box. Except for those like Mrs. W, the school administration didn't make much of an attempt to understand what was wrong. To be honest, no one seemed to care much or to even notice my quick descent into depression. Their unfortunate solution was simply to ignore the mean spirited treatment that I received from some of the bullies and even from some of the staff. Like most students who are different, I was ignored and allowed to fall through the cracks. My class participation diminished drastically. I became petrified to be called upon and my nervous anticipation only made my stuttering more pronounced.

My pronounced stutter was a crushing blow to my already fragile ego. One of my life's paths is to be heard. Just imagine trying to express your thoughts with a vice grip clamping down upon your throat. The more I tried to speak, the tighter the noose became around my neck. The harder it was to communicate, the more terrified I became that I wouldn't be able to spit the words out of my mouth. My growing fear about expressing myself energetically started to develop into a full-blown, paranoid phobia of speaking in public. I had an even bigger fear that I might blurt my thoughts out loud involuntarily.

My stutter would stay with me until almost sixteen years later. (I explain my the origins of my stutter and how I finally overcame it in detail in a separate chapter of this book.)

END OF JRHS

During the course of junior high school, my Spirit guides could see that the overwhelming intensity of my intuitive levels was literally driving me to a suicidal position. I begged for it all to stop. I was tired of feeling overburdened by the constant stream of unbridled intuitive messages. I didn't want to hear other people's thoughts anymore. I didn't want to constantly see and talk to dead people anymore. I just wanted to be a normal kid, so people would find it easy to become friends with me. I had had enough time alone, and as a target for humiliation. I just wanted all the psychic stuff to be gone. And if that meant dying ... so be it ...

My Spirit guides came to me. I begged them to please help me to transform myself into the person I wanted to be. I asked them to help me with the gift. They put a protective shield around me, which would help block out other people's emotions and thoughts. By the time I graduated from junior high school, they had begun to help me integrate and to start getting a handle on my abilities.

That summer was very transformational for me. I had finally been paroled from the emotional prison that I had created for myself in junior high school. I was going to start high school in the fall. My mom, dad and grandma all sat down with me for a long inspirational talk. Each of them separately explained that I was going to be starting a whole new school. This was the perfect opportunity for a new beginning. This was my chance to change everything that I had hated about junior high school. I had to pull myself together and prepare for my new adventure in high school.

Anything that had happened to me in junior high that I didn't like would not have to continue in my next school. Everybody would be entering the school at the 9th grade level together. It would be a new school for everyone and they would all be just as nervous as I would be. This was the pivotal time to reinvent myself. If I presented myself in a way that expressed how I wanted and expected to be treated, then I would no longer be tormented or teased.

My Dad told me to go after the biggest kid I could find, or somebody who had tormented me in my other school. From day one, I should stand up for myself and not take anybody's bullshit any more. He taught me how to throw a punch and how to defend myself. When somebody tried to intimidate me, I would now know how to defend myself. He told me to walk with my head held high in a commanding way.

Watching one of my favorite icons, Bea Arthur, I learned that I could fit in better if I showed people that I actually had a keen sense of humor. I remember one time watching a rerun of Maude when, right then and there, something just shifted and things started to click. Maude never took crap from anybody! I wanted to have the balls that she had.

By the end of the summer, the severity of my sense of devastation had lessened considerably. With the help of my family and Spirit Guides, I actually started to like being an intuitive psychic medium.

That summer the messages my Spirit guides relayed to me were very clear:

They told me that I had a special intensified gift. They told me everything was going to make sense soon enough. They made it clear that my intuitive abilities were indeed something to embrace. They were going to help me get a better understanding of my abilities.

They were going to reveal the reasons why I was able to communicate with souls living and deceased.

They were going to diminish my abilities a bit for the time being, but would gradually increase it when they felt I was better prepared.

My gifts were special and needed to be nurtured, not despised. They were going to help improve my self-confidence.

I would always have access to my guides anytime I needed them.

It was time to let go of the tears and pain that I had been carrying all this time. Not all of the pain was mine and I needed to let my Spirit guides assist in lifting it from me.

They would show me how to separate myself from the different energies that I would encounter.

The whole summer my Spirit guides worked with me. I started feeling so much better.

Thank You Spirit!

HIGH SCHOOL

In high school, I got a fresh start. Since I hated my birth name, Harvey, in junior high I had already begun to call myself H. As is customary in the Jewish faith, a baby is named after someone who has passed. Babies are usually given the exact same name, or they are given a name with the same initial. I was named for my Grandfather's brother Harris, who had passed away well before I was born. I didn't want to disrespect him, so I started calling myself H. I figured I would eventually find a name I wanted to be called later and somehow incorporate the H into it. That is exactly what I did!! Harvey graduated high school as H.

Right before school started, I went out and bought a rubber stamp with my new identity "H." Schaeffer. I began stamping my name on everything. This was my way of stomping out HARVEY and declaring myself as H to the whole world. If someone asked me my name, I would proudly say H and stamp something. This was an about face from junior high school, where I used to write my name in the smallest possible way whenever we marked each other's papers in class, just wishing I could disappear.

I knew from the first step into high school, that it was going to be so much different. In the past, just the idea of walking up to somebody and striking up a conversation was enough to send me into a panic. I had always tried to bury those fears internally. Well, at least I thought I was hiding them. I never realized how transparent my frenetic panic always was.

Now it was a whole different world. I was no longer the strange new kid to those classmates from junior high. Instead, I was someone that they recognized—a familiar face in a whole new environment full of strangers. It felt wonderful. My Spirit guides supported me energetically. I was able to project confidence and approachability. I now had much better control of my psychic senses. I was still getting impressions, but thankfully, I was no longer overwhelmed by them. This helped out enormously.

In elementary school and junior high, fitting in was the most important thing. But high school was all about the exploration of individuality. Standing out in a crowd was no longer cause for crucifixion. Weird was now cool! I was transformed from being the strange outcast to being one of the eccentric cool kids that people wanted to know.

On one of my first days in high school, I encountered a couple of my old classmates who had tormented me. I remembered what I had learned during the transformational summer. I could hear my father's voice telling me, "Just walk right up to them." It didn't matter if I was afraid. I needed to do this in order to truly start high school with a clean slate. I could not allow myself to cower away and act defenseless, as my knee jerk reaction would have prescribed in the past. Energetically, I needed to set a precedent of how I would allow myself to be treated from now on.

I confidently walked right up to them and laid down my new rules. This was a new school and I was not going to take their teasing again.

I firmly demanded, "Cut the crap and treat me with respect. I have had enough of it."

They laughed and said, okay okay. In junior high, we were only joking around. You made yourself an easy target and you never fought back. If only you would have stood up for yourself then, you would not have been picked on so much. We all agreed it was a new school and it was time to start fresh. They introduced themselves to me and I introduced myself to them officially as H. From that moment on, I have never let anyone pick on me again.

Through my transformational process from an insecure child to a self-confident adult, I have been able to move past these painful experiences. In high school, I was able to truly open up and enjoy a very popular life. I actually became friends with many from the past. My college years allowed me to openly self-explore the many different aspects of who I am. I now totally understand why everything was supposed to happen as it did. Those challenges forced me to finally deal with countless issues I have carried around for many lifetimes. I never fully understood these lessons in prior lifetimes. This was the lifetime I would have the opportunity to finally confront these challenges and transform them to the light.

I hold absolutely no malice towards anybody from those days. Why should I? In fact, I am very grateful. They helped me become the H, who I am today. Who hasn't had a lot of crap they had to deal with growing up? As an adult, I can now look back and see I really had many more friends then I thought I did. Blindly I was too overwhelmed with my own inner turmoil, which totally blocked me from having the ability to see this then. Thanks to Facebook, I am now friendly with so many of these special people who I grew up with. H is for what? H is for Healing!

GRANDMA—MY HERO

Grandma, my Mother and my father were an integral part of helping me to see my inner shine, even when I could not see anything but a dark void. I love my parents who are absolutely wonderful people and beautiful souls. When I was growing up, they had a rough time trying to understand me. Raising any child can be a difficult task in itself. But when that child, like myself, just happens to be extremely intuitive and empathic, it can make the challenge ever more complicated. Like all parents, they had ideals, which they wanted for all their children. My parents were very supportive and gave me their all, but, I might as well have been speaking Aramaic-Klingon. I was as foreign as I could possibly be.

It is easier for a grandparent, since they have already raised their own children. My Grandma was on a totally different level. She didn't have to mold me into anything. She just helped me to be the best at who I was.

When I was young, there was no one in my life that understood my gift more than my Grandma. We always shared an intense understanding. Instinctively I knew that I could learn from her incredible, self-taught nursing abilities, her abilities as a natural healer. She never spoke metaphysically, nor did she ever consider herself to be an intuitive or a healer. As she explained it to me, she did just what came naturally to her. Her hands were always hot to the touch, a sure sign of a healer. The more intense the heat became, the more powerful it was. At times, Grandma's hands were practically on fire. When somebody was ill, she would instinctively place her hands upon them and send them love.

My Grandma's parents had emigrated from Poland with their oldest daughter in the early part of the 1900s. They settled into a small farm on the lower east side of Manhattan, and started their own coal business. That is where my Grandma was born. My great aunts and uncles would have been the first to agree that my grandmother was the co-matriarch in their family, alongside their own mother. My great grandmother, who later in life would develop diabetes and endure amputations, had never been a well woman.

So from the time my Grandma was a just a few years old, she was already helping her mother take care of their household. She helped with the cooking and cleaning, as well as taking care of her brothers and sisters. She even helped my great grandmother during her spells of illness. Grandma would crawl into bed with her mother and lay her hands on her, generating intense body heat, easing her sickness and pain. There really was nothing she wasn't capable of doing, learning or trying. She even assisted her father with the farm animals and helped to run their coal business.

Straight out of high school, Grandma began working for *Consumer Reports* magazine. She started in the mailroom and quickly worked her way up to managing supervisor. The company had originally been located in Manhattan, but like many businesses, they moved out of the city to a more economical location in Orangeburg, NY. Her commute went from being forty-five minutes to almost two and a half hours each way. She schlepped all the way from Brooklyn to Orangeburg everyday for over thirty years. Her work ethic was impeccable. In all the years of that exhausting commute, you never once heard a single complaint out of her. She was extremely maternal with her co-workers who affectionately referred to her as Mom. When one of the employees had a headache, she was known to place her golden hands upon him or her and send love and light. Before they knew it, the headache would be gone. Any time someone had a stomachache or wasn't feeling well, Grandma had one of her remedies. Believe me, her old school remedies usually did the trick! After she retired from *Consumer Reports*, her co-workers still kept in regular contact with their second mother. Many expressed to me how she had been there for them, when their own families had not.

In many senses, Grandma was like the Mother Teresa of Brooklyn. When family members, friends and neighbors got sick, she was there at their bedside. She even took many of them into her own home, and nursed them back to health or eased their passage to the other side.

Grandma had a keen ability to accurately judge someone's character by a mere glance. She always called it her common sense. My father calls it his gut instinct. But it really was her dynamic gift of being able to see inside somebody, to the core of his or her soul. Whenever she saw a golden beacon of light in someone's soul, no matter how buried, she was always able to help bring it up to the surface.

I couldn't have picked a better soul to be my grandmother. She unconditionally believed in me, even when I didn't believe in myself. She went out of her way to be the sun, moon, stars, and universe for me. She carefully geared me towards self-love as she helped me to understand myself. Whenever I felt like the world was caving in around me, she always was able to help me to see beyond that. She taught me how to quiet the nonsensical chatter in my head, the kind that tries to undermine everything in life.

When I wanted to check out, she would always pull me back and assist in my fortitude to go on. She always had been and always will be my guardian angel. She brought me back from the edge of suicide more times than she knew of. When the harshness of the adolescence and teen years beat me down, Grandma was always there to pick me up and wipe away the tears. When people would ridicule me, she would help them to see through my webs of insecurities and confusion. This would help them to see my inner bright light and understand how I ticked inside. Nothing will stand in her way of always being an amazingly loving and powerful force in my life.

My Grandma was an absolute angel. She would allow me to take ten minutes if need be, to speak one sentence without even an ounce of impatience or agitation. She allowed me to just be me. And if I stuttered or stammered in between words, she never gave me anything but her 100% attention. Importantly, she never told me to talk slowly nor did she try to correct me. She just let me express myself, which gave me a level of confidence I surely was lacking. Her beautiful warming love was a huge security blanket for me. Her love surrounded me with a wall of encouragement. She helped give me the courage to not give up on this world, or myself.

As I write this, Grandma comes to me. She says she never did anything extraordinary that somebody else in that position wouldn't do.

Even in spirit, she is as modest as ever. What an inspiration! She was incredibly self-sacrificing and hardly ever took credit for her many deeds. She never asked or ever expected anything in return. She felt she was just doing God's will.

I grew up in the 80's. It was a time when hair was wild, crazy, punk and gothic clothing was in style. The androgynous look was all the rage. During this time I actively explored many sides of myself, and was very self-expressive. As outlandish as most of my outfits were back then, my grandma was never embarrassed to be seen with me, not even once. And believe me, my wardrobe was way, way out there. I once showed up for a family function in one of my outrageous getups. My grandmother thought nothing of it. She walked me over to all the other tables and proudly introduced me as her grandson to relatives I hadn't seen since I was a young child. She was always very proud of me. She would say to the critics, "Mr. H is young. Just allow him to be." No ifs, ands, or buts, my grandmother single-handedly made sure I was unconditionally accepted in our extended family. From early on, my whole family recognized that I was different from most others and came to accept who I was and what I was all about. To be honest, just about everybody knew I was gay many years before I knew it myself. One of my Aunts told me recently, "I knew you were gay since you were a little boy. We all knew it was just a matter of time before you knew it."

The first time Grandma saw me wearing black eyeliner, she called me over to the sink. She washed it off and then showed me how to apply it correctly. Even though it might not have been her taste, she certainly wasn't going to deny my right to wear it. I went through a period when I wore a lot of vintage tuxedos and formalwear with my wild wardrobe. Many times, I would go to Grandma's house and she would have a vintage jacket waiting on her bed for me. She most definitely had her own flair for fashion. She showed me pictures of clothing styles from different eras. Most importantly, she taught me how to find a good deal. She had incredible bargaining skills. By the time she had finished grooming me, I was a world-class haggler. She helped me to understand the value of a dollar and a hard day's work. Whenever my ego would begin to get a little out of hand, she would gently help me tone it down a few notches.

When I was eighteen years old, I legally and officially changed my name to

H. Most of the family was a bit confused at first.

What?? … You changed your name to a letter? What kind of nonsense is that?" This was a familiar chorus at family gatherings. I can't blame them. Most people found it a little strange that I had changed my first name to a letter. But not Grandma. Never Grandma. She was the first person to acknowledge my new name. She showed me the world of respect. From that point on, she referred to me as Mr. H. It was that type of respect with which she treated people. She was millenniums ahead of her time.

Grandma never had a problem relating to me. She always was able to get through to me, when I felt that nobody else could understand. She never made assumptions about my lifestyle. She felt that would be too judgmental. Instead, she accepted me as I was. She respected and supported all of me. If something didn't sit well with her, she would gently help me to see things from another viewpoint. She encouraged me to channel my anger into creativity.

The motto by which she lived her life was LOVE! DON'T JUDGE! "You give with warm hands," was a favorite expression of hers. She taught us that you didn't need to wait until you had passed, to share what you have with your loved ones. By giving while you are alive, you are able to share with your loved ones, and see them enjoying it.

Grandma truly was one of my best friends. She was and still is my life's biggest inspiration. As a tribute, one day I gave her a framed picture of the two of us with the inscription, "You are my hero." She cherished that picture more than words could say. This picture now sits on the antique mantle that she left to me. My computer at home bears her image as the screensaver. I talk to both pictures everyday. And she actually does communicate with me in her own way. She was my guardian angel in life and is absolutely my guardian angel now in Spirit.

Before I announced to my family that I was planning to go to Boston to marry my soon-to-be-husband Michael, I told Grandma first. She was wonderful. She didn't miss a beat and rallied the support of the rest of my family. How many gay couples can say, they had both immediate families happily attend their wedding? There are so many gay people whose families have disowned them. Michael and I are truly fortunate to have the love and support of both sets of our parents, as well as our brothers and sisters.

At a zestful 91-1/2 years old, Grandma spoke at our wedding. Her amazing, loving presence was the best gift I could have asked for. She was definitely the Belle of the Ball. My friends were all smitten with this incredible woman. They couldn't get over how youthful she looked. She was one of those rare people that actually deserved the pedestal upon which everybody had put her on. To know her was to love her. She truly embodied those extra special loving qualities we all look for in a grandmother.

One of my girlfriends remarked how Grandma and I had an electric connection with each other. With just a mere glance between us, we knew exactly what the other was thinking. There was no generation gap at all. How lucky we were to have had a connection as special as that. My friend said that it was beautiful to witness and experience the special connection we shared. How lucky we were to have it! Yes we were! And still are to this day!

In the end, Grandma still had one last major lesson to teach me. One I had actively been trying to avoid. The time had come for her to teach me about death, and the dignity in dying.

Only a few months after my wedding, she was diagnosed with cancer. Those words I had dreaded and feared my whole life had finally intruded upon my reality. Despite her age, she underwent two separate rounds of chemotherapy, which she bravely endured. The doctors didn't give her much of a chance. They obviously had never met Mrs. Sallee Berlin. The cancer went into remission.

A couple of months later, she called me late at night. She was having trouble breathing and was in severe pain. Michael and I rushed over see her. I went with her in the ambulance and my family met us at the hospital. The doctors told us that she should have died that night. But she was such a fighter—a powerhouse in a tiny frame. She was not ready. Her condition was upgraded.

A few months later we were all in her room, when the doctor entered. Her cancer had comeback and spread. He gave her a few months, at most, a year to live. In her final months, she taught us how to be courageous when it would have been so easy to just give up. How truly important the love of family and friends is in someone's life. She carried herself with such dignity, despite the terrible pain she was experiencing. Her mind was as sharp as a tack and she was very conscious all the way up to the end. My brother and I stayed very close through all this and Grandma was delighted. She had been able to see her dysfunctional grandson grow from an insecure child to a strong, vital, happily married man.

One week before our first wedding anniversary, in the hospital, Grandma gave Michael and me an anniversary gift. She explained that she wanted to give it to us then because she wasn't sure if she would be around for our anniversary. This brave woman was fighting the monster, cancer, like a warrior, but she was still thinking about us. She hadn't forgotten my anniversary and she wanted to share it with us. In return, I gave her a plant for long life and two stuffed hearts with angel wings. It was then that she said, "Please no more presents." I knew something was up, but tried to put it out of my mind. If I didn't think about it, my hope was that it just wouldn't happen.

A few days later, my incredibly strong, loving mother called me. There was such immense pain in her voice. She was hardly able to speak. Grandma had taken a turn for the worse. She told me I should go see her immediately. My parents had been by my grandmother's side throughout the whole ordeal. No daughter and son in-law could ever have been more attentive to an ailing mother. Michael and I rushed to Grandma's side. She was lying in bed and looked just like an angel. She had a luminous glow all around her. She could barely speak because of all the morphine they had given her. When she saw us enter the room, her eyes became as clear as a bell. I couldn't hear what she was saying, but I could feel the love. I knew she had been fighting the cancer in order to be there with all of us.

She was self-sacrificing to the very end. I knew she was in tremendous pain and would not recover this time. It was now my turn to be self-sacrificing and put her needs ahead of my own. She had done everything for us. She had never retired to Florida, just so she could be close to us. She had given us her all and now it was my time to give something back.

It was then that I did the hardest thing that I have ever had to do in this lifetime. It was something that I never would have wanted to happen and never would be ready for. How can you ever be ready to say goodbye to somebody who you love so much?

As I have tried to write this, I have stopped several times because it is still so excruciating. Even proof reading it is torture. You never get over this. But you keep going on.

Michael gently told me it wasn't looking good. I understood it was time to say goodbye. I know that we never really die, we just move on to the astral plane. But there never were, or ever been, any guarantees. The idea that Grandma would not physically be with me anymore was a concept I just didn't want to grasp. Her terminal illness forced me to confront some of my feelings about life and death. Her prolonged illness had allowed me to let the shock set in slowly.

Even though I communicate with spirits on a regular basis, I was still afraid. Would I ever see or be with her again? Was my gift just some kind of psychosis that prevented me from thinking about death? I knew Grandma did not want to die. I knew she would keep fighting until her final breath. But now the time had come to trust in Spirit and believe that everything was truly going to be for the highest good. I had to say good-bye.

My tears flowed like a river. The words finally started to pour out. I told Grandma that she was the most amazing person I had ever known and that I loved her with every fiber of my existence. I knew she loved me the same way. I told her, she was one of my best friends and soulmates. How she was so incredibly giving of herself. How blessed I was to have had her as my Grandmother. How she was and will always be my hero and inspiration. How her exemplary life was an example that I hoped to live up to. How she had helped me to become who I am today. I promised not to disappoint her. I thanked her for helping make my wedding happen. I told her, I never wanted to let her go, but I knew I couldn't be selfish anymore. It just wasn't fair.

I promised her, "I will take care of your baby (my mother). I will never let anything ever happen to her. I will protect her and love her. I don't want you to ever leave me, but I know you are ready. If you are ready to leave, I give you my permission. It is okay. But only if you promise to visit me everyday for the rest of my life, until it is my time to join you and you will come for me. I love you with all of my heart, body, soul and spirit. I am so blessed to have had you in my life. You must visit me and let me know that you made it back home safely. I promise to keep you proud of me and to always take care of your baby. I love you."

I kissed her goodbye and left the room. Michael then had his talk with her. They had become so very close in the couple of years that they had shared together. I had promised to take care of my mother. He promised that he would take care of her other baby, me. With that, Michael left her room and would be the last person to see her alive. My Mother called the next morning. She didn't have to say a word. I just knew Grandma was gone and my heart has been broken ever since. She had even made sure not to pass on my anniversary. She was always thinking about her special grandson.

Later that day, I received a visitation as clear as I had ever had experienced before. My Grandma came to me in a vision. She was dressed like an Egyptian Goddess, and bathed in a golden glow. She looked absolutely beautiful. She said, "I love you. I have made it home perfectly". She regally glided up to the sky and slowly faded away. If anyone could break through, I knew she would. It then hit me. This was now the only way I would be able to communicate with her.

Her funeral was very surreal. I gave the first of many eulogies. I knew she was there. I could feel her as I entered the funeral parlor. She had lived her life with dignity and her elegant service reflected that.

In the Jewish tradition, one year after the person has passed, there is an unveiling service at the gravesite. A veil is put over the headstone. Prayers are said and the new stone is unveiled to our world. It serves as a tribute to the living memory of the loved one. The role of the Rabbi or any other religious or spiritual leader is to honor those who are no longer with us and to bring comfort to the living. Unfortunately, Grandma's unveiling was anything but settling.

The presiding rabbi was of the Jewish Orthodox faith. He lived his life strictly by the book and expected all others to do the same. At her gravesite, he was going over what he intended to say. In a very demeaning way, he claimed that since my grandmother had not been ultra orthodox, there was no guarantee that she would go to heaven. Excuse me?

My Aunt, who has been my mother's best friend since they were three years old, could not contain her contempt for this hypocritical man. I also became enraged. How dare this judgmental, supposed man of God, spew out this religious garbage.

I regrettably have to admit that my subsequent behavior was not the most dignified, albeit justified. My heart was in the right place, but I let my grieving emotions take over. My delivery was as raw as the loss I was feeling. I literally grabbed the Rabbi and turned him physically around. He was not going to face Grandma's headstone as he spoke his misconceived words.

I bluntly told him, "You mean to tell me, that just because my Grandmother never did it through a sheet that she is not going to heaven? Are you kidding me? This Woman was the epitome of a good soul. How dare you. We don't need you. If you cannot see what a spectacular soul Sallee Berlin was, you have no business being here. I am a minister, I can do this myself."

My whole family united and we agreed that he was not going to dishonor this great Lady with his outdated, narrow-minded jargon. When he saw he was about to be dismissed, he magically realized the error of his ways and had a sudden change of heart. He quickly modified his words and the service was delivered briskly and briefly. Our entire united family defended her honor passionately. Just like Grandma, we are all very feisty too.

For days afterward, I was horrified at how I had reacted at the unveiling. But I just couldn't let that man say those hypocritical words about somebody he had barely met. I was tortured by the nagging voice in the back of my mind, which loves to make me doubt myself. In my gut, I knew Grandma had agreed with me and didn't mind my coming to her defense one bit. She even found a way to assure me of that. Grandma made her presence known, while I was in a therapy session with Dr. Deva. (Dr Deva is my wonderful therapist you will read about later.)

She conveyed to us that she understood, and was honored that I had defended her memory. Of course she wouldn't have used the same exact words, but she knew it was all done out of love. Dr Deva said Grandma actually found the whole thing rather amusing and loved to see her fighting Spirit live within me.

Grandma showed up regularly at my Dr Deva therapy sessions for quite awhile. She assisted Dr Deva in helping me to shift back into gear. She still does show up every now and then. Never once when I have needed her to show up, has she ever disappointed me. She may not be in her body any longer, but she is still keeping very busy...

As I continue writing this, Grandma comes to me again. As you can tell through my writing, I miss her terribly. She comes to me everyday and I vividly can see, feel, hear and smell her. We still have our conversations and I am grateful for that. But what I wouldn't do to feel those angelic arms holding me in the physical once again. God bless her!!

ANGELIC VISITATIONS

My Grandma was my guardian angel. Now let me tell you about my personal experiences with other guardian angels.

{#1} ARCHANGEL MICHAEL VISITATION

On February 19th, 1991, accompanied by two dear friends, I was blessed with a soul-affirming experience, which has forever changed my life. Anyone with whom I have shared this experience has also been deeply affected by it.

Being born with the blessed gift, I have been able to see, feel and communicate with subtle-energetic beings such as angels, spirits and loved ones who have passed on.

Like most people, there was a point in my life when I began to question the true existence of God/Spirit. I especially questioned the visions and interactions that I had with spirits, as well as the feelings that would come through me. Though I had my doubts, I still continued to pray and meditate deeply. I specifically asked to be sent a sign, a very clear sign, not something that could be mistaken for anything else! What you shall ask for, you shall receive, only if it's for the highest good. And, oh boy, did Spirit hear me loud and clear.

On that February day, though it was snowing, my friends Karen, Nova, and I felt an overwhelming need to walk outside, around the corner to Washington Cemetery. Washington Cemetery is one of the oldest cemeteries in Brooklyn, NY. As we entered the cemetery, there was a funeral in progress. In order not to interfere with the funeral or be disrespectful, we walked down the road in the other direction. After we had walked a bit, a beautiful, ever so bright being appeared from behind a tree. He later revealed himself to be the Archangel Michael. He was dressed in clothing from a variety of time periods. He had Roman gladiator sandals on his feet, and an ancient frock on his body. He was carrying an exquisite, café colored parasol decorated with delicate lotus blossoms. His mouth appeared to resemble the letter S and he had an almost blinding, golden halo of curls.

Though it was snowing, we did not get wet. Instead, we were drenched with the beautiful feeling of the most immense Love. It resonated in every part of my being. I have never experienced such an overwhelming magnitude of Divine Love ever before. There was no denying or fighting it. At that moment, I was able to truly feel pure Unconditional Love from the highest of realms.

We began to walk toward the new part of the cemetery. But we kept feeling Archangel Michael pulling us back into the old section. He brought us up to a mausoleum, which had been defamed and misused for ungodly worship. As we approached it, with each step further toward it, I was able to feel myself facing intense darkness and fear. Glass was shattered and broken on the outside of the mausoleum, as if something had tried to break out. The interior was in pristine condition, as if it had just been sealed the day before, though the date engraved on the outside was 1924. Terrifying emotions engulfed me, but Archangel Michael's love helped me to transcend and rise above them.

It was then that I was separated from my friends. Archangel Michael led each of us in a different direction. I was lead through a path of graves that brought chills up and down my spine. When I reached the end, there was a tombstone with a similar spelling of my last name. Archangel Michael looked directly into my soul, we were now one. I felt only the greatest healing from all the pain I had been carrying. All my life's spiritual doubts were instantly removed. I was able to feel the true essence of the Divine Love. His energy was, and has been, one of the strongest stabilizing forces in my life. I am glad to be able to share the story of Archangel Michael's gift with you.

When I rejoined my friends, I found out that each of them had had a similar experience. Michael had been able to help each of us face that which had been preventing a direct experience of God/Spirit in our lives.

Michael looked directly at the three of us, and we all looked at him. We heard a loud noise and turned away for just a second. When we turned back, Michael, and also the funeral procession, had vanished into thin air.

{#2} A FUNNY THING HAPPENED ON MY WAY FROM THE COLISEUM

According to Buddhist tradition, highly enlightened beings, such as the Buddha, have routinely revisited the Earth in the form of disheveled homeless people. The same person, who is looked down upon as one of the derelicts of society, might actually be a highly enlightened being or an Angel in human disguise. Skeptics may think this is total bullshit. But my very own experiences have verified that it is most definitely the truth.

In 1985/86, I used to work for a company in midtown Manhattan. Everyday on my way to work, I used to pass the now defunct Coliseum bookstore on W.57 Street. Every single time I walked by, I would see this homeless man outside of the bookstore. We would exchange pleasantries and salutations. When I had some extra time, I would usually have a conversation with him. People would stare at him judgmentally. Granted, he normally reeked of alcohol, among other things, but I couldn't have cared less. I found him to be a very fascinating individual who always had a smile on his face. Over the course of time that I worked in Midtown, I used to look forward to our conversations. My friends thought I was absolutely insane. Why would I want to talk to something as grotesque as that? Well, he was not a "that." He was a person who had become my friend. I just found it disgusting how cruel and insensitive society was toward him. Sometimes he would talk to me about his troubles and I would gladly offer whatever advice I could. Sometimes I would curse somebody out, when they said horrible things to him.

We would talk about how cruel some human beings could be. The funny thing about it all was that I was always so much more bothered by their denigration than he was. He would just tell me to try not to pay attention to it. Most of them were like sick animals and I should just pray for them. Most people were blind and only special souls like myself could see with compassion. Everybody was just a few steps away from the bottom—the ground. They just didn't know it until they had fallen down hard.

He always gave me gems of wisdom to ponder. I felt like he was living in different world than ours. At times, his world seemed a whole lot better.

One day, I saw him sitting on the sidewalk in front of Coliseum books. Something just didn't feel right. His coloring was very grey and his aura was very murky. I sat down next to him on the ground to talk to him. He told me he was just very tired. He was going to go on a trip very far away and would not be coming back. I knew exactly what he was referring to … suicide.

I am strongly opposed to anybody prematurely ending their life, instead of trying to see their problems out to the end. Before we were born, we made an agreement with Spirit to work on certain karmic and energetic issues. Yes, during our human life, we can renegotiate our agreement. But we cannot break it completely.

We all reach a point when things feel so apocalyptic, that we just might want to check out of here for good. During these times, we can ask Spirit to let us learn these lessons less harshly. We can ask Spirit to let us have gentler and easier lessons.

I explained to my friend that no matter how dark his life seemed right then, there was a bright light at the end of his path. If he gave up before he had completed the lessons, he would only be returning to relive the same lessons. The next time, they would be of a much harsher, and crueler magnitude. He looked at me and his glassy eyes transformed back into crystal clear right before my eyes.

He said, "Okay you have convinced me. I am going to stay and work it out."

His smile came back and his coloring started brightening right in front of me. He looked me straight in the face and said, "So Harvey Lewis Schaeffer, now I have a message for you."

As soon as he called me by my birth name, my mind was completely blown. I was absolutely shell shocked. Ever since I had changed my name to H, I had kept my birth name a secret, more tightly guarded than Fort Knox. I no longer had anything with my birth name on it. Back then, I would have practically fractured somebody's jaw if they had come close to using that name. Nobody except my family or my pre-college friends, knew that name. There was no way in the world that he could have known about that name.

He saw that he had just knocked one out of the park with that one.

"Yes, you heard me, Harvey Lewis Schaeffer" he said smiling. "I knew that would get your attention. You have wondered your whole life, are you going to make it? Are you going to be successful? Well the answer is YES. But no way near as fast as you would like, or in what capacity you think. You have certain lessons and experiences you will need to go through first. Plus your newly confident ego will also need to be put in check first. We have been watching you and will continue to watch you your whole life. Your gifts will increasingly magnify and in time all this will make complete sense to you. We love you, Harvey Lewis Schaeffer. So now H, it is time for you to love Harvey as much as we do."

We were still sitting on the dirty sidewalk when I heard this loud crackling noise. I turned my head for just a split second to see what the noise was all about. When I turned my head back, my friend was gone. There was no way he could have picked himself up and run away that quickly. There was absolutely no trace of him whatsoever.

I intuitively heard him tell me, "Harvey Lewis Schaeffer, you will never be alone. We will always be with you and we will always be here to assist you. And we will make occasional visitations when the time is right."

I ran around the corner looking in vain for my friend. My friend truly was an angel disguised in human form. I never saw my angel friend again after that day. But I am comforted in knowing that he is still watching over me.

One day, during one of my daily intuitive conversations with the spirit of my Grandma, I asked her about my angel friend. Grandma confirmed that he really was an angel and she had now lovingly joined him in watching over me.

This had not been my first angelic encounter. I knew it would not be my last.

{#3} HELLO, H, WE ARE TALKING TO YOU!

In 1996, I had applied for a job at the phone company and was scheduled to take their entrance exam. I had been out of town and had flown back to NYC just to take this test. It was a miserable day. It was raining relentlessly and very grey outside. I rushed from the airport to the phone company's building, where they were giving the entrance exam. Naturally, I was running late and arrived at the building exactly two minutes late. Though it was only two minutes, the guards had locked the front door and refused to let me in. I was informed that I would have to call again to reschedule another exam. I was stunned. I had rushed like a madman from the airport, and it was all in vain. I was extremely disappointed and really pissed off. I thought I had just totally blown my chances for the job at a company that had excellent benefits. Being a psychic has certain perks, but health insurance is not one of them.

I was really hard on myself and felt like a complete moron. I walked around the city roaming aimlessly in the rain, having a pity party for myself. In my wanderings, I came across a homeless man standing under scaffolding. He had a blanket laid on the ground with books he was trying to sell. As I glanced at the blanket, one book started glowing to me. I began to feel like it was a magnet and it was pulling me closer to it. I finally picked up the book.

The homeless man looked up at me and smiled. "Harvey Lewis, this book is for you."

I just stared at him. "Yes Harvey, this book is for you."

I was taken back once again by somebody calling me by my birth name. I practically jumped down his throat. Why do you people keep calling me by that name?

He calmly replied, "How else would you know it is us?"

True. Point well taken. He went on to tell me to please continue my intuitive healing practice. He said my healing practice was necessary, as part of the healing of our planet. I was going to soon be working in the corporate telecommunications world as well, which would serve several purposes. It would allow me a steady income. So I could be very selective in whom I would take on as a client in my private healing practice. Spirit would be sending me many souls that needed my help. There would be some who could easily afford to pay for my services. As well as others who also needed my work, but had no means to pay me. Some souls would be in a living body. Others would have already passed away and be in need of assistance before they could cross over. Little did I imagine, he was referring to my work as an intuitive healer associated for the 9/11 tragedy five years later.

I thanked him for the book and his insightful messages. I knew right then and there that my job with the phone company would be no accident. As I was walking away he told me I had an important phone call to make in three days. Exactly three days later, I spoke with the phone company to reschedule my entrance exam. I passed the test and got the job.

You just never know what impact your actions will ever have on someone else. So I think it's important to always be as compassionate as possible. Always try to fill the role of the angel yourself, whenever you are presented with the opportunity.

All angels were very much around us during the horror we now know as 9/11/01. As a 9/11 survivor, I know I was protected that day. Next are my experiences what I personally went through during that frightful day.

9/11 AND CAROLINE MYSS

Several weeks before 9/11/01, I went with two of my girlfriends to a TV taping for Caroline Myss. Caroline Myss is one of the pioneers of energy medicine. Her books are absolutely wonderful and I recommend them to everybody. Caroline is a world renowned medical intuitive and one of the trailblazers in the field. Caroline Myss is by no means a meek, mild doormat without any backbone. She is feisty and tenacious. Her bedside manner is about as blunt as being hit over the head with a two-by-four. Caroline does not mince words. She doesn't beat around the bush. Caroline just tells it how it is.

She was taping a short series for the Oxygen cable network. For several months before the taping, my practice had been going through a major metamorphosis. I had recently been ordained as an interfaith minister by the New Seminary of New York. I thought my practice would now be overflowing with clients as a result. Instead the complete opposite was happening. Many of my steady clients had been disappearing. My practice was going through a very slow period. To make things worse, many of the intuitive messages I was getting around that time just weren't making any sense. I knew Spirit must have planned this for me. I trusted that Spirit was working in my best interests. But I needed to know what that was. And I wanted to know in a New York minute.

When I heard Caroline was taping a few shows, I knew I had to go to see her. If anybody could help me make sense of things, I knew Caroline could. During that time, I literally felt like I was living in two worlds. I was in between our physical world and the spiritual world. My grounding was off kilter. I could sense my abilities were metamorphosing and I wasn't sure into what. I had so many spirits around me that I had unknowingly started referring to myself as WE.

So off I went to the taping of Caroline Myss's show. As soon as we entered the studio, I could sense her powerful energy. She began the taping and it was very enjoyable. I was waiting for my chance to ask Caroline what was going on with me. She finally opened up her questions and answers segment with the audience. Several people asked her questions. Finally she came around to where I was sitting and looked directly at me. We met eye-to-eye and I could feel the chills of energy up and down my spine. Caroline knew I wanted to ask her something and didn't wait for me to raise my hand. She came right up and asked for my question. I explained that I was a healer whose practice seemed to be radically changing. I needed clarity about where my practice and my path were headed.

Caroline collected herself for a minute and tapped into my energy field. She said I needed to get a grip on myself. I was beginning to sound like the British royalty referring to myself as WE, as if I was speaking to my royal subjects. Intuitively, she explained that I had always been a healer constantly in the healer's role. My abilities and my practice were indeed going through a dynamic change.

The change was necessary because Spirit was preparing me for my next major collaborative role in our planet's transformation to the light. I have always been the one to be the healer. No matter what situation, I was there to help people with their problems. Caroline further explained that I would be in the center of something major league and it would be extremely traumatic. My natural instinct would be to stay behind and play my familiar role as healer. But this time, I was to do the opposite. It would be my duty to step aside and allow other people to be the healers.

Caroline was very specific. "You need to just GET OUT. This time you will not be the healer. You will need to allow this to happen. Just keep saying to yourself Get Out, Get Out! Everything will make sense and fall into place after this major traumatic event."

I wasn't sure what Caroline was referring to, but I was sure I would be finding out pretty soon.

In 1993, by Spirit's fate, I happened to have been at the WTC the day before the first bombing. I sensed that something just wasn't right. I could intuitively sense dark clouds looming. I could hear loud noises. I wasn't able to decipher what they were. I just knew trouble was brewing and I wasn't going to hang around to find out. I went home sick to my stomach. The very next day, the WTC was bombed. I thought that had to be what I had been sensing. Little had I known that would just be the tip of the horrific iceberg.

One week before 9/11, I started having terrific migraines. I knew the migraines were intuitively based. I thought, "Great … this is just what I need." I then walked into the graveyard across from the WTC. This place had always given me comfort and the spirits in residence there were always wonderfully helpful. I asked the spirits to help lift the intense pain. The loving spirits did as I asked and helped lift the migraines. I thanked and blessed them. I sent them loving reiki healing energy.

One of my co-workers reminded me of what I had been doing during the week before 9/11. Evidently, I had been walking around the office like Chicken Little pointing up to the ceiling, saying, "Look, look, the sky is falling." She said I had kept repeating it the whole week before 9/11. I had a conversation with one of our customers at Cantor Fitzgerald. We both had felt a strange vibe was in the air. In hindsight, we had both unconsciously been sensing the impending danger that was to take place the very next day.

I had been scheduled to attend an 8:30am meeting with Cantor Fitzgerald on the 105th floor of the World Trade Center on 9/11/01. At the very last minute, the meeting had been postponed to later in the day. When I woke up that morning, I just didn't feel right. I couldn't put my finger on it. My spirit guides weren't talking to me that morning.

I had figured, "Oh well… I'm sure they will check in with me later."

Before I left my apartment, Caroline Myss's book *Anatomy of a Spirit* suddenly leapt out of my bookcase and dropped in front of me. Okay, somebody was trying to talk to me, but still nobody was speaking.

"When they are ready to communicate with me, they will know where I am," I thought to myself.

I left my house and walked to the train. It was an absolutely beautiful day. The weather was picture-perfect. Little did I know, I would soon find out what a horrific day it would turn out to be.

Since the 8:30 meeting with Cantor Fitzgerald had been pushed back till later in the day, I took my time getting to work. As usual, I took the train to the Fulton St train station one block from the WTC. As I exited the train station at Broadway and John St, I could just sense that everything that I had known was now completely changed. From the moment I stepped out onto the street, I felt like I had just stepped out of a time machine into a whole new world.

The surroundings were the same, but everything was completely different. I looked up and my heart collapsed like a ton of bricks. I glanced upon the WTC and I saw the fiery gaping hole spewing smoke from one of the towers. My first thought was that some stupid stunt pilot must have screwed up and crashed into one of the twin towers. There was a deafening silence. Everybody, including myself, was just stunned looking up at the smoky WTC tower. It felt very surreal. This couldn't be happening. Especially not my twin towers. One of my childhood friends, the World Trade Center, had just been injured and all I could do was watch helplessly. I collected myself and started walking down the block. All of a sudden, a toxic evil wave came over me. I heard a terrible noise. I looked up to see the second plane. It looked like a deadly piranha soaring through the sky. It then turned and intentionally crashed into the second tower. My body convulsed from the worst type of evil I had ever experienced. I knew this was no accident. This was a terrorist attack. This was WAR.

The unsettling feeling I had always sensed had come to fruition. Damn, how I wish I hadn't been right this time. Everybody was running in every direction in fear for their very lives. As I ran into a nearby Chase Bank, the front window shattered in front of me slicing through the face of a female passerby. Blood was gushing from her face. It was terrible.

I started to hear Caroline Myss telling me, "GET OUT … GET OUT. You are not to be the healer this time." Suddenly, everything Caroline had told me all made sense.

In a moment of relative calm, I unsuccessfully tried to use my cell phone. I wanted to call my girlfriend who worked in the WTC and tell her not to come down to the madness. I had no signal at all. Without hesitation, I quickly ran down Barkley Street to the phone company building at 140 West St, across from the WTC. I walked through the side service entrance and took an elevator up to my office on the 13th floor. I had no idea that my building had already been evacuated. I calmly went to my desk and called my Mom to tell her I was okay. My mother said that it had been the longest hour in her life while she was waiting for me to call. After I called my Mom, my office phone rang. It was a close friend of mine who lived in Brooklyn, a few blocks away from the Brooklyn Bridge. He told me to hang up the phone and get out! He wanted me to walk over the bridge and come to his house immediately.

I saw one of my co-workers walking around the office. I joined him. We were looking through the windows at the WTC. We could see people jumping from the towers. I saw a couple holding hands as they hurled to their deaths. A supervisor, checking to see that everybody had evacuated, saw us. He told us to get the hell out of the building immediately. No problem!

I wasn't thinking. I didn't bother to grab anything from my desk. I couldn't imagine anything else happening. Little did I know that hours after the towers fell, the ceiling of my office would completely collapse. If I had known that, I would have grabbed the original picture of Agela that I kept at my desk.

My co-worker and I exited the building and walked back down the street toward City Hall. We passed by one of the plane's engines lying in the street. We could distantly see people still jumping and could hear the horrible thuds of the bodies hitting the pavement.

We walked to City Hall. I kept hearing the voice of Caroline Myss echoing, "Get Out, Get Out!" I knew in every fiber of my body, I had to get off the island of Manhattan immediately. The Brooklyn Bridge was right there across the street. The Brooklyn Bridge had been another childhood friend of mine. For several years I had walked across the bridge to Brooklyn several times a week after work. But this time was different. I could sense that even more terror was about to be unleashed. It was time to get out! I told my co-worker to cross the bridge with me, but he wanted to hang around and watch what was going on. We wished each other luck, and off I went.

Walking across the bridge had become a wonderful ritual for me. The bridge had been the perfect spot for me to meditate. I could feel all four elements Earth, Air, Water, and Fire. The magnetic vibration of the bridge was an amazing conductor for channeling. It was an excellent place to ground myself.

But on this day, the opposite was true. The bridge had become a terror filled vessel on which to escape the darkest, carnal forces of evil. The bridge was packed with a sea of people. I could sense the cornucopia of different feelings people were experiencing. Some people were relatively calm. Others were in various stages of anxiety, fear and despair. I just kept hearing Caroline Myss echoing, "Get Out, Get Out!" There was a looming paranoia that the terrorists would attack the bridge next. I knew I had to get off the bridge as fast as my legs could carry me. I started to speed walk through the maze of people. Many people were stopped dead in their tracks from panic. I quickly wove my way through the crowd.

All of a sudden, I intuitively heard a blood-curdling scream. I turned around just in time to witness what would be the last moments of tower two imploded its way into history's past. First there was an excruciating silence. Intuitively I saw a huge cloud of spirits rising from the building up to the higher realms. There was a rumbling sound. Everybody on the bridge was glued into their shoes. All of a sudden, there was smoke. The building started collapsing down upon itself, like the tower of Babel. The building came down quickly. Everybody was now hysterically screaming.

I immediately started running and just hauled ass. I made it over the bridge safely and sat down on a nearby street. I was just trying to take in what I had just witnessed. This could not be happening. I could not have just witnessed the destruction of one of the towers. How could any of this be possible? I had seen a huge cloud of the souls rising as a whole up to Spirit.

I collected myself and walked over to my friend's nearby apartment. He had the News on when I walked in. I sat for a minute, but the newscast threw me into a sudden shock. By the time I had made it to my friend's apartment, the remaining tower had also collapsed. The WTC had just been assassinated by a terrorist attack. I had witnessed it from only one block away. The graceful towering twins had fallen where they once stood. The carnage was unimaginable. I knew thousands of people had just lost their lives. I had witnessed the single most fatal attack in American history. All the impending impressions I had been having now made perfect sense. Just like Caroline had said.

Whatever you might have seen of the tragedy is nothing compared to how gory it was witnessing it first hand. Fortunately, I had listened to Caroline and had gotten off Manhattan Island before that toxic dust cloud covered everyone and everything around. My co-worker, who had stayed behind, was caught up in this cloud. He had respiratory problems for a few days afterwards. But he was eventually okay. I also found out later, that the Cantor Fitzgerald employee, who I had been friendly with, was safe. Thankfully he was still with us. He just happened to have missed his train. Fortunately, he had been late for work. I was elated. We spoke shortly after the tragedy, and have been cool ever since.

As a result of my own survival experience on 9/11, I have been able to counsel the victims of severe trauma. Having gone through it myself, it has provided me with an extra special window into their particular pain and anguish. I have been able to make major progress with my clients, where conventional and traditional treatments have failed.

There are countless people across the world, who have suffered, or still are suffering, from post-traumatic syndrome, anxieties, panic attacks and other 9/11 related illnesses. You didn't have to be right there to experience it. You didn't need to be in New York, Washington D.C. or Pennsylvania. You just had to be alive on

9/11/2001 to be affected by that bloody carnage.

The morning after 9/11, I woke up to find over 100 spirits of the victims of 9/11 waiting for me in my apartment. The lost souls had intuitively come to me. It would be June 2002, nine months later, before the 9/11 souls stopped coming to my apartment.

Usually spirits come to me in fully intact bodies. The 9/11 lost souls appeared in all stages of disembodiment. I could perceive the stench and see the gory sights. They had no idea what was going on. They were not aware that they had died the day before. These poor souls were in various stages of confusion and denial. Some were aware that the planes had crashed into the WTC. Others had no concept of the 9/11 tragedies at all. They wanted to know what was going on. Some souls were stuck in an ongoing loop, continually repeating what they had been doing before the planes crashed.

Like all intuitive-medium healers, I am a beacon of bright light to disincarnate souls. They were instantly drawn to me. Many of the phone company's fallen customers would come to me in the next nine months. Even several, who were supposed to have been at the postponed meeting, came to me. I intuitively recognized them. I frequently visited ground zero and always encountered lost souls. I still do to this day. I still counsel these lost souls, just as I counsel my living clients. The only difference is that they are not in a human body any longer.

PHOTO ALBUM: PART ONE

THROUGH THE AGES

AGE 2, UPSTATE NEW YORK
MY FATHER THOUGHT IT WAS CUTE THAT
I WAS PLAYING WITH CHARCOAL AND GOT IT
ALL OVER ME.

YES, I LOVED THE 80s.
PHOTO BELOW, RIGHT, MY ACTUAL COLLEGE
GRADUATION SHOT.

PHOTO, TOP: MY PRENATAL WORK WITH
LILITH HELPED HER TO GET OVER HER
INHERITED FEAR OF CHILDBIRTH.
PHOTO, RIGHT: DALILA KRIHELI TOOK MY
PHOTO FOR THE COVER OF THIS BOOK AND
IS LIKE MY KID SISTER. SEE HER WORK AT
ROCKSTARPIX.COM

MY HEALING PATH: TRANSFORMATIONAL STEPS FROM SELF-HELL TO SELF-HEALING

PANIC ATTACKS

Paranoia, panic attacks and bouts with nervous jolts of anxiety used to wreak havoc with my stability and my very sanity. Panic attacks would totally undermine anything I tried to do. My heart would start racing and I would begin to sweat. My ego, or whatever was left of it, would be decimated, completely kicked to the curb.

I could be having a great time one minute, then something inside would get triggered. My nerves would become Pacman, slowly eating away whatever parts of me that was still solid and stable. I might appear to have a seemingly calm demeanor on the outside. However, inside I would feel as if I was beginning to collapse, terrified. Sometimes I had visions of crowds of people chasing after me with torches, swords, rocks and fists. They would stone me until I lost consciousness and then everything would just go blank.

My self-confidence, self-respect and self-love were always damaged by these blitzkriegs. For a time, it was really bad, and with my extremely noticeable stutter, it crippled whatever shred of self-worth I still had, and exacerbated the whole cycle. An anxiety cloud would come upon me like a tidal wave, crashing against the very rocks of my fragile, insecure world.

Devastation is exactly what panic attacks create, causing you to scrutinize and second-guess everything in your life. Doubts about every aspect of yourself ensue.

Panic attacks are the knee jerk reactions of our subconscious. Their purpose is to insulate us from anything that might inflict pain upon us. That's funny. The panic attack's true purpose is to protect us, to take us away from whatever it is that our psyches deem harmful, be it a situation, person, place or emotion. In reality, the attack causes more harm than the original alarming stimulus would have.

When the threshold of what you are able to endure has exceeded your resources, your resistance is depleted. Things quickly begin to feel extremely overwhelming. For some it feels like being hit by a Mack-truck. Others become fetal.

There is always an underlying root cause as to why the attacks occur at all. People usually have one or two prevalent themes that are the reason for their existence in the first place. When anxiety comes into play, the causes and reactions might be different per individual, but the energetic vibrations are the same. When an upsetting situation arises, a part of that person doesn't want to have to go through that experience again. Ergo, a panic attack ensues. This makes it almost impossible to pay attention to and deal with the upsetting situation.

Consider yourself an energy being. If there is a short circuit or loose wire somewhere, the body will not function 100%. The more continuous the malfunctions, the more the system will breakdown and repairs will be necessary.

Say for instance, when you were six years old and riding your tricycle, you decided to be bold, daring, and tried to ride a bicycle. You stumbled, fell head first off the bike, suffering from humiliation and physical pain. Maybe in the delicate mind of a six year old, this was a sign that every time you would try new things, you were doomed to failure and it would hurt very much. As you grew older, this stigma would always be in the back of your mind, unconsciously building fear. As you grew into an adult, you stayed extremely resistant to risk. You avoid any situation where you have to confront your fear. Even when you see that really cute guy/girl in the elevator everyday who always has smiling eyes for you, you refuse to take the chance. The possibility of being rejected and hurt is just too devastating. You may say linking these two events is far fetched, but actually they are more connected than you think. In many ways you are still looking at these life situations through the eyes of that terrified and humiliated six year old.

In growing up, nothing is more crucial than developing one's self-identity. This is what separates you from the crowd. Yes, we are all of the One. But this physical plane we call Earth is where we are to express ourselves. If your self-identity is fractured, so will your outlook on yourself and your life. That is why it is so important when we are growing up to have other people help us adjust to understanding how to live in our own skin. And eventually find our place in this complex society.

If these early fractures are not repaired, they will eventually compromise the foundations of your soul. Just like a building, if the foundation is compromised, cracks can eventually cause the building to fail. We as humans are no better. If the foundation of who you are is fractured, then your outlook and perspective will also be disjointed until you are able to deal with it and repair it.

For a good deal of my childhood, adolescence and early adulthood, I felt I was living in both our physical and the ethereal world. I felt like I was being pulled between both worlds. And to be honest, sometimes I wasn't sure which side was more comfortable being on. As I grew into the gift, I came to realize I had to work on the balance of living in these two worlds. This was something that would be a recurring theme in my life.

Once you are able to confront the causes of the panic attacks, you are able to start being your whole, true self. You will see past your fears, reclaiming your power and existence over them. All the energy that was invested into blocking the incidents is now released, which you can now use towards empowerment. The fears in many ways are jailors, and once you are free, you can live a life where you are not a prisoner of them.

My own experiences have helped me to formulate my healing practice and the techniques, steps, stages and procedures that I follow to this day. There are several different methods that I show you throughout this book, which can help you further understand all about anxiety and panic attacks and how you can regain control of this phenomenon. As a healer, I am able to see and feel the core of these energy patterns and help create an environment. Where these malfunctioning energy patterns can be repaired and transformed, restoring the energy body and person back to fully functional being.

When a panic attack first hits you, what do you do? My methods will help you to get past the story behind things and arrive at the energetic patterns, of the cause of the disturbance. Through the true aspect of Spirit, we are able to transform all blocks that we encounter and allow a true healing on all levels of our beings. Life will then offer you the possibilities of everything, with no limitations on your happiness or your ability to love and to be loved. The frequency and severity of my panic attacks have decreased considerably since I've learned to recognize the early warnings and to significantly alleviate the symptoms early on.

MEDITATION TO PREVENT OR STOP A PANIC ATTACK

The secret lies within the pranic breath. The ancients called it the breath of life and considered it to contain "prana," the life-force energy of our universe.

When you start to feel a panic attack coming on, the best thing is to try to stop it before it turns into a full blown episode. Panic attacks are electrical, so you need to try and ground yourself.

M E D I T A T I O N

First stand or sit still with your back straight up. Begin by closing your eyes and taking three deep pranic breaths. Inhaling from your nose carrying that breath all the way to your solar plexus located just above your belly button. Then slowly exhale through your mouth. Allow yourself to picture a circle of white light all around you. Ask for only those who come in the path of the light/God/Spirit, for the highest of good to be allowed to come to you. Continue with your pranic breaths from your nose down to your solar plexus and slowly exhaling thru your mouth. With each breath, you begin to become one with the white light. With each breath, you are becoming more solid and less anxiety filled.

Now imagine there is a spiral of Ultra-Violet (UV) light, the light of unconditional love at the highest of forms around you. With each deep breath, the spiral of UV light begins to enter your body through the left side of your ribcage. This spiral spins counterclockwise, as it continues to travel through your body and slowly exits out from the right side of your ribcage. This is what the wonderful healer Lillie O'Brien coined as "spinning", to help cleanse your body's energy fields. With each deep breath, the UV light continues to spin from the left side of your body and exiting out through the right side. This counterclockwise spinning is how you can energetically cleanse yourself and just about anybody or anything else of negative disturbances or patterns. The more you continue to spin, your body starts to automatically spin the UV light throughout your body.

Once you cleanse, you must also send positive energy back to refill that space. Otherwise, the negative energies will creep back in. Once your body is automatically spinning counterclockwise the UV light of unconditional love, it is time to spin the UV light clockwise back through the right side to empower yourself. This is exactly what you've just done from the left side, but you are simply reversing it.

With each breath, imagine the spiral of UV light entering your body spinning clockwise from the right side and exiting out the left side of your ribcage.

With each breath both spirals will continue automatically. Continue this spinning that clears and then empowers your body. Now your body is automatically spinning out the negative energies from you and replacing that with empowering positive healing energies.

Now imagine there is a beam of UV light that can travel all the way from your solar plexus up to the sky, to a sparking crystal star. This star is a group of enlightened beings always there to assist you. With each breath, this beam of UV light travels all the way up to this crystal star. You are now connected with this enlightened group. Allow yourself to imagine a beam of UV light traveling from this star back to your solar plexus. This UV light travels from your solar plexus all the way down to the center of the earth to ground you. Allow this beam of light to return from the center of the earth to your solar plexus. So you have now successfully become a channel in between the grounding energies of the center of the earth to the crystal star of enlightened beings. Stay with this as long as you like and then slowly open up your eyes. When you are finished, you will have successfully stopped the panic attack from happening. If you were already in a flown blown panic attack, this will help it to stop.

MY STAMMERING STUTTER AND HOW I OVERCAME IT

When someone develops a stutter or speech impediment, it is a very horrifying time. Surprisingly, the cause in many cases is electrical. We are all electrical beings. When one part of the body has an electrical block, in my case my throat, it short circuit's the rest of your body's equilibrium. Consider your body as one electrical connection with many intricate wires running along it. Once there is a blockage, the rest of the electrical connection is thrown off. The more the blockage builds, the stronger the tendencies for a short circuit. There was an energetic block in my throat chakra, which was blocking the direct current for normal speech pattern. In my case, I would not be able to tap into this blockage until later down the road, sixteen years later.

When a client comes to me, I am able to scan their body and their subsequent energy fields. I am then able to detect if there is a blockage in any area of the body's energy meridians. As common sense would rule, it is much easier to sense a blockage in somebody else then ourselves. I have never been quite able to give myself a complete reading. My emotions undoubtedly interfere with getting an unbiased take.

The majority of intuitives, psychics, mediums and healers will agree. It is one thing to be unaffected by another person's issues. It's a whole different ballgame to be able to completely detach from yourself and unbiasedly read yourself, as if you are a separate person. That is hard. I have only been able to do this on rare occasions. Surgeons cannot operate on themselves. The same goes for us.

My stutter added to the fear of expressing myself, which started to develop into a full-blown paranoia of speaking in public. This developed into an even bigger fear that I would start expressing my thoughts out loud. Besides being able to feel what people's true thoughts were—not the socially polite garbage they would mask it with—I now couldn't even talk to someone without it being a battle between me and my energetically blocked throat. Oh yeah! I was a real happy camper.

I am a sound believer in, and certified practitioner of, hypnosis and past life regression. Many of the paths we take in our current lives are more or less associated with our previous incarnations, when our souls walked upon this planet in different bodies. What I discovered was that my stutter was actually an energetic block that had been created in some of my past lives.

Days before my stutter first reared its ugly head, my brother and I had gone to the movies to see The Lincoln Conspiracy. Everything was fine until the scene in which the conspirators were all hung. When I saw the cloth being put over their heads, my heart sank and my throat clenched. The bottom dropped out from beneath the prisoners and their lifeless bodies hung in the air. It felt like a nuclear explosion had just gone off in my mind, body and soul, striking a major cord throughout my entire being.

I had a very strong déjà vu experience. I could actually feel the cloth go over my head. The hangman's noose tightened around my throat and then the trap door opened. Over the years, this was a recurring image that would pop up in my mind. Each time the vision reappeared I would become completely unglued. Over time, I learned how to internalize it all. I tried very hard not to show anything externally. This further exacerbated my stutter.

As my practice progressed, the gift became stronger. I began working with auras and chakras. I was now able to sense that my throat chakra was blocked. That was a no brainer for someone with a stutter. As I had grown older, my stutter had been reduced to a stammer, which had become part of my normal speech pattern. Some people noticed it, some didn't.

As I explored more of the psychological realm, hypnosis became a subject that fascinated me. I read everything I could find about hypnosis. At that time it was mostly used as entertainment. Like many alternative practices back then, it was looked upon very cynically, but I instinctively knew hypnosis was an excellent tool that would serve me well.

Past life regression really rang a bell for me. Actually, it was more like a five-alarm siren. I was in my late-twenties when I finally made an appointment with a hypnotherapist Rev. Celeste. I discussed the issue of my stutter. We agreed upon three sessions for past life regression hypnosis. As with many people, the first session took much longer than anticipated. Going into a deep meditative trance had never been an issue for me. What was an issue, was releasing the control. I had the normal apprehensions that anybody else would have had. A surgeon can perform one hundred operations without an inkling of doubt. But when the surgeon himself needs surgery, he will of course be nervous. It was the same thing for me with hypnosis. I am intuitive, but I still had apprehensions about somebody else having free access to my innermost sacredness.

As with all new experiences, I entered the session with no expectations. Coming into a situation with no expectations clears the way for endless possibilities to happen. When you walk into a situation with preconceived notions, you set limits upon the field of possibilities. Expectations can easily tarnish your entire experience.

I asked my guides, angels and spirits for protection. I asked the four Archangels to help assist in lifting all that could be lifted, and healing all that could be healed or transformed. It took a while for me to allow myself to go under. But once I let go and let Spirit, I sunk like a rock into the deep realm of unconsciousness.

The first past life experience that surfaced was my life as a Bedouin named IJAMAL. My father in my present life was also my father in that lifetime. He didn't look like he does now, but I just knew it was him. We were craft vendors who traveled from village to village peddling our goods. We sold crafts, elixirs and potions to all who were interested. Some of our potions, which were made by combining natural herbs and oils, went against what was readily accepted. Our potions helped promote natural healing for whoever used them.

The political and religious leaders of those communities had deemed our ways as blasphemous. Blasphemous my butt! We were blasphemous because we had refused to give those very same leaders a cut of our profits. I publicly spoke out against the establishment, their greed and corruption. The leaders did not like this. I was arrested on trumped-up charges. My trial lasted only a few minutes. They made an example of me to discourage any further dissent. I was found guilty and executed by public hanging. We revisited this incarnation and energetically changed the outcome of that lifetime.

The next two sessions flowed much more easily than the first one had. I was able to allow myself to enter into a deepened trance rather quickly, anxious to discover the origins of my stutter and the blockages in my throat chakra.

In my third regression, I was taken to a past life somewhere around the late 1700's, maybe early 1800's. I was a male from a very affluent family in the United Kingdom. I was a good son but I hadn't been living up to the expectations that my very masculine, disciplinarian of a father had for me. My father had been born into old money. He felt I was too lackadaisical and lacked ambition. This was unacceptable to him. He also thought I was a bit too soft. In order to remedy the situation, he forced my enlistment into the British Navy. My mother was dead-set against it. But my father felt the navy would toughen me up and make a man out of me.

I served my duty and quickly grew up to be a strapping young man, just as my tough-as-nails father had thought I would. I always had a smart mouth and a lively sense of humor. Most surprisingly, even then, I already had a little bit of a stutter. In the navy, I got along with just about everybody and I could easily put a smile on a disgruntled crewman's face. I had grown to be well respected by my shipmates.

The Captain was a cantankerous, crotchety seadog who had been weather-beaten by life. He was adept at instilling fear into the crew and was how he kept everybody in check. He was a short-tempered drunk who argued excessively with anyone who disagreed with him.

One night, the Captain got into a nasty spat with one of his officers. They both had a bit too much rum from the Captain's secret stash. They grew argumentative. Fueled by dark rum, the argument quickly escalated into aggression. The two drunken men soon locked horns. There was a struggle. While scuffling, the Captain shoved his officer down an open bay door. The officer plunged through the opening, snapped his neck, and died instantly.

Surprise surprise. I had witnessed the whole thing. Figures! Lucky me! Once the Captain realized that I had been there and witnessed the entire event, he immediately accused me. "Look what you have done. You killed him."

"Are you joking?" I snapped back at him. "I just saw everything. I saw you push him down the open bay door. You are not going to blame this on me. Are you bloody crazy?"

But that is exactly what the Captain did. He lied. He fabricated a story that made it look like I had been the one who had killed him in a fight. Nobody believed him. But he was the Captain, and on the seas, his word was law. The Captain court-martialed me at sea, and led a bogus investigation against me. He hated me. Unlike him, I was well liked by the crew, which only fueled his ire. Since he was the judge, jury and executioner, I was found guilty of murder and treason. My sentence was death by hanging, to be executed immediately.

The crew was deeply saddened as the noose was tied to the highest pole and was lowered around my neck. The Captain laughed as he cut the rope. My body catapulted into the air and hung swinging in the wind. I did not die instantly. It took a few horrific minutes before I finally passed.

Although I was not aware of it at the time of the regression, I would later discover this particular life's fascinating connection.

It was after this final regression with Rev. Celeste, when I remembered an earlier session I previously had with the gifted intuitive Lille O'Brien. During her throat chakra channeling class, she was the first to tell me of this significant past life and the infamous connection. You see the late American author Herman Melville had learned of this tragic life and had loosely based his best selling classic novel, *Billy Budd* upon it.

After Rev. Celeste, several other psychics would also tell me of this same lifetime and confirmed the same story. When I finally read *Billy Budd*, I cried terribly. I had many painful flashbacks to the horror I had endured in that short, but pivotal lifetime. The infamy of this life lives on.

In those past life regression hypnosis sessions, I learned that I have a huge need to speak the truth. I especially need to be heard, even when it is not popular. In some wonderfully intense, liberating lifetimes my speaking-up meant freedom. But on the flipside, there were a number of past lives where I had been killed or disgraced for speaking up. These memories had subconsciously remained in my energy field. The deep-rooted fear that this might happen again had been clamping down on my throat just like a hangman's noose. With my throat muscles clenched, it had not been very easy to speak my mind, or to speak at all, for that matter. In a sense, my subconscious was trying to insulate me from the same possible outcome that had occurred before, when revealing my true feelings about something. My subconscious was trying to protect me from bringing about another violent, gruesome death, which seemed to be the usual result of not going along with the status quo.

It was obvious where the energetic patterns of my stutter had originated. Now I needed a way to transform and heal these disjointed patterns and finally get over it. The way I was able to transform those stifled energy patterns was by changing the outcome. Under hypnosis, I simply reinvented the endings of those lives. Instead of death by hanging, I saw myself live happily to a ripe old age. The violence had been transformed to a positive, long, and loving life. This helped expose the darkness to the light of unconditional love, which in turn cleared those blockages from my soul, as well as the throat chakra of my physical body.

Almost sixteen years of stuttering had come to an end, virtually overnight. The elephant was now off my back. I had been freed from the hangman's noose once and for all. With that, the nervousness was gone. Words now flowed from my mouth, free as a bird. I was no longer embarrassed or fearful to speak my mind. My big mouth has not shut up since.

PAIN IN THE NECK

Several years ago, I had severe pains running up and down my neck, shoulders and back. I went to a neurologist and had an MRI performed. The MRI showed that I had a double herniated disc in my cervical vertebrae. Without missing a beat, the doctor informed me that I would need to come back to schedule for surgery. He insisted that surgery was my only option. I had a sour feeling in my stomach. Every time I get this sour feeling, I know it is a signal telling me that something is not right. I listened to my higher self instead of the doctor. I had visions of myself with a chiropractor and a massage therapist. I asked the doctor about those options.

He snarled at me, "Don't be ridiculous. Those are only temporary fixes!"

It is my body. I listen to what my body tells me first. I asked the doctor to explain the x-rays, and to show me where the problem existed. He showed me on the x-rays that the fourth and sixth discs in the neck had both been herniated, and the fifth disc had been sublimated. I asked him to demonstrate on the intern exactly where the discs were located.

"Why, you think you can heal yourself?" He sarcastically quipped.

"Absolutely," I snapped back at him.

He wished me luck and scheduled my follow-up for one year later.

During that year, I found two amazing chiropractors and a massage therapist who were all open to my holistic, alternative energy medicine as accompaniment to their treatments. They were already familiar with me and knew the kind of work I did. I explained that I wanted to achieve a complete healing and I needed their help with this transformation. Before they would work on me, I would perform reiki on the office, as well as on them. I asked them to visualize a chlorophyll green healing light all around my body. Then I asked them to imagine my discs healing and regenerating. During my actual treatments, I would be channeling reiki. They were all excited about it.

I had three sessions a week for the next year. Slowly but surely, my discs began to regenerate. The constant pain was gradually decreasing. At home, I gave myself additional reiki treatments daily. I actually talked to my herniated discs, telling them how I loved them and that we would heal back together as a whole. Consistency was crucial. In a short time, my neck started to feel much better.

One year passed and I went to my follow up visit with the Neurologist. He greeted me sarcastically.

"I thought you were going to heal yourself. I knew you would be back. Glad to see you finally came to your senses and forgot about that alternative treatment nonsense. Anybody can hang up a shingle and claim to be able to heal. But how many have actually gone to medical school or even finished high school for that matter."

I told him, my neck felt great.

"Oh really." he scoffed. "Lets first take some tests and then we will see about that."

He wanted me to take that wretched electrode test again, where they shoot electrodes that course throughout your body. During this procedure the pain coud be almost unbearable at times.

On my initial visit, the doctor had performed this test with his intern's assistance. As the electrodes were surging through my body, this unfeeling, cold-hearted intern kept asking the doctor questions, instead of completing the test first. He had argued with the doctor, and, just to prove a point, had proceeded to send the electrodes several more unnecessary times throughout my body. It hurt like hell. I had enough of being a test dummy for this desensitized medical numbnut. I pushed him away and pulled the probes off. I had then ordered the intern out of the room. My doctor had never asked my permission for the intern to have been there in the first place.

As a patient, you have every right to say who can and cannot be present during your exams. This intern had absolutely no compassion or feeling whatsoever about me as a patient, or as a human being. It hadn't mattered to him, that his obsequious questioning had been causing me extreme pain unnecessarily. I had refused to allow myself to be a pincushion or an anatomy cadaver for this fool. Neither should you. If something does not feel right, and your solar plexus tells you NO, listen to your solar plexus. Remember, it's your body and you should never feel intimidated or afraid to speak up for yourself.

The doctor remembered what had happened a year before when I had first taken the test.

"No interns for you," he said. "You hurt his feelings."

Okay. Well, if his intern had tried poking me some more, I would have wanted to hurt more than his feelings. Lol.

The doctor performed the tests again. This time, it showed that there was absolutely nothing wrong with my neck. Both discs were no longer herniated. As a matter of fact, the tests and MRI showed no signs of any disc problems at all. The doctor was dumbfounded. He had me retake all the tests again just to be sure. When the results came back, it was the same. They showed my body had no signs of any prior or current disc problems. The doctor didn't know how I had accomplished this, but the herniated and sublimated discs had realigned and were perfect once again.

If I had listened, I could have had an unnecessary operation. This may not always be the case for everybody, but a healing had taken place for me. I had aligned with Spirit and co-healed myself. This was when I was in my early thirties and, thankfully, not a single neck problem has recurred. Keep in mind doctors are not always right. Go with your gut.

My grandfather was a perfect example of how someone's strong will and soul can overcome just about anything. My grandfather, Papa Irving was an extremely upbeat, joyfully charismatic man. He reveled in singing and dancing at any opportunity. He was an extremely talented craftsman, who used to make and cut dress patterns. As he toiled away, hard at work, he always sang or whistled. He was the favorite of his grandchildren. He used to tell us about the southern supermarket chain called Piggly Wiggly. It had a big oinking pig, whose eyes would light up as you entered the store. As he told the tale, he had an extraordinary ability to wiggle his ears. We never tired of asking him to wiggle those ears. As I write this, he comes to me still wiggling his ears.

When he was in his early 70's, his eyesight deteriorated and he eventually became partially blind. One day, as he was crossing the street independently, as he always did, a car struck him. Papa Irving was hurled into the air and smacked down onto the pavement. He was rushed to the hospital, where he lay dying. Doctors told us, he had lost 3/4 of the blood in his body. He had also suffered many broken bones and ribs.

This elderly man's prognosis was less than a twenty percent chance of survival. The doctors told my family they should think about making the final arrangements. The doctors had written him off. There was just one thing they had forgotten to add into the equation: my grandpa had the will and constitution of a strong and stubborn ox. He was not going anywhere. Grandpop wanted to live. He beat the odds and recovered to live another sixteen plus years.

It is possible for a living being's will to overcome almost anything. The doctors had Grandpa ready for the dirt nap. But his strong will to live pulled him through against such insurmountable odds. It earned him the label of The Miracle Man. Sometimes you need to think outside the box. You can't give up on yourself or you might well be wrenched away prematurely. Your Spirit can help lift you above when your life feels or appears to be hopeless.

The medical and religious communities are not God. We as living beings of this planet, all have divineness running through our veins. The medical community provides us with incredible advancements to achieving our optimal health. But just because someone has an M.D. on his license plate, this does not mean his or her word is an indisputable fact or law. As human beings, we are all susceptible to mistakes. Listen to your higher self and you will know what feel right for you and what does not.

DR. QUACK

These days, it seems the medical community has another designer disorder diagnosis every other week. Doesn't it seem like they are coming out as frequently as the fashion industry comes out with another designer perfume? Not all children have ADD. Not all adults have chronic fatigue syndrome. Granted there are many cases where this diagnosis is legitimate. But I'm sorry, not every patient who seeks help from doctors suffers from one of these disorders.

Anti-depressants are extremely helpful in treating biological, chemical and emotional imbalances. When prescribed and carefully managed, they have amazing results. But they should not be dispensed like aspirin. Not everyone needs to take everything a doctor tries to prescribe for him or her either. Listen to your higher self and you will know what feels right and wrong. For some doctors, medications have become a quick fix, a band-aid they use, instead of actually trying to help cure the condition.

My personal belief is that everybody should go into some form of counseling or therapy at some point in his or her life. All therapists are required to enter into therapy as part of their certification. I for one am no exception. My problem was, and still is, the fact that the medical and psychological communities don't have a strong regard for psychics or mediums. Nor any of the other alternative healing practices outside the box.

Without meaning to generalize, the medical community seems a bit too quick to hand you a handful of prescriptions, label you and be done with the whole matter. Of course, there are numerous doctors who still practice medicine with compassion. But these fabulous, old school doctors are starting to become more rare. This is a very disturbing trend. To me it almost seems like these pharmaceutically-geared medical schools are vicious vampires, draining the humanity and compassion out of their new medical students. Isn't it scary that most of us will have to entrust our very lives into the cold hands of these emotionless Stepford medical drones?

Keep in mind, this is not always the case. It is not the entire medical community that falls into the mold of the Stepford medical drone. I'm simply making an observation about a growing trend. I for one, can tell you that all of my doctors are wonderful, compassionate souls. They actually treat their patients in the same manner that they would want their loved ones or themselves to be treated when seeking medical care. But I have to admit, it did take going through quite a few of the Stepford medical drones, before Spirit led me to my current doctors. You have to do your homework, but it is well worth the effort.

In the psychiatric community, there is a clear-cut difference between psychiatrists and the psychologists, therapists, counselors, and social workers. Obviously psychiatrists went to medical school and can prescribe medicine. But many psychiatrists are no longer therapy-oriented. The medical school drones are more likely to label you, hand out a stack of prescriptions and send you on your way. Many psychiatrists are now starting to lean more toward neutralizing or numbing the symptomatic problems. On the other hand psychologists, therapists, counselors and social workers are more therapy based toward actually helping the patient understand his or her problems. Medications can be a very good thing. But, they need to be combined with a therapy-based program. They will assist you with acquiring the necessary tools, the ones required to put you on the road to recovery.

With the first psychiatrist I found, I had a very bad experience. I felt no connection with him at all. Fortunately, I later found Dr Bodi, an excellent psychiatrist with the right balance and energy who actually understood me. For Dr Bodi, being a psychic didn't mean that I was delusional and needed to be institutionalized. He practices with compassion and intuitiveness.

Let me tell you first hand of my unfortunate personal experiences with a horrible quack, before I finally found the right fit. Being a psychic isn't the easiest egg in the basket. After long thought, I made a conscious decision to enter into therapy. A good friend at the time noticed I was in a great deal of torment. So he made me an appointment with his own psychiatrist, whom I shall call Dr. Central Park Quack or Dr. Quack for short.

Dr. Quack was well respected in his field. On my initial visit, Dr. Quack asked what had brought me to see him. I explained that I am a psychic, an intuitive, a medium and a spiritual healer. I could communicate with the living, as well as communicate with those in Spirit. But that was not my problem. I went on to tell him what was troubling me at the time.

He couldn't move past the psychic part. His hand kept writing. I thought his hand was going to break. Each time I would talk about the real problems that had led me to his office, he would give me a half smile. He would then immediately go right back to the part about me being a psychic. I kept telling him that being psychic was not my problem. Dealing with the living was my problem.

He asked me to demonstrate my psychic abilities. He asked me to just humor him a little. I had no problem with this, as long as it was going to help move the whole thing along. I immediately tapped into an older female spirit, his late mother. She was a sweet lady who still loved wearing her moth eaten powder blue sweater and her perfume was a strong Ombre' Rose. I told him some other details, which made him chuckle.

Dr. Quack smiled as I continued reading for him. When I was finished, he complimented me on my accuracy. The he proceeded to ask me if I had a few weeks to check into a facility, so that I could be properly observed and examined. In plain English, he thought I was freakin out of my mind and wanted to commit me on the spot. What? Absolutely not!

He went on to give me a preliminary diagnosis: Borderline Manic-

Depressive, with Severe Hallucinatory Disorder and possible Acute Schizophrenia. He handed me a stack of prescriptions, almost the highest of doses, and scheduled appointments for me with one of his therapists. By the time it was over, I had been diagnosed with several labels, all stemming from just telling him that I was psychic. He lived in a cut-and-dry world. For him, just my saying that I was psychic was the same thing as declaring myself cuckoo for cocoa puffs.

Since Dr. Quack was well recognized, I reluctantly filled all the prescriptions and went to his therapist for a couple of months. The meds he had prescribed literally numbed me of almost all emotions and feelings. I felt like I was a robotic vegetable. My family and friends all told me that I was just not acting like myself. They said I looked like a walking zombie.

The therapist he had recommended spent most of the sessions trying to explore my need to claim I had psychic communications. She asked how long I had these hallucinations. No matter what I discussed, every single time the conversation was steered back to my being a psychic. She felt that I had Schizoid Hallucinations and a God-Like Complex. Shortly thereafter, I realized this therapy was leading me nowhere. I told her that I was extremely disappointed by my sessions with her as well as those with Dr. Quack. I felt I was being over medicated and was not comfortable with that. She insisted that my dosage should be elevated to the maximum legal level. That was the final straw!

I told her this was nothing but a crock of bull. This so called therapy that she practiced was nothing short of brain washing nonsense. She and Dr.Quack were absolutely ill prepared to help me in any way. In fact, I felt worse now than I had felt before I had first come there. I explained to her for the 100th time, being psychic and communicating with dead people was not my problem. Having to deal with the living was.

I then gave her a fierce impromptu reading. I called her out on most of the extreme details of her life. I spewed names, dates, places, everything. I could see that she was shocked. I was dead-on and she knew it. This went completely against everything she had been taught in school and everything that the medical community readily accepted.

When I left the office her mouth was wide open. Dr. Quack contacted me once again. He insisted that I was severely disturbed and needed voluntary reevaluation. I told him of my extreme displeasure with his practice. He had been of no service to me. He had actually done me more of a disservice. I went on to call him a quack and I told him that I would report him. He laughed and told me I'd be back.

I began the procedure of filing a complaint against Dr. Quack. I was interviewed. I told them of the disservice I had been given. It was evident that my complaint would not be taken seriously. I was disregarded as disgruntled and unstable. My complaint was dismissed and never filed. It had been virtually ignored.

DR. DEVA ... AT LAST

Just remember, one apple doesn't spoil the whole bunch. Just because I had encountered a bad psychiatrist and a useless therapist, didn't mean that all psychiatrists and therapists were bad. That would be ridiculous. Years later, right after 9/11, I decided to actively pursue finding the right therapist once and for all.

I wrote down on a piece of paper exactly what I was looking for in a therapist. I wanted to make sure that this time we would have a better relationship. I preferred a female, who was gay friendly. She had to believe that being gay is not a choice, but a matter of birth. Just like we are born with ten fingers and ten toes, our sexuality is something that is innate. She had to at least be psychic friendly and have some knowledge of the intuitive world. I wanted a therapist who actually understood and embraced the extraordinary sense perceptions of the psychic world. She had to believe that being intuitive was a gift and not a matter of schizophrenic episodes. It would be ideal if she also had the gift herself. That would be a perfect match. Someone with those qualifications would be able to understand what was going on with me and know how to assist me better. I actively sent my request out to the universe and left the rest up to Spirit.

One day my dear friend, a fellow minister from the Interfaith Seminary, called me. She herself was a very compassionate psychologist in her own right. She had thought of a fellow therapist who would be a perfect match for me. Chills ran up and down my spine when I heard about her. Unlike Dr. Quack, I could just feel that this would be the right person for me. I called Dr. Deva right away. In the few minutes we spoke on the phone, I experienced an instant connection. I believed that I had finally found the therapist I had been seeking. She had all of my specifications: a female psychologist, gay friendly, and had a keen intuitive psychic gift she kept on the down low.

At last my search was over. There was instantaneous mutual respect between us. I was thrilled to finally find an intuitive psychologist. She was excited about the possibilities our sessions would present for her to finally be able to be forth coming with her intuitive gift. I was going to be her first of many intuitive clients. Now this additional element would become part of her practice with anyone who was actively pursuing intuitive input.

Since beginning therapy with Dr. Deva, we have done some amazing work together. It was such a breath of fresh air to finally be with a therapist who embraced my gift, instead of crucifying me for it. Dr. Deva was exactly what I needed. What I had really been looking for was someone who could be the kind of healer for me that I had always been for others. During almost twenty-five years as an intuitive therapist, I have successfully combined the psychic element with psychotherapy, hypnosis, reiki, numerology and a variety of other alternative spiritual healing practices. Just like I conduct sessions as a healer, Dr. Deva incorporates intuition with many profound psychotherapy practices. Dr. Deva was just what the doctor had ordered.

With me, when a client is not forthcoming about certain things, I am able to intuitively tap into their whole being. I can help unlock areas that they have blocked off from themselves. In many instances, I can assist with the details provided by the client's deceased loved ones, guardians, guides, angels and devas. Instead of just hearing about their difficulties, I can actually experience them as well. Countless times, many of us just don't know how to talk about a troubling issue. It is just not that easy to be able to express it clearly. We often have huge mental blocks about extremely traumatic episodes. I can assist by tapping into the block. I can help my client to see and feel what their unconscious is holding back from them. I can help them to see what they can't see for themselves.

Dr. Deva has been able to tap into my own blocks stemming from this lifetime, as well as prior lifetimes, where certain problems first arose. This has sped up the healing process considerably.

For quite a long time, I have been able to directly relate to lost spirits who have come to me. Because most people can't even see them, they walk around feeling invisible. They are not recognized by anyone, until they come across somebody like myself. Not only can I see them, but also capable of assisting in their healing. I can counsel them, even though they no longer reside in a physical body. I too, felt similar feelings. The world had been unable to see me for who I was. With Dr. Deva, I could be seen, heard and assisted with my own healing. To be able to find someone who could be as strong a therapist and intuitive to me, as I am to my clients, has been a sheer blessing.

After the horrific trauma I experienced as a 9/11 survivor, I don't know what I would have done without Dr. Deva. 9/11 really rattled my cage, like it had never been rattled before. I was able to be an excellent intuitive, therapist, medium, and healer for my clients and friends after 9/11. Not to mention all the poor lost spirits seeking my help. But I found it too overwhelming to help myself with certain personal issues, as well as my issues pertaining to 9/11. That is where Dr. Deva came through.

Sessions with her were very instrumental in grounding me. She helped me to bridge the insurmountable gap of living in both the spiritual world and our physical world.

Dr. Deva was able to tap into my entire being's past, present and future. She was then able to see where I was energetically, mentally, emotionally and physically. She could see where I was fractured and where I was complete. She helped me to regroup my whole being and synthesize the fractured parts of my psyche and soul. Her work has played an integral part in putting my focus back on track in all areas of my life, especially in writing this book. I suspect our sessions have been as therapeutic for her as they were for myself.

Dr. Deva's work is truly trailblazing.

In recent years, I have also been led to a wonderful psychiatrist, Dr Bodi. Dr Bodi himself is not psychic, but is open to the intuitive gift, as well as different forms of meditation. He is a very compassionate man who is not averse to thinking outside of the box. He has respect for my work and has also been instrumental in my internal and external biochemistry balancing. What a difference the right doctors can make!!!

LILLE O'BRIEN: AWAKENING MY HEALER ROOTS

Lille O'Brien is an incredibly talented woman with an extraordinary, special gift. She became my first teacher in the realm of intricate healing energies. She taught me how to channel, to astral travel, and to communicate and work with higher energy beings. She taught me about distinct energy levels, known as kingdoms, and how to work with higher beings on each level.

There had always been many different things that I was able to do, but could never quite explain what I was doing. Lille helped me clarify and codify my methods, and put names on my techniques. She recognized my abilities as a natural channeler and healer, as well as my knack for numerology and suggested I take her numerology and reiki workshops.

Lille's approach to the healing arts was very no-nonsense. She has a wonderfully compassionate heart and the voice of an angel. Her classes were very much like a wonderfully-blessed spiritual boot camp. Her work is eons ahead of its time. Lille is a woman of complete, upfront honesty. How truly refreshing!

I was already established in my practice as a professional intuitive consultant and healer, when I decided to go for some formalized training. Of the many so-called intuitive healers I had met, some were incredibly gifted. But I had also come across more flakes than a snowstorm. I have always believed that when the student is ready, the teacher appears.

I prayed out loud to Spirit, "Please lead me to the right person to help me harness and make sense of my gifts."

I was an accurate, effective intuitive healer. But I just knew that there was so much I could learn, or shall I say re-learn. I was thirsty for knowledge. I had read stacks of books. Now I needed the personal instructions of a physical human being. This was something the pages in a book could never give me. I decided to pick up a local new-age newspaper and glanced through the classifieds. As I flicked through the pages, something caught my attention. I saw this small, four-line advertisement. It started glowing like the North Star. As I ran my fingers over the advertisement, I experienced rushes of energy pulsate through my hand. This was enough of a sign for me. I knew I had to call this woman. Spirit had made this all perfectly clear.

I dialed the number and the answering machine picked up. The voice of an angel began speaking and I was immediately captivated. Lille called me back and she told me about her introductory seven-chakra class starting soon. I signed up on the spot. I have always listened to my higher self. Your higher self will tell you if somebody is right or wrong for you in every situation. My higher self didn't beat around the bush this time. I had asked for a formal teacher of energy medicine and Lille O'Brien was their answer.

Whenever you entered Lille's apartment, it felt like you were entering into another dimension, outside of time and space, as we know it. The energy was incredibly comforting. It felt as safe and secure as a mother's womb. There were always several wonderful higher beings, spirits and angels present. Just sitting in her apartment was enough to send you into a state of blissful joy! There was never a time when I entered Lille's apartment, when I wasn't able to quickly go into a deep meditative transcendental state. Once experienced, the joys of Lille's apartment were very hard to leave. Even the spirit of her late, beloved dog would come back for a visit. He was a very loving, playful spirit and a delight to encounter.

Let me say this very clearly. If you ever have the opportunity to book a private session or attend classes with the incredible Lille O'Brien—run, don't walk—to sign up! She has a heart of gold, a New Yorker's edge and is honest as the day is long. She can see bullshit a mile away and she will calmly call you on it. Plus you will thank her for doing so. When I came to Lille, I was still somewhat of a rookie. She helped transform me into a solid professional.

The first set of classes I took with Lille was a series of seven lessons pertaining to the seven chakras. Each class taught you how to tune into one of the chakras. You learned how to sense each of them and to clear any blockages that you or your client might have in that particular chakra.

Once I was comfortable working with the chakras, I was ready for her on-going advanced group. In this group, the energy work was very intricate. She guided us to actively make energetic connections with the higher energy realms and with the many higher beings. She helped teach us how to astral travel out of our bodies to the plane of the higher light beings. Once we were comfortable traveling to the City of Lights, Lille introduced and initiated us to the energy kingdom of the four Archangels and other high level energy beings. It is here, interacting and connecting energetically with the four Archangels, that absolute transformational healing can take place.

Granted, I already had many gifts at my disposal. But Lille was the person who actually taught me about spiritual and energetic tools and how to use them. She guided me through the integration of my physical and higher self. She helped me to understand the intricate mechanisms of energy medicine and the chakra system.

Before Lille, I had been able to communicate with spirits and angels. I was already well suited to assist in healings. But, I had no idea how I did what I did, nor how to control or strengthen my healing capabilities. It had been like driving from one destination to another, without a map. Lille taught me how to become my own GPS system. Once I learned how to astral travel, I could go anywhere and connect to anyone or anything. Through Lille, I gained structure, which allowed me to take my work to the next level. I have incorporated Lille 's meditation techniques into many of my guided meditations and channeling sessions. I gladly give credit, where credit is due. Lille was an inspiration.

It was with Lille that I studied reiki and was attuned as a reikimaster. She helped explain to me what I had been doing my whole life. In a sense, she handed me an energetic instruction manual. She is just a dynamo.

As I previously mentioned earlier, in her throat chakra channeling class, Lille was the very first intuitive to tap into one of my past lives. It was this lifetime, in which I had been the real-life person upon whom Herman Melville loosely based his literary classic, *Billy Budd* on. In trance, Lille told me some details about that past life. Unknowingly, I further explored this previous lifetime through a later past regression I had with Rev. Celeste. During this regression, I could re-visualize and experience that infamous life Lille had brought to my attention, once again very clearly.

Lillie's advanced classes were a weekly group session in which we collectively traveled together to the different corners of various universes. In her advanced class, I met some very incredible people who are still my friends. It was a blessing to have been able to share this experience with such spiritually evolved souls. My girlfriend Marie is wonderfully strong, yet very compassionate. She reminds me of one of the fiercely strong, amazon women whom you would expect to be living on Paradise Island with Wonder Woman. Another girlfriend, Raven, is also a gifted healer. She is like a breath of fresh air. Raven has performed reiki along side Dr. Oz of Columbia Presbyterian during several of his open-heart surgeries. Lille really attracted some of the most gifted souls around. Our group was amazing and I loved every minute of it.

In all the years I have done spirit energy work, I have never met a person as humble as Lille O'Brien. I can honestly say Lille helped me achieve my spiritual voice. I am ever so thankful this wonderfully gifted healer entered my life. She gave me direction when I was not steady on my intuitive healer's feet. As I have said before, she is a healer's healer. Through her training, I can now proudly say I too am now considered a healer's healer.

Eventually the time had come for me to move on. This little birdie was now ready to leave the nest. I could now fly through a hailstorm unscathed. I could now tap into the center core of this hailstorm, clear its disruptive energetic patterns and transform the hail into a rainbow of Ultra-Violet light of unconditional love of the highest of forms. I was now able to achieve this all due to the guidance of the one and only Lille O'Brien.

H (really now) was for healing.

SECTION 3
SESSION SECRETS

PSYCHIC 101

Looking at your life from a psychic point of view can lead to many twists and turns. The road can lead you to the deepest core of your being. By revealing these experiences and energetic patterns that have shaped and created you, it will shed light onto who you truly are.

In many cases, the psychic gene doesn't fall far from the family tree. It might be your parent, grandparent, aunt, uncle, your butternut squash… Whoever. But I can assure you, somewhere in your bloodline, one of your relatives has the heightened antennae and receives messages as a channel between our physical world and the world of Spirit. My dad for instance doesn't attest to having any extrasensory abilities, or even understand much of the topic himself. But, he will always talk about listening to his gut instinct. As he has said numerous times every time he goes against his gut instinct, things have always gone awry. My grandma used to call it her common sense. Her father, my great grandfather not only believed in reincarnation, but also always led his life by his instincts. He emigrated from Poland with barely the clothes on his back. He followed his intuition and eventually went on to become an extremely successful businessman. Call it what you will. Your gut instinct, strong commonsense, street smarts, etc. Most people are not comfortable with the psychic label. I can easily understand.

We are all intuitive and psychic to a certain degree. It's just some like myself have a higher evolved antenna. With meditation, dedication, and the mastering of how to allow yourself to go completely blank, everybody can strengthen their intuitive abilities enormously. Follow many of the mediations I have written throughout this book and your own inner antenna will be strengthened considerably.

The word psychic is a name, adjective and verb, which over the years has taken on a negative connotation. When you hear the word psychic, a number of derogatory images come to mind: a corrupted gypsy fortune teller, a swindler con-artist, an air-headed flake whose head is so far in the clouds that reality is a far distant place for them. Maybe some 800 pound lady who eats only sticks and berries and stares into crystal balls, etc. I'm sure we all have our own, not so pretty picture. Hollywood's portrayal certainly hasn't helped any. Granted there are definitely some deceptive people out there who do not have your best interests. But there are also many genuine individuals who have truly remarkable gifts. Just because there are unscrupulous ones, doesn't mean that all psychics or new-agers are charlatans. There are definite ways to scope out these barnacles and prevent yourself from being duped by their deceptive money-grubbing schemes.

(1) If the so-called practitioners tell you that unless you pay them a great deal of money something quite horrible will happen, they are likely running a

scam. All curses, evil spells, hexes, vexes, the boogieman and what ever other garbage they are trying to scare you into giving them all of your money and energy are all utterly powerless and quite simply bullshit! As being a beacon of light, all negative diversities have absolutely no power or control over you, unless you allow it. As long as you know light energy is always stronger over the darker energies, it can never harm you or even come near you.

Simply visualize a circle of white light all around you and ask for only the highest of lights, those that come to you in the path of Spirit/God, for the highest of good, are allowed to come near you. Those that are dark and wish you harm, gently but respectfully leave at once...

(2) Beware of a person who is being extremely judgmental with you. Particularly with your gender, color, sexual orientation, religion, body shape, etc. They are usually preaching that their way is the only way. You are a sinner and are doomed unless you listen and obey their every word. Walk away immediately. This type of person may indeed have some form of the gift. But their own holier-than-thou righteousness and grandiose, megalomaniac ego is going to block them from a pure message. They can only speak from their own insecure need for superiority. Turn away and just leave their madness at once. Spirit does not discriminate. As long as you are of the light, all is welcome.

(3) If a person is insisting you must convert to their religious/ spiritual practices, leave immediately. He or she is nothing more than a religious nut trying to actively shove their beliefs down your throat. God's/Spirit's way doesn't have to force. It should come to you as natural as breathing oxygen.

(4) If the person or group claims to be from another planet, galaxy or universe, I wouldn't support them. By some remote chance this may be true. Many of our souls in very early past lives, may in fact have originated from someplace other than earth. But then this person also might be a few crackers short of a stack and I wouldn't want to be the one to find out.

WHAT GOES ON IN ONE OF MY SESSIONS

Just as in the medical community, some doctors are general practitioners and others specialize according to their expertise. I do the same. When I first starting doing sessions, most people would come to me for my matchmaking/love counseling talents.

The answer to many relationship questions is a need to look inward. To give ourselves the unconditional love and passion, we think only someone else can give us. People are magnets. We attract whatever we are sending out. When we are confused or distracted, that is what comes back to us. If we send out a nasty, shady vibe, it will certainly come back when least expected. If we send out powerful positive energy, we will definitely receive this back. Don't sit at home waiting, looking at the calendar thinking, "When is this going to happen?" Keep in mind, we are going by Spirit's time, not our own. Be careful, and think before speaking. Always be as clear as possible. The more crisp the focus in the messages we send out as well as the clarity of the language we use, the more precise the energy will be that comes back.

After my own experience with past-life regression hypnosis, I decided to become a certified hypnotherapist, and began regularly incorporating hypnosis into my practice. Over the years I have developed my own special form of hypnosis and regression therapy. I serve as the conduit for Spirit to give very specific, soul-path advice. Those who pay attention and follow the advice, have the opportunity to dissolve many of the blocks that are impeding their progress. Over the years, my practice has evolved to include intensive, heavy-duty healing. Everyone who comes for a reading, also gets a deep, soul-elixir session.

When someone comes to me for intuitive therapy, there are usually one or two specific issues the client wants to work on. I always ask for the exact name and date on your birth certificate. I ask for you to send me a list of questions. To be quite honest, I do not even look at them until maybe an hour before the session. It's not like I am going to Google your answers. Lol. When you write down your questions to paper, it forces you to focus more on the nature of the questions. This actually moves this energy from your thoughts into the physical, allowing fruition to your questions.

In preparations for a session, I will meditate, open myself up and begin channeling. The questions you send help me to fine tune the frequencies of the energy coming to me. In many ways, it's similar to radio stations. Each radio station has its own frequencies and different messages. Each question vibrates to its own with the energetic patterns.

I focus my visions to help discover where pertinent issues first appeared physically, as well as energetically. I begin working in the present lifetime. In order to feel the true essence of what is happening, I allow myself to experience in my own body, the very same problems that the client is undergoing. I need to feel what it's like inside their skin, how they are actually experiencing things. It is important for me to truly understand how they are processing their feelings. I make these feelings my own for a short period of time.

I ask Spirit to take me to the origins of these disturbing energetic patterns. I ask to return to the past life where they first manifested. This way, I can know from whence they first arose. Next, I experience that lifetime myself in order to understand how a particular incident or series of incidents affected that particular lifetime. I then follow the energetic patterns to see how those incidents are subsequently responsible for the blockages and problems experienced in this current life.

I always ask for assistance from my guardians, spirit guides, angels and devas, as well those of my client to help remove and release whatever can be released. It is then up to the person, to allow the blockages to be lifted. I am able to create an environment that is conducive for healing and transformation. But it is up to each individual to co-create his or her own new life. I can assist in their healing, but they are truly the only ones who can allow it to happen.

LILITH

Prenatal energy work has inadvertently become one of my specialties. By working energetically with pregnant women, I am able to link the spirits of the unborn children up with the mothers before the births.

Lilith is a friend of mine. It was while giving Lilith a reiki session while she was carrying her daughter MJ, that I first worked on a pregnant woman. There have been many women in her family who have had major issues while giving birth, including some who have died. This created a lot of karmic imbalance. Naturally, Lilith was very anxious about the impending delivery.

Lilith is an excellent massage therapist and a gifted energy worker in her own right. She understands all the energy terminology, but it doesn't make her resistance any easier to overcome. In fact, with more knowledge comes more complicated responsibility. I was prepared for it all.

That first session with Lilith was amazing. I was able to tap into the spirit of her unborn baby MJ and communicate with her. I was able to see the unborn child's energy patterns. I was able to tell that MJ was going to be an extremely bright, creative individual. MJ would have a unique dynamic about her that will bring her success in whatever paths she will choose in her life.

MJ would have a very magnetic personality. Yes, I was even able to tap into an unborn child's personality. After all, our personality, as well many aspects of ourselves, are carried along with each lifetime we experience here in our physical world.

I could see MJ had a star-like quality. Throughout her life, she will draw major attention from others. If and when she puts her undivided focus towards a specific direction or goal, MJ will surely obtain it. She was an old soul, who would be almost grown up by the time she was born. I felt an immediate bond with her. She reminded me a lot of myself. MJ was going to be a force to be reckoned with. She already had taught me quite a few things and she wasn't even born yet.

When MJ was born, she was a very happy baby. She was well adjusted, emotionally, mentally, physically and spiritually. When I saw MJ for the first time, she recognized her Uncle H instantly.

I also worked even more extensively with Lilith during her second pregnancy with her son David. In these sessions together, I would energetically create a specially channeled healing space in the higher realms for her. It is in this wonderful space, where you can be at one with your higher self and achieve true inner peace. I would channel in many high-energy healing lights such as St Germaine, Padre Pio, the eternal mother Gaia and Jesus. These amazing beings are the spiritual lights of love, life and the transformations of misaligned energies to unconditional love in the highest of forms. It was here in this sacred space, where I energetically connected Lilith and the unborn David with all of these special high-energy beings.

Within this space, David could intuitively show me the past life connections he previously had had with his mother. David would also intuitively tell me about the lessons, he would be exploring with his beautiful Mother in this lifetime.

With pre-natal energy sessions, we are able to influence the unborn child's development and energetic patterns, which are still being formed inside the womb. Lilith reminded the soul of her unborn son David of all the wonderful and helpful qualities that he should remember to bring into this lifetime. By reinforcing positive traits while the unborn child is still in the womb, it helps the incoming soul to incorporate those qualities before the amnesia of being born erases the memory of this knowledge. Since babies are still so fresh from the other side, they still have paranormal abilities and they can maintain these abilities if they are encouraged to do so.

Through my assistance, David was able to assure his mother, that he would be helping her with his entire birth transition. She would not be doing this alone. They would be doing it together. Lilith could now feel that she wasn't going to be doing it alone and was ecstatic. This strengthened their bond with each other.

The day before she was to go in for a scheduled C-section, we had a very intensive session. We began talking about the possible complications involved. Whether she should have a spinal or epidural. Adding in the fact that although David, like most babies, had hated the amniocentesis, but had liked the ultra sound.

Then we did a healing meditation. I surrounded Lilith in a cloud of Ultra-Violet light. We gently had the cloud energetically lift her to the temple of the Divine Mother, where she was greeted by the elders: Gaia, Eve, Mary, Kwan Yin, Isis, Hathor, Aphrodite and all the other divine mother figures. A rainbow of crystal light wrapped around Lilith and adhered to her being. This light is like a spiritual epidural, an intravenous drip from the divine. Lilith was given controls—the left thumb and pointer fingers when pressed together would increase the crystal light and take away pain, discomfort, and fears. The right thumb and pointer fingers when pressed together would reduce the light. I told her that the elders would take control of everything and that she should just let go and enjoy the experience. I purposely didn't bring her back down completely from this higher spiritual realm. She was nursed, comforted and supported by the ancestors. She was totally at peace.

Then something very surprising happened, just as I was about to bring Lilith out of the meditation. Her late grandmother, who had died during the birth of Lilith's own mother made an appearance. To be honest, I have never tried to hold back information that I receive. I never deny the presence of a spirit who is dropping by to make an appearance during my sessions. But this time, I wanted to break my own code of ethics. I tried to hold back. I didn't think it would be good for Lilith to have any knowledge of her grandmother's presence. This was much too delicate a time. I was afraid this sudden visitation might send her into a tailspin. I didn't want to create the least bit of excitement, especially since she would be giving birth the next day. The whole experience of giving birth was already traumatic enough for her.

However, her Grandmother's spirit was extremely forceful. She was not about to have some human telephone pole stand between herself, her beautiful granddaughter, and the precious experience of the birth of her dynamic great grandson. She didn't even give me a choice in the matter. She practically took control of my speech and I was forced to tell Lilith of her appearance.

As soon as I mentioned her grandmother, Lilith's energy sank like a stone. I explained that Lilith's Grandmother was there to ask for forgiveness for the pain that her death during childbirth had caused all her loved ones. Lilith always had the fear in the back of her mind. Maybe the childbirth death syndrome had skipped a generation, and that her fate would be the same as her grandmother's. The impending C-section and the presence of her grandmother brought everything to a head. But Grandmother was there to lighten Lilith's load and to reassure her that she was not destined to suffer the same fate. Grandmother was there to help to take care of her great grandson. As a result, Lilith overcame her fears and gave birth to David, a beautiful, healthy boy.

Children who have had prenatal energetic work seem to be extremely well adjusted. They have the most incredibly adult dispositions. The energy work really seems to help propel the children and give them that special edge that we all wish we had while growing up.

This work excites me to no end. Just imagine being coached on what special traits to bring into this life! Wow!! Working with pre-natal feels so completely natural for me. It has become a very strong component of my healing practice.

ALICE: THROUGH THE LOOKING GLASS

I met Alice when she was still in high school. We happened to have been standing next to each other on line for The Black Crowes rock concert tickets. We started talking and had many things in common. Our kinship was instant. I became her wild big brother who she could come talk to about anything and everything. I was there to guide her through her transition from a teenager to a full-fledged woman.

Alice had come from a family of museum quality artists. Her mother easily is the greatest living painter I have ever seen and have had the privilege of sitting for. Alice is an exceptionally talented artist in her own right. Her photography skills are extraordinary. The images and new points of view she captured through her camera lenses, undeniably forced you to look at her subjects in another fascinating new way. Looking at Alice's photos allowed you to see another aspect of life. One that was right in front of your face. But something you never bothered paying attention to.

From teenage through adulthood, Alice had her share of empty ended relationships where the prospect was over before it started. Since her high school graduation, there was very little time when she was not involved in some kind of relationship.

There was a part of her that was afraid of being alone by herself. Like most of us, there was a part of Alice that was fractured. This energetic fracture occurred during her childhood and she never had the chance to fully address and heal from it. This caused her strong distrust and non-belief in God or any religious faction. She was even unsure if there was even any higher energy force or realms beyond the physical world that we lived in.

In entering into an empty-ended relationship, it allowed Alice to avoid being alone. Being by herself would eventually force her to confront these inner deep seeded insecurities which blocked her from finding true, long love. The benefit of a nowhere relationship also allowed her the freedom to leave without much hesitation or resistance. Especially when the thrill was gone with nothing left but the aches, pains and sorrows of a broken heart. Since all these relationships had no permanence, she could easily block out the possibilities of life existing outside of our physical world. Life could be viewed just like these relationships. It would have a beginning, middle and definite end and that would be it.

On the flip side, from day one Alice knew I had the gift. She completely believed in my abilities. This strongly conflicted with some of her other solemn views. So I always knew when Alice was ready, I would be able reach her.

At one point, she was not involved in a relationship. She was confused about her life's experiences and her place in the scheme of life. She was at a crossroads where her younger disbeliefs no longer served a purpose. Her finite views of the spiritual realms had become antiquated and didn't work for her anymore. She was at the threshold for an epiphany—ready to embrace the possibility that life exists beyond this world that we know. Alice just needed my guidance. She trusted me and felt safe. She knew I would never do anything to harm her. She was a loving soul who was ready to give and receive true love.

I received the call from Alice. She was ready for a session and open to the insights I could provide her. So I set up to meet Alice in Central Park, to be accompanied by her good friend Penelope. Penelope was a wonderfully loving friend whose positive spirituality influenced Alice into broadening some of her finite points of view. Intuitively I knew the glorious nature of Central Park would help create the perfect environment for her spiritual transformation.

And boy was I right!

It was a very triumphant day that I met up with Alice and her friend Penelope in Central Park. I wanted to find the perfect space within this huge outdoor sanctuary. When in doubt, I always let it up to Spirit to guide me to the optimal location spot. So I intuitively opened myself for direction. Spirit took the lead and we followed.

I needed music, but had forgotten to take speakers with me. As Spirit led us up past the bike path, we started to hear tribal drums. A sure sign that we were headed in the right direction. We followed the sound of the drums which led us to a perfect spot, just within earshot. We could immediately smell burning sage and sandalwood incense. A sacred space was being created for us. It was time to open the channel and get to work.

It was the first time that I used my portable table in public in a session, and it worked wonderfully. Spirit takes all the guesswork, paranoia and performance anxiety away whenever I channel. Information flows from me like a babbling brook, and boy, can this brook babble.

Alice was ready to finally deal with some of her issues. She wanted to know why everything was such a struggle for her. She was over the empty relationships. She was ready to open herself up for a real soulmate connection. But she wasn't sure how.

We talked about a friend who had entered her life. He was definitely a magic man. As she described it, at times he would enter her dreams and into her spiritual body, as if she was getting spiritual head (pardon my frankness). In order to be around him, she would be forced into exploring her spiritual self. She could only protect herself if she allowed the Light of Spirit to enter into her life.

I gently guided Alice through a meditation.

HOW TO HOW TO FREE UP PAST KARMA AND RE-NEGOTIATE YOUR LIFE'S
KARMIC LESSONS

Close your eyes and begin by taking three deep breaths. Inhale through
the nose all the way to the diaphragm, your solar plexus. Now slowly exhale
through your mouth.

Allow yourself to imagine there is a circle of Ultra-Violet light, the energy
of unconditional love in the highest of forms. The circle of Ultra-Violet light
surrounds you. As you continue to inhale, you begin to breathe in this wonderful
light of unconditional love. As you exhale, you begin to become one with this
wonderful light of unconditional love in the highest of forms. The more you
inhale and exhale, the more you are one with this light. You can no longer feel
your body. You now are this light. Imagine that you can float around like a
weightless cloud. You can float and arise above your body. You continue to float
higher up and then through the clouds. The higher you go, the lighter you feel.
You see a glowing rainbow star. You can feel yourself being drawn to this
rainbow star. The closer you get to this rainbow star, the more unconditional
love you feel. You feel so safe. So comfortable ... so loved.

You are pulled closer until you land on this rainbow star. You can now see
this beautiful garden. This garden is the most exquisite you have ever seen. Stop
and smell the enchanting fragrances. Don't they smell, just incredible? You see
this golden path. You follow this golden path and you are lead to this fabulous
gazebo. There is a bench and you sit down. There is this violet mist that
surrounds you. This violet mist cleanses all the things you are ready to let go of.
All the pain and heartache, the troubles, anxieties and worries all gone. You now
have never felt lighter.

Isn't this amazing. And the best part is this wonderful loving light
beaming from this garden is all you. Our bodies are just envelopes to contain all
this vastness about ourselves. We are now in a place beyond time and space, as
you know it.

This is a place where you can receive healings of the highest of levels, all
for the highest of good. Allow yourself to feel this electric light of Spirit embrace
you. It feels amazing, yet so familiar doesn't it?

You are at a place in your life where you are ready to let go of everything
that is holding you back from being able to feel this electrical spiritual light all
the time.

You have so much love emanating from you. Your love has created this
exquisite garden. You can co-create anything and everything you focus your
attention to. All for the highest of good. You no longer need these empty
relationships. They have well worn out their welcome. You are now so ready to

open yourself up to a real relationship based on true love in the highest of forms. You are so beautiful. It is time to finally allow the world to see your majestic loving beauty and allow this to enter your world.

How can someone get to know you if you don't even know your spiritual self? This loving ecstasy is a very integral part of your higher spiritual self. It is time to take down some of the shields to let your higher self shine through. You have so much love waiting from others to share with you.

The casual friend entering your life was not accidental. You have mentioned by first meeting you felt an immediate connection. You instantly knew him. But he was holding back from letting you see the complete picture. The connection you are feeling is genuine. It stems from a past life you shared together as lovers. The bond you shared together was intense and explosive. Together you roamed the European continent sharing your artistic ways wherever you went. In many ways you were like gypsies with no set plans. You both traveled where the winds took you. This relationship was extremely passionate, but explosive at the sametime. When it was good, it was so positive for the both of you. But when it was bad, it brought out the worst in both of you as well. You both enjoyed to party and intoxification was the norm. But as times started getting rough, the intoxification increased excessively. His drinking and drugging became increasingly dark and addictive.

He introduced and forced you to participate with his addictions. It caused him to abandon his morals and frequently step outside of the relationship. He began dabbling into the darker realms, causing major havoc to your relationship and your self-esteem. You both strayed away from the higher lights of Spirit and towards the darker energies. He actively delved deep into the darker arts. He tried to force you into that, but he was not successful.

Tragically, he was misguided into making a toxic mixture. He tricked you into taking this concoction with him. It was a lethal mixture. You made a last ditch effort by praying to the light to help heal you. Unfortunately you slowly went to sleep and never woke up. What you might not have realized was that your praying saved you from painfully experiencing the excruciating effects from this lethal cocktail. He was not so lucky. He wretched in pain until he was dead.

He made an agreement with you after death in the higher realms that would make up for the dark path he tried to lead you down.

When you met up again in this life, he would help to gear you back to opening up and exploring your spiritual lightness. Your spirit guides also made sure to put enough issues between both of you, to prevent any reoccurrences of the past happening again.

You have now learned about your connection with him and your uncomfortableness with any form of the higher light energies. Now that we have relearned this lesson, it is time to rewrite this past to cleanse and free up your own spirit to pursue the lighter and loving beauty of life.

In this life, he would still be into exploring the mystic arts, but this time he would be exploring the light energies. You will be soul friends. There will be temptations to reunite, but that will never fully come to fruition this time around. He has learned from his past mistakes. He will be best as just a soul friend for you. You have so much to explore and create with your extremely talented artistic gift.

His re-emergence into your life will provoke past feelings and temptations. But he has already agreed with Spirit not to cross those boundaries with you again. But his temptations will direct you into exploring your own spirituality.

Now I want you to imagine there is a crystal podium with a book that is emanating the rainbow lights. This is your book of past, present and future. You approach the book and by thought, it automatically turns to this past life with him. The pages at the end of this chapter are dark. Now allow yourself to imagine your former self not drink that toxic cocktail. Neither of you drink it. Instead, the toxic cocktail begins to turn color. It starts to glow. The power of love and light pour into this mixture, transforming it to a drink of love and light. You both drink it. Your bodies instantly start transforming. All the heartache, the pain, the dark destructive deathness fades away. You are both now glowing in this rainbow light. Everything is now so light and love is flowing everywhere. Now picture you both growing older, happy and healthy. When you are both a ripe old age, together you both ascend up to the light.

Now imagine the book closing and sealing itself.

You have just sent major transformation healing energy to change those dark destructive patterns to light in the highest of forms. By freeing up your past patterns, this frees up your present to allow endless wonderful possibilities for your future.

Now it is time to come back. Allow yourself to imagine an elevator made of rainbow light. You enter and the doors close behind you. As the elevator lowers, you can start to feel your body again. The elevator doors finally open. Your gently glide out and back into your body.

Stay with this as long as you like. When you are ready, open your eyes.

The healing meditation helped clear all the dysfunctional ties between them, to allow the possibilities of healthy now ones to emerge. Alice was able to have peace with her friend once and for all. They went their separate ways on the best terms.

Like many people, Alice was disillusioned by spirituality, religion and the whole concept of God. In situations like this, it is best to handle things in the most delicate way. There are certain words, which pertain to God that won't alienate clients like Alice. By simply using these words instead of the others, such clients would feel more comfortable. Instead of the word God, Yahweh, Jesus and Buddha, I used the terms Spirit, the Light and the Higher Realms. When the uncomfortable words are replaced by more palatable ones, the person is more likely to be open to the new concepts, without animosity towards them.

It seems that more and more of the clients that are coming to me have a stronger awareness of their own gifts. Spirit allows me to help them ignite their desire to work with their gifts and with Spirit. But it takes dedication, concentration and the best of intentions for the channel to flow. The girls commented that I make it look so easy. Through my guidance, I was able to show them that they can access their talents and gifts just as easily.

Here is an actual testimonial from Alice herself:

"I used to walk with my head hanging, and the values and confidence that you instilled in me made me feel fierce and so comfortable in my skin... I was able to walk with my head up high and feel like I carried myself with a purpose and I mattered... And when people were turning their heads it wasn't to point and laugh, it was to say... WHO IS THAT? She must be SOMEBODY! Great feeling. I carry that around with me every day.

Thank you!!! Love U, H! :)"

JANET: THE CONTROL FACTOR

I had a client whom we shall call Janet. Janet didn't understand why her health had been deteriorating. She took her vitamins, maintained a healthy diet and exercised regularly. Her weight had always been in normal range and she was very careful about what she put into her body. She never smoked and rarely even indulged in glass of wine.

But ever since her career, as well as her life, had become very successful, her health had started a downward spiral. She had been diagnosed with MS (multiple sclerosis). She took extra care of herself because of that. Unfortunately, the disease was progressing quickly. She came to me to find out the energetic cause of her disease.

I scanned her energy field, the aura around her. I was able to detect several holes in her energy field. These were vulnerabilities. I decided to investigate further. I allowed myself to tap into her soul energy. I opened myself up to perceive the blocks in Janet's soul that had been causing problems with her health. I was intuitively shown glimpses of some of her past lives, as well as how she was conducting her current life. I could sense a definite pattern, which was consistent in all of her lives, past and present.

Control was a major factor influencing Janet. She had to be in control in every facet of her life. She was currently the owner of a consulting company. Her diet was highly regimented. Her meal portions were measured to the centigram. Her husband was very docile and passive. She completely controlled their entire marriage, especially in the bedroom. Her greatest problem was that she was unable to relinquish control. Even at the dentist, she always refused Novocain or any other anesthetic. If she were under the influence of a drug, someone else would have temporary control over her. That was out of the question. Not even for a root canal would she acquiesce. She preferred to endure the pain, to control her own tolerance of the pain, than to allow someone else to have control over her for even an hour.

In her past lives, she had been no different. In one of them, she had been a general in charge of an entire army during the days of the Roman Empire. This general had beheaded one of the officers for disobeying his command in front of other soldiers.

During another lifetime, she had been a British soldier during the colonial days in the 1700's. His assignment had been to keep the royal colonies in line and to make sure that they obeyed King George's orders. When a colonist got out of line, he would be sent to the stockades for disobeying orders. Control had been the most important aspect of this soldier's life. Disobeyed orders were a threat to his control over the colonists.

The pattern she had carried with her throughout her lifetimes was, in fact, control. Everyone or everything had to obey her commands or they would be disciplined. Now in this lifetime, she was still unable to relinquish control for even a split second. Janet needed to learn the lesson:

YOU CANNOT BE IN CONTROL ALL THE TIME, THE ONLY THING THAT REMAINS CONSTANT IN LIFE IS CHANGE.

As a result, the universe had presented her with a learning opportunity. She had developed and manifested MS. MS fights the central nervous system. As the disease progresses, one has less and less control over his/her own body. Because she had not been able to learn how to relinquish control over anything, this time the lesson would have to be extremely harsh. She needed to endure the crippling effects of MS, so she would eventually not have a choice but to let go of the reigns of control she held so tightly. She had fought this lesson every step of the way. If only she would have allowed somebody else to help her. If she had ever allowed someone else to have any control over any aspect of her life, she might not have had to learn her soul lesson so harshly.

When I told Janet my intuitive diagnosis, at first she was quite confrontational. "You expect me to believe that just because I am such a tight-ass, because I must have full control over my life, this is why I have MS? That's a load of crap."

The ringing of her cell phone interrupted her defensive explosion. Her husband had called to ask about their plans for the weekend. She scolded him like a child and dictated the weekend's itinerary hour-by-hour. Everything was rigidly set. I couldn't tell if she was speaking to her husband, or if she was barking out a command as the General to one of her officers. But she had no control issues. Yeah, right!

I asked her to just humor me and let me guide her through a simple meditation. She would not cooperate. She was not going to make this easy.

As a rule, I will never force my practice, methods, or exercises on anybody. Everybody has his or her own free will. If someone chooses to agree and follow along, that's great. If they sit with their hands folded and refuse, that's fine too.

But as I often have to tell my clients, "Don't shoot the messenger!" It's not my fault if you don't like the message.

I am just the human telephone poll between the physical world and the Divine. I am here to deliver Spirit's message. I assist and facilitate in creating a healing environment, one that is conducive for healing at the highest and deepest of levels of your being. If a person doesn't want any part of it or is simply not ready, I do not take it personally. In actuality, it really has nothing to do with me. However, at times, staying balanced can get very tricky. In those situations, I have to keep reminding myself that I am just the medium, the mediator, and the messenger.

Janet kept looking at her watch, a sure sign that nothing I was saying was sinking in. She was getting ready to bolt. Spirit had brought Janet to me, so I asked Spirit for assistance with her. All of a sudden, the spirit of an older gentleman in his early 70's, about five foot ten or eleven, with a medium build, empathically came to me.

I relayed his message to Janet. Didn't you learn anything from Sammy? Then he told me to make a slithering sound, like Hannibal Lecter sipping his Chianti with fava beans, which I did.

Janet stopped cold in her tracks. She looked like a deer caught in the headlights. Her eyes bulged open. "What did you say?"

I explained, "An older male spirit is here and he is insisting that I ask you, didn't you learn anything from Sammy?"

"And the sound?" He insisted, so I made the slithering sound once again.

Bulls-eye! Her wall of ice just melted. Instantly, she burst into tears. All those years she had had of keeping such a tight vice grip on her emotions and feelings began to wash away as the tears steadily flowed. This was a healing cry, a release. It was something she hadn't done for a long time. I gently placed my hands on her shoulders sending waves of Ultra-Violet light, the highest form of transformational, unconditional love. UV light is the light of transformation for the highest of good.

The elder gentleman told me he was her father. He explained the significance of the message I had communicated on his behalf. You see Sammy was the pet snake that Janet had had when she was a little girl. Like all reptiles, Sammy had begun to shed his old skin in order to uncover his new skin. But Sammy wasn't shedding fast enough for her. She wanted to control this, too. She started peeling off his old skin. By the time she had finished, all of poor Sammy's old skin had been peeled off and his new skin was exposed. Most of his new skin wasn't fully developed yet. Sammy quickly went into shock. The exposed skin became infected and he was gone by the morning.

Janet had now reverted back to being the little girl that she had locked away, deep inside, so long ago.

She called out, "Sammy, Sammy. I'm so sorry. I didn't want him to die. I just wanted that ugly shedding to stop. My poor baby. I just wanted to make him better."

Her father opened his jacket and there was Sammy, all happily slithering and hissing lovingly. My client started to feel something wiggling around her arm. She instantly remembered what had made those sensations. That was the same feeling she used to feel as a little girl, when Sammy would crawl up her arm. She asked if that was Sammy. Yes it was. Even pets can be reunited with us and can help with our healing process. The Janet that had walked into the apartment was not the same Janet that walked out. She was so much lighter. I had helped transform some of her blockages and her aura was so much brighter.

I heard from Janet again almost eight months later. She called to schedule a session. She went on to tell me everything that had taken place in her life, since our last healing session. She sounded so much happier.

She thanked me, "HL, you were so right. Life used to be just one big control knob for me. In order for me to feel safe, I had to be in control of everything and everyone. The life I led before your session was so rigid and so damn constrictive."

"Everything you told me was so on target. I was just too stubborn to admit it. Just too scared to allow myself to actually see another point of view besides my own. My father passed a few years ago. He always tried to help me ease my obsessive, compulsive control over life. It was just like him to bring Sammy back with him. To be honest, I had completely forgotten about Sammy until you mentioned him."

"My poor Sammy," she continued. "I had to be in the driver's seat, even as a child. I couldn't even let my snake shed his own skin. It brought everything back to me. All of a sudden, I had such clarity about my life. How my obsessive control issues was destroying it, as well as making it unbearable for everyone around me."

"It took time," she admitted. "First, I started allowing my husband to actually do things for me. Not by ordering him around like a servant, but actually treating him like a husband. Then I started to not be so controlling of others too. When I finally relinquished control, I started feeling so much better. I was feeling great. I went to the doctor's for a routine visit. We took tests and by some miracle, my MS was now in remission. Instead of fighting the doctors, I simply listened to them. I allowed the doctors to doctor me and not me doctor the doctors. I am still a work in progress. But such a happier work at that."

In our next few sessions, we did past life regressions and soul retrieval to help further her understanding and to free up those energy patterns from the past. By healing the past, you are able to change your present and open up your future to all possibilities.

Remember, disease is the physical manifestation of dysfunctional energy patterns. Every body and every case is different. By my client understanding her major blocks and changing her mindset, she was able to change her whole life. In her case, her MS went into remission and is to this day.

There are no guarantees, but the possibilities we have in life are endless.

THE CORPORATE INTUITIVE CONSULTANT

HOW I GOT STARTED

Isn't it funny how life always seems to turn out differently than you expect? When I was young, if anyone had told me that one day I would be working in the corporate world, I would have laughed in their face. If they had told me that I would be sought after by several major companies, specifically for my intuitive abilities, I would have thought I was on Candid Camera and I would have been looking for Alan Funt to jump out and yell "Gotcha!" But, in addition to having a regular job at the phone company, I have also been retained as a professional intuitive consultant by several corporations.

The great financier J.P. Morgan once said, "Millionaires do not use astrologers, billionaires do." Over the years, in addition to astrologers, Wall Street has employed more psychics and intuitives than Dionne Warwick's Psychic Friends Network. But this secret is buried deeper than Jimmy Hoffa.

I first started working as a professional intuitive during my days in the entertainment field. My very first paid booking was for an actor that was in the film I was working on at the time. During the actual production of a film, there is always plenty of downtime. During these long breaks, I would occupy myself by giving fellow cast and crewmembers readings. One day an actor came out of his trailer and approached me for a session. He had heard that I had given a number of readings to some of the others, and the buzz was very good. He asked if I would be available for private a session, off the set. I agreed, but we never really discussed a fee. I left it up to Spirit to work out the financial stuff. To be honest, I don't really remember many of the session's details. I advised him on career direction, as well as inner emotional and spiritual focusing. When it came time for him to compensate me for the session, he had no hesitation. He was happy with the reading and paid me what he usually paid for sessions. He referred many fellow actors to me.

As time went on, there was a very costly film strike in New York, which resulted in the exodus of many production companies. Since many New York films were now being shot elsewhere, I wasn't getting as many film jobs, either in front of, or behind, the camera. Instead, I was starting to get more private bookings for my intuitive work. Before I knew it, most of my phone calls were for private sessions. Eventually I just stopped looking for film jobs and only booked intuitive work.

I have been asked, why do I charge for my services? My answer is very simple. You are not paying for the message. You are paying for the messenger.

THE MODEL AGENCY

In one of my film jobs as a movie extra, I made a very interesting connection. Spirit had slowly been leading people to me, who needed my work. I struck up an instant bond with another extra who we will call Tom. Within minutes of meeting Tom, I intuitively sensed the presence of his grandmother. Without trying to spook him out, I explained to him that I had intuitive abilities. I then asked his permission to relay to him the messages his grandmother was giving me. Tom nodded and I quickly went into a semi-trance state and gave him a very personal reading. When I was finished, his eyes had welled up. Tom warmly thanked me for the messages.

His grandmother had passed a few months earlier and he had been really missing her advice. They had been very close. His grandmother's message gave him encouragement on his current relationship, as well as his career path. His grandmother said there would first be rough waters, before there would be a beautiful, loving calm.

"Don't run away from this relationship, like you have routinely done before," I told him on her behalf. She showed me Tom with many cameras, surrounded by many headshots of other people. She pointed to a picture of a sign, which said, "Go for it."

Tom confirmed that he was having difficulties in his current relationship. His grandmother was correct. He usually ended his relationships at the first sign of difficulty. But he was going to listen to her advice and try to work through the problems.

Career wise, Tom was trying to start up his own model agency. He had made many connections through his film work and wanted to network them. He was slowly starting up his agency, but was waiting for a sign about when to put all of his energy into it. His message from his grandmother was everything he had been waiting to hear.

A few months passed before I heard from Tom. He once again thanked me for his impromptu reading, for he had been missing his grandmother terribly and had asked for a sign that she was okay. And there I was with precise details that only could have come from her. He had been getting cold feet about his decision to put all of his focus on the model agency. His grandmother's message had answered many of his impending questions about himself and his agency. In fact, it had crystallized the direction his agency should go.

Tom scheduled regular sessions with me, and his grandmother intuitively communicated her messages through me to her grandson. As his model agency began to take off, he put me on retainer as an intuitive consultant. Tom would have me present at business meetings. Afterwards we would privately discuss my impressions of what had actually transpired. Before any prospective new model would be signed, Tom first consulted with me. This is how this worked. Tom would hand me a sealed envelope with a picture inside of a new model, a client or whatever else he wanted to know about. I would hold the sealed envelope and use psychometry to pick up the energy inside the envelope. Psychometry is a method of reading the vibrational energy of an object that is held in one's hand. I would clear my mind of everything and hold each envelope with my left hand. The left hand is the receiving hand for energy. The right hand is the one that sends energy out. As I would hold the envelope, various images, impressions and messages would come to me. I never forced it. I just let the energy do its thing and tell me the story of the contents of the envelope.

I remember one incident, where I picked up horrific suicidal thoughts and extremely violent episodes. As I sat with this energy, the darkness of the images only intensified. There was absolutely nothing positive about anything I was feeling. I strongly recommended that this model, Ms. Thing be rejected. She was going to be nothing but a nightmare of trouble. Tom was confused. He opened the envelope to reveal a picture of an incredibly photogenic, beautiful girl. Ms. Thing had been naturally blessed with a gorgeous outside, but her inside was simply dreadful. Her whole life, she had used her beauty to manipulate, deceive and denigrate everyone to get whatever she wanted. I just knew that Ms. Thing was nothing but pure trouble. Tom listened to my advice, but signed her anyway.

Her first two assignments went very well. Tom joked that I must be losing my touch. My crystal ball must be broken, and I needed to take it into the shop for repairs. OK. Whatever. Undaunted, my impressions never changed about her. It was on her third assignment when Ms. Thing's demon-child self surfaced. The photographer was very strict and methodically disciplined. He ran his photo shoots like an Army commander. This just rubbed her the wrong way. He didn't cater to her pampered whims at all. Instead, in his mind, models were essentially walking coat hangers. To him their silence was golden. This did not sit well with Ms. Thing at all. She wouldn't cooperate with him. She pulled a diva tantrum.

Without missing a beat, the photographer told her, "Either shut up or ship out!"

Ms. Thing's eyes saw red and she just went wild. She started screaming and cursing. She violently kicked over some very expensive equipment. This beautiful girl had turned into an ugly Medusa. The photographer immediately stopped the shoot and had security escort her from the premises. Ms. Thing went home and in her rage, began cutting herself. She made deep gashes to her arms and wrists. A neighbor called an ambulance and she was taken to a psychiatric hospital. Tom called me up to tell me what had gone down with Ms. Thing. Her actions had cost Tom and the agency plenty. The photographer billed the agency for the loss of equipment and the cost of the studio rental. Tom's agency was never booked again for anything remotely related to this photographer.

Another time, Tom handed me a sealed envelope and my hand just started buzzing. This person was going to be BIG. Still a diamond in the rough, but with time, patience and tutoring, this model was destined to be a star. Once again, my reading confused Tom. This model's pictures were nothing special and Tom only photo-tested her as a joke. Well, this joke was absolutely destined for stardom. Tom agreed to sign this model to a short-term contract, but he had major reservations. I sensed that the model needed my assistance with a few emotional problems. In six sessions, along with an abundance of my energy healing work, she was able to come to grips with many of her problems. Now, with the emotions under control, her true star quality essence began to blossom. The agency got a last-minute model request for the casting of a commercial. Nobody else was available at such short notice. Tom reluctantly sent her to the casting. I went along to help keep the energy positive. From the minute the model arrived, the client was in love. The test shots went amazingly smooth. The commercial only required a few takes and the director wrapped up the shoot. A couple of weeks later, the client called Tom. The print ads and the commercial had come out incredibly well. The model was immediately booked for a series of national and international campaigns.

Tom was stunned. His agency received a very lucrative commission and he was a very happy camper. Within the next year, this model booked several highly important jobs and raised the agency's profile considerably. The model eventually left Tom's agency and signed with one of the largest model agencies in the world. I have purposely not given the model's name to protect her privacy. She has since branched out into several areas of the entertainment industry. Tom's agency still continues to be very profitable.

THE RECORD COMPANY

Ever since I was a child, I had an uncanny knack of being able to tell what music would be a huge success and what would be a dud. I have always been able to hear a song on the radio just once and know if it is going to be a hit or not. I have been consistently able to spot what artist or group was going to be the next big thing. At first, my friends would laugh at my choices. But time usually proved me correct. Sometimes, when I hear or see an artist, group or whatever, I will experience major jolts of energy throughout my body. I will intuitively see stars and the stars will explode into even bigger stars. I only experience this when the artist, group, product, company, etc., will be successful. The more stars I see and the more powerful the energy jolts I experience, the more successful the subject will be.

One day I received a phone call from a friend of mine, whom we shall call Gina. She scheduled a private session with me. Her session went very well. We worked on her personal, professional, emotional, mental, physical, and spiritual selves. When her session was finished, talk turned to business. Since I had helped her in virtually all areas in her life, she asked if I would be interested in coming down to help with her job at a record company. The company had recently gone through a major restructuring and they were bringing some new blood into the mix, my girlfriend included. She was in charge of discovering, signing, and developing new talent for the record company. She wondered if I would be interested in consulting about some of the raw talent that passed through the office. I thought she was offering me a desk job, but that was not what she had in mind. She wanted me to be an independent, intuitive consultant who would help her in the process of deciding which new talent and products to sign.

Using the same process I did for the model agency, I was given sealed envelopes containing the names of prospective new acts and asked for my intuitive insight on each. In order to use psychometry, I cleared myself of everything and became an empty slate. I then took several deep pranic breaths and held each envelope in my left hand. Gina recorded and wrote down all of my impressions. The next step of my consulting was very interesting. The prospective talent would be called into a waiting room, where I was already seated. The talent had no idea who I was or what I was doing there. The majority of the time, the talent would think that I was just another artist trying to get a record contract. I would calmly scan their energy field and tap into their souls. I would then write down my impressions and whatever information Spirit would have given me about them. I had conversations with them, while I simultaneously read them intuitively to myself. When I was finished, I would head to Gina's office to report on my findings. Without ever actually having heard any music from an artist, I was able to give Gina unbiased details about the artist's mind, body, soul, and spirit. I could tell her about any long-standing or upcoming mental or physical issues. I could tell Gina of any present drug or alcohol problems, as well as a potential susceptibility to that. Being a medical intuitive, I could sense any physical health issues, past, present or future. Finally, I would then actually listen to their music or read their songs. All this information factored in, and assisted Gina in determining whom to sign to a contract and whom to reject.

I remember one artist in particular that the record company was thinking of signing. They intended to invest a large sum of money in this artist as well. When I held the sealed envelope, my lungs began feeling very tight. The longer I held the envelope, the tighter my lungs became. This made it a bit difficult to breathe. I was given intuitive information about an impending liver malfunction and deterioration. I wanted to know why, so I tapped into the energy field further. This person had had a major drug and alcohol addiction for several years, but had been able to conceal it from the public. This person was very much a serious addict but had the ability to appear quite normal on the surface. This addiction was soon going to get the best of this person. My recommendation was to pass on the artist for several reasons. An active addict is still an addict, no matter how you slice it. The artist's body was beginning to deteriorate internally from the years of abuse and the grasp on reality was thin at best. An impending breakdown was inevitable within one to two years. This deterioration was siphoning away the creativity of the artist, who would never be able to produce any music close to the potential shown on the demo tape, which had been recorded several years earlier. I strongly recommended that Gina should advise this person to seek medical attention immediately.

Gina took my advice and passed on the artist. She did advise the artist to seek medical attention, but the advice was immediately shrugged off. Another record company signed the artist shortly afterward, and subsequently invested a load of money. The artist never sought any medical attention and continued to party hard. Between one and two years later, the artist overdosed in the recording studio and died the following morning. Sadly the addiction had been so strong, none of the recorded material was even salvageable. Gina later told me that I had saved her record company the $800,000 that had been allotted toward that artist.

Another time with another envelope, I sensed a group with major potential for success. I could sense that the band was a tight, well-oiled machine with one exception, the lead singer. The lead singer was like a toxic cancer that would destroy the band's dynamics and creativity. If they changed the singer, stardom was very likely. Coincidently, my hand immediately gravitated toward another envelope. I held this envelope alone, and then held both envelopes together. My body experienced jolts of energy and I saw the exploding stars. The person in the second envelope needed to replace the lead singer of the band. If they made the switch, the chemistry would be phenomenal. I didn't even need to meet the band or the other singer. I told Gina to have the band record a demo with the other singer.

At first, she was reluctant. But the investment in a demo tape was very minimal. So she proposed the new demo audition with the band and the other singer. The original lead singer was rightfully furious, but the band was willing to record a new demo with the other singer. In the studio, the new band's chemistry was fantastic. They gelled with the new singer like they had been together for twenty years. They recorded five songs and felt very good about it. Gina played the demo and signed the new band's lineup on the spot. The record company was so impressed with the demo, they released it as an EP mini album. With minimal publicity, radio stations began to play the band's songs. Within no time, the EP sold well and the band was a hit. Their first complete album also sold strongly and they became quite successful.

The entertainment industry is very fickle. Corporate restructuring is a constant reality. Gina's record company went through another major restructuring and Gina, along with many others was let go. She thanked me for my work, but decided to leave the music business altogether. Since my intuitive consultations were not common knowledge, the new management did not retain my services. Before she left, though, she let me know that my intuitive consultations had made and saved the record company a considerable amount of money.

WALL STREET FORTUNE 500 COMPANY

Like many others with the gift, on occasion I have worked local psychic fairs. At one particular psychic fair, I gave a reading for a very bohemian looking man whom we shall call Sky. I scanned his body and immediately picked up a very sensitive stomach with bouts of colitis. I went into detail about how with energy therapy, he could control and possibly heal his condition. He showed me a photograph of a beautiful female and wanted to know more. He said he had admired her from afar and wanted to date her. My intuition told me something different. He was not interested in dating her, but her twin brother. I went into details about the brother's appearance and how over-protective she was with him. Sky had been friends with the woman for years, but she had only recently mentioned that she had a twin brother. When he had finally met her brother at a dinner party, there were undeniable sparks. But she was against her brother getting involved with any of her friends, Sky included.

After I told Sky my impressions, he laughed joyfully. He confirmed that I was completely on the money. The picture had been his trick to see what I would say. I did recommend the he should listen to his girlfriend and not pursue her brother any further. It would destroy their friendship, and that was very important in his life. His relationship with the brother would only turn out to be for unsatisfying, short-term sex that wasn't worth the loss of a friendship. Sometimes window-shopping is much more satisfying than actually getting what you are looking at.

Sky was impressed and thanked me for my honesty. He commented on my accuracy and asked if I would be interested in doing some private intuitive consultations for his company. Sky was an executive for a large Wall Street Fortune 500 corporation. He oversaw many corporate decisions. I explained how I worked with psychometry previously in the corporate world. Sky set up a session for the following week. He insisted that my work was to be kept secret from his fellow workers. Wall Street has always had many intuitive consultants working for them. They just like to keep that bit of information very much under wraps, Sky included.

Sky placed several sealed envelopes on the table and let me go to work. With each envelope, I would read its energy and be able to tell him: Yes! Go with this. No, this is a bomb! Or, Wait! Hold off for now, this is not the right time. And then I would tell him when that time would be.

I specifically never wanted to know any information at all about the subjects that were in the envelopes. This preserved my ability to be unbiased and allowed my impressions to be that much more thorough. I would place the envelopes in the yes, no or hold off piles and write my intuitive notes or time frame for each envelope's subject. Some envelopes would feel red hot, which told me, Yes, this is going to be good and for how long. Other times, I would get a horrible feeling. The more extreme the pain, the quicker Sky needed to get rid of it. I would also advise Sky when certain planetary energy patterns were very ripe for aggressive actions, or when the energy was erratic and to hold off on any sudden movements. I would warn him in advance before any Mercury retrogrades. As all astrologers know, the planet Mercury is all about communication. When Mercury's orbit is retrograde, all communications will be very erratic.

Before Mercury retrogrades, I would tell Sky to turn on the back up systems. And as I had predicted, when many of his electronic and telecommunication systems would experience periods of failure, he would be protected. I convinced him to avoid signing any important contracts during Mercury retrograde. During a Mercury Retrograde, you should try not to start anything new. Try to hold off buying anything new. Please try to avoid signing a contract or any documents at all costs. Expect appointment times to go astray and plans to suddenly fall through. During retrograde, there are always many mishaps and failures with electrical devices, especially those related to communication, like telephones and computers. A good way to think of Mercury retrograde is to think of a full dinner plate. During this time, it is best to finish up what is on your plate, before you add something new to it.

As part of Sky's job, he would have to make regular speeches to large crowds. Secretly, Sky was terrified of making these speeches. But he never let anybody see him sweat. Before the speech, Sky would get so panicked that he usually threw up. I conducted a series of hypnosis sessions with Sky to address these specific issues. Through regression hypnosis, I was able to take him to the core of his phobia. When he was a little boy, he had an obnoxious uncle who had an even more obnoxious mouth. Every time little Sky would try to speak, the uncle would interrupt, laugh, and cruelly criticize him. This belittlement had stayed in the back of Sky's mind and the fear of this reoccurring would surface just before he was to make any speech in public.

Through regression hypnosis, I was able to help him silence this loud mouth uncle's criticism once and for all. I gave Sky suggestive tools to use when he felt these panic attacks coming on. This helped him tremendously. Eventually his nervousness about public speaking disappeared completely. Over time, Sky secretly sent many people on his staff for private sessions with me.

When Sky decided to retire, my work was completed. Sky told me that I had saved or made the company a considerable amount of money. He was very grateful and occasionally still came to me for private sessions.

THE HIP HOSTESS NYC

The Hip Hostess NYC (HHNYC) is an innately creative powerhouse who is naturally cutting edge. She loves to plan creative parties and is the quintessential hostess with the mostess. She has the uncanny knack of discovering raw talent of every industry, field or area. With her innovative eye, the HHNYC always discovers the best gadgets and inventions, people, products, places or things. She first tests them all out to see if they meet her very high standards—which does not always mean the most luxurious. Those successful candidates, ideas, talent, products, philosophies, etc. become part of the focused theme of her next series of fabulous themed parties, or subjects of her column and blog.

As she formulated each step of her new business venture, my intuitive input was used as one of her valuable resources. When it was came time for the HHNYC to film her TV pitch, she let me loose to do my magic.

She was engulfed by the choices for casting her TV pitch. Curious to the medium herself, I had coached HHNYC in the method I use to make recommendations. I told her to do a printout, including a photo, on all the candidates, and then fold the paper to hide the identity. Next, I instructed her to clear her mind, open up to the spirit, and hold her hand over each piece of paper. I advised her, write down whatever comes into your mind, no matter how ridiculous it may seem—a word, a feeling, a color, a smell. The dozen candidates got narrowed down to two as her favorites. Being new at this, she wanted to check her results, so she then had me interact with the twelve photos, without giving me the slightest bit of information. Using the gift, I opened myself up and allowed Spirit to empower the decisions. I scanned the photos and quickly put ten in the rejected pile. My last two photos just happened to be her exact two favorite candidates. I opened myself and further connected with their energy patterns. As I tapped deeper into the first candidate, I started getting an awful feeling. I picked up sneaky, unreliable and would not interact well with the HHNYC on camera. I also picked up an attitude with too much ego that showed little respect for others that couldn't boost his career. My answer was absolutely NO. Food with no love just is not worth eating.

I cleared myself and tapped deeper into the energy patterns of the second candidate. This one was just a true character, full of exuberant passion and a real zest for his craft. He had a brilliant mind and loved to incorporate a multitude of many components into his delicious food. I could tell his energy would blend perfectly with the HHNYC. He was a true artist—not some cocky, headstrong egomaniac. He was without a shadow of a doubt, the right person to appear on the TV pitch. After I finished my selection process, the HHNYC had a wonderfully pleased smile on her face. My candidate choice just happened to also be her top candidate choice. This confirmation sealed the deal.

Prior to this filming, the HHNYC had filmed two other versions for her TV pitch. But both just seemed to be a little off from what she was trying to achieve. Each had its own very good points. But in the end, the HHNYC decided to go in another direction. The main distinction: she was now front and center on camera. Secretly a shy person, this step made her extremely nervous, and she began to fret over it. I assured her that all would go well, and I would help her by being present on the set of this taping.

As a start, I energetically cleared the space where we would be shooting. Once the space was clean, I channeled in an amazingly calm, empowerment light. This energy helped bring in an encouraging confidence, while keeping out any chaos that naturally comes with any film shoot. I also helped calm the HHNYC with a necklace that not only looked great on camera, but was charged with calming energies. HHNYC said she felt a difference as soon as she put it on. With the absence of this disruptive chaos, we could get down to business and let The HHNYC and the chef's natural creative juices flow uninterrupted.

This happens to be one of my special abilities that helped keep my own sanity, during my past career as a film production coordinator. In film, time is money. The longer it takes for the production to be filmed, the higher the budgets would grow. That was never a good thing. I also found that on a disruptive set, creatively would be stifled. Our equipment would have constant operating difficulties, repeatedly freezing up in the middle of shots. There would be unnecessary discourse with the cast and crew and the production would take many more hours, days, weeks even months to complete. When I did my energy work, none of this would ever happen. On all of my sets, the only drama allowed was in front of the camera. My sets are always very relaxed, with my cast and crews coming together like a well-oiled machine. This has saved producers and film studios countless dollars. Most of the time, nobody would be aware of what I was energetically doing. It was not apparent until the shooting was wrapped, several hours earlier before it normally would have taken.

The difference of having energy work done on a set is quite considerable. I was not part of either of the two earlier TV pitch film shoots for HHNYC. The talent was excellent, but both productions ran into the same obstacles that can coincide with film shoots. The right cohesiveness was missing. Both shooting times went several hours over schedule and budget. Most importantly the HHNYC experienced unnecessary tension: egos colliding, equipment snafus, and a loss of control over the presenters.

In the final shooting for the pitch, there were none of these issues. When our shoot wrapped, everything fit seamlessly. The HHNYC was not drained. In fact, she was energized and was glowing. Her nervousness was a thing of the past. We wrapped the shoot early enough, that we had ample time to go over some future casting for another part of her production.

I was very protective over HHNYC and made sure her show's vision came to light. With her nerves totally settled, this allowed her star qualities to shine as bright as a Christmas tree. Stay tuned for more developments on this project.

THE NIGHTCLUB OWNER

In addition to my intuitive consultations, I have also done energy work in the corporate world. Being a healer, I am able to channel energy and infuse it into people, places, and things. We have all walked into a room where it just did not feel comfortable. Spaces are like sponges. A space will absorb and retain the various energies that have occupied it. When an uplifting event takes place, the room will vibrate joyously long after it is over. The space can also hold onto negative energy just as easily. This is why after having an argument, it is best to light a candle or maybe some incense to dispel the subtle, negative vibes that remain.

In my younger days, I enjoyed a vigorous nightlife. I was always going to clubs, bars, restaurants, etc. During this time certain club owners began to take notice of my abilities as a healer. They witnessed noticeable positive changes in their patrons after having had interactions with me. I was able to transform the energy of the confused, depressed and misguided that came to me over time. One night a visibly upset clubber approached me. She had been going through a very emotional episode. With her permission, I placed my hands upon her and began channeling positive, transformational energy. As I continued to raise and change the energy within and around her, I could feel the depressive clouds lifting. When I finished, she was noticeably much lighter in spirit. The gloomy-doomies seemed to have released her. She was very grateful for my assistance and asked for my card.

A few weeks later, I received a phone call from her for a consultation. She happened to work for one of the largest club owners around, whom we shall call Raul. She had told Raul about me and he was fascinated. He wanted a private session. The consultation went very well. He was intrigued by my energy work. I gave him insight into his personal and professional affairs. The energy in his office felt very restrictive to me. So I channeled, cleared and transformed it. When I was finished, Raul could feel the tremendous difference in the atmosphere. The restrictive vibe in his office was gone. It now felt invigorating instead. Raul's interest was piqued. He wondered if I could transform the energy of his clubs, as I had done for his office.

Absolutely!! I replied enthusiastically.

And that is exactly what I did for Raul. A few days a week, I would go to his one of his clubs in the afternoon, several hours before it opened. I would tap into the energy of the space and see what was going on. Then I would create a sacred space and clear out all of the club's lingering energetic residue. Once the space was clear, I would channel a wonderfully joyful and electrically uplifting energy. This made the space feel terrific and inviting to all the clubbers that would arrive later in the evening.

Within a short period of time, Raul's clubs were booming. The volume of his business had increased much more than he had expected. He was delighted by the results. Our arrangement was very discreet. Not even any of my close friends had any idea about this. For the next couple of years, I continued to work privately for him, cleansing the energy of his different properties. Eventually Raul grew tired of the whole club business and sold everything. He acknowledged that my energy work had had a very positive effect on his business. He thanked me for my work and expressed the respect he had for it. Since then, I have discreetly done this type of work for a variety of other businesses, restaurants, theaters, entertainment production companies, professional television and film sets, as well as private homes.

THE BOOK TOUR

The time I was called for jury duty turned out to be a very interesting experience. My goal was to be released immediately from having to serve. So when the court asked what my occupation was, I answered that I was a psychic. The assistant district attorney gave me a perturbed look, but the defense attorney was happy. She knew, as an intuitive, I might be able to see that her client was innocent. The judge calmly asked if my impressions would hamper my ability to distinguish right from wrong. I replied that my abilities would not impede my judgment. I was selected as an alternative juror. The case lasted for six and half weeks. The court proceedings were very interesting.

One of my fellow jurors was a new author who had recently been published. Without much publicity, out of the box, her book had made the New York Times Bestsellers list. We quickly bonded during the course of the trial. She found my work fascinating. She loved being a writer, but had some difficulty with the public appearances it entailed. That was where I came in. I gave her several readings and also did healing energy work on her.

She invited me to one of her book-reading appearances. I arrived early to do some energy work on her. During her appearance, I continued to channel energy into the bookstore, creating a very safe and secure environment for her. As a result, she did not experience her usual nervousness. Instead, she felt empowered. I continued to flood the space with positive energy, as she read from her book. Afterwards, she felt triumphant. She had been able to feel the energy the entire time that I had been channeling.

This appearance had been the easiest and most pleasant one that she had ever experienced. Convinced of my abilities, we discussed the possibility of me accompanying her on some dates on her book tour. Unfortunately, our conflicting schedules would not permit it. However, I was still able to help her by sending her long distance healing energy for the duration of her book tour. She let me know that she could feel my presence at each public reading, which helped to make the tour very enjoyable for her. She thanked me for all my help.

THE HILL: THE INVESTIGATION

I was working at The Red Salon in the West Village, doing readings and healing work, when I first met my friend Shirlei. Shirlei is fierce. She is one of the nicest sweethearts I know and a phenomenal chef. This hot Brazilian Mama can turn a plate of leftovers into a gourmet feast. I was invited to Shirlei's birthday party. It was going to be at her friend Elle's house up in the Catskills. I was invited for the whole weekend and promised to give a few readings while I was there.

Within seconds of meeting Elle, I knew immediately she was someone from my soul group. The feeling was mutual. After about ten minutes I felt like I had known her for 1000 years. Elle can be described in one word, fabulous. I have always called her, the female Andy Warhol, with a wonderfully real personality, a heart and soul.

Elle's house and surrounding property is affectionately known as The Hill. It literally sits up on top of a hill. In order to get up to the house, you have to drive up a long and winding dirt road. This road reminded me of a smaller version of the twisting road, which takes you up to The Hearst Castle in San Simeon.

The Hill is an entity unto itself. It sits on top of more than 200 acres of land. There is a lake, as well as a pond for the pets to swim. It was once a farm. Before that, it had been a ceremonial center for Native Americans to communicate as one with nature. The vital energy on The Hill can be devastating for some people. It is a vortex for all kinds of transformation, a magical place. I have experienced numerous paranormal/spiritual activities there. There are a bunch of different spirits that inhabit or visit from time to time. During your stay, you might encounter the spirits of three little girls, to name a few.

Just like when they recorded We Are The World, everyone who is invited to The Hill is forced to leave their ego and everyday bullshit down at the bottom before they arrive. As you ascend the slow drive up the dirt road, you start to feel much lighter. By the time you reach the house at the top you feel absolutely energetically lighter and clearer.

The first time my husband Michael and I took Precious (she is my wonderfully loving furry little child—part Bichon Frise, part Westland Terrier, 100 % diva) to The Hill, she had the best time. She was playing and racing all over the place. She even jumped right into the pond, her first time ever swimming. Animals are the best judges of good and bad. They have a much keener set of senses than we do. They can sense if something is very right, or if things are very wrong. If you take your pet somewhere and they are happy, having a great time, of course this tells you thumbs up. If your pet wants no part of the place and wants to leave quickly, for sure there is something not in your best interest lurking around and it's time to go. Precious gave The Hill a happily barking two paws up.

The house at The Hill has three floors. Upon my first visit, when I entered the house, I was automatically drawn straight to the top room front center from the staircase. Over the years, some guests have experienced unusual things, which they couldn't explain, particularly while staying in that room. It was never anything bad. A lot of times strange things occurred or someone had feelings they just couldn't exactly put their finger on. I was drawn to this room, which has since been named The H Room. As I first entered the room, my spider senses immediately tingled.

I heard laughs and giggles, very much like children's laughter. It was little girls' laughter to be more specific. I looked around the floor to see whose kids were up there and what they were up to. To my amused surprise, there were no children on The Hill that particular weekend.

The giggling got increasingly louder. I felt someone tug on the bottom of my leg and pull at my trademark spiked hair. I opened myself up for communication and three little girls immediately came through. All three were between the ages of seven to nine. Like most girls that age, they were very precocious. They giggled constantly. There was no question about it. The girls knew I could see them. They asked what my name was.

My name is H, just the letter H.

They started jumping up and down and playing hide and seek with me. I referred to them as the girls.

I firmly called to them. Girls, girls, we can play later.

They giggled again and disappeared.

I left the room and went to wash up. I left my unopened bag on the bed. When I came back to the room a short time later, my bag had been opened. All my clothes were scattered around the room.

Girls ... Girls... I firmly spoke to them. H does not play that way. Now play nice.

I heard giggles again. That was just the beginning. I continued to have contact with the girls every time I went up to The Hill.

For those who resist letting go of fear or any of those things that hold someone back, time on The Hill can be a very uncomfortable struggle. There are usually one or two people each time Elle invites a group of friends. Somehow something happens to cause them to scurry away.

I once worked with a film crew that wanted to film a paranormal investigation of the house on The Hill. The crew heard some of the stories through the grapevine and wanted to shoot there. Elle had asked me what I thought. I tuned into The Hill's energy and the answer was an astounding YES. The Hill wanted some well-deserved time in the spotlight. As its resident intuitive medium/healer/human telephone pole, it was up to me to be The Hill's spiritual voice and guardian. There have been many deceptive people over the years, who have wanted something from The Hill. It was usually for some form of ego gratification. Their projects usually did not have The Hill's best interest at heart. I wasn't going to allow anything like that to happen.

A few days before the shoot, one of the little girls from the house, who I know as Amelia, came through to me. She was very excited, but nervous at the same time. Her nervousness overtook me like an opened floodgate. I had to separate myself from her feelings, in order to determine if the nervousness was Amelia's or my own. I took several deep pranic breaths (inhaling through the nose, breathing all the way down to the diaphragm, and then exhaling through the mouth.) This is a very good way to center and clear yourself.

After centering myself, I tapped into the nervousness once again. I asked myself, is this nervousness mine? Nope. Is this Amelia's? Yes. I knew right then and there, that there was definitely going to be something buzzing during the film shoot.

I had an extensive film production background before I worked at the phone company, even before my days as a professional intuitive. As a matter of fact, I received a BA in film production from good old Brooklyn College. I also earned my psychology degree there. I had worked in various capacities in the film industry, virtually every area, both in front of, and especially behind the camera. I had experience directing, producing, pre- and post-production, wardrobe, make-up, set design, continuity, etc. Most often I enjoyed regular employment as a production coordinator. I was the glue that held it all together and made things run smoothly on and off the film set. A production coordinator is the person who channels the director's vision, and holds the crew and cast cohesively together. It's kind of like what I do when I communicate between the physical and the spiritual realms.

I felt it was crucial not to portray The Hill as a haunted place. The word haunted instantly evokes a sense of darkness and evil. I wasn't going to allow my special friend, The Hill, to be attached to any such connotations. The crew was a pretty cool bunch of guys, with whom I could easily knock down a beer or two after the filming. They all were very excited and little overcome by The Hill, simply because it was The Hill. The atmosphere was very laid back, but everyone was as excited as Amelia to get things going. Originally, I had been told that there would be five other psychics. But when I arrived, it was revealed, that I would pretty much be the Grand Pubbah of mystics. I am glad that I didn't know this before hand. I prefer to know as little as possible, to be spontaneous, and just let things flow as they come.

At midnight, the filming began. I welcomed the viewers to The Hill. I made it a point to explain it all very clearly.

The Hill is a transformational vortex, where many spirits happen to reside. Originally, it was a big farm with fields of crops and many animals. Many centuries before that, The Hill used to be a central place where Native American Indians used to hold and perform ceremonial rituals to give thanks to Mother Earth and many of the higher energy beings. The Hill is not haunted. It is inhabited. There is a difference. Haunted brings a negative vibration which is the furthest from what The Hill energy is all about.

With the cameras in tow, I walked through the house, room by room. I opened myself up to each individual space and the separate, intricate energies each room held within its walls. In this kind of work, the breath is the control knob. The breath can be used to deepen an experience, to clear energy, and to center oneself. By deepening the breath, you can go even deeper into the experience. There are other ways the breath can be used to clear energy or take you away from an experience.

As soon as I stepped into one of the first rooms, I felt isolated. A deep, sadness and gloom filled my being. I deepened my breath to further explore this isolating sadness. I began to see and feel the spirit of a short woman, maybe 4'9 – 4'10 inches tall. She so wants to get out of the life of hardship she is leading. She revealed to me that she is the cook, who has to slave over preparing everyone's meals. Nobody appreciates her. She never even hears a thank you. As I delved deeper into her energy, I was able to see the lighted path that she longed for. She so much wanted to be in the main house, to be the one who is waited upon hand and foot. She is stuck in a never-ending cycle of beating herself down. She feels her existence is insignificant and dreams about how much better it could be. She is very frustrated because she doesn't know how to bring her dreams and desires to fruition. She is trapped in a seemingly endless circle of self-torment. She isn't even aware that she has passed. She isn't even aware of my presence. Until she will allow herself to recognize another being, person, or spirit, I can't help her. I ask Spirit to lift all that can be lifted from her and to help her to move toward the light and eventual peace.

We entered another room. I was instantly familiar with the energy. This was the energy and presence of a seven-year-old girl, who I affectionately know as Amelia. Amelia was very excited to see me. She was all smiles and giggles. As I explored deeper, I was able to see through the smile and truly understand what that smile was covering up. How many of the funniest comedians fill you up with jokes and laughter, but behind the laughs are deep-rooted pain and anguish? As I looked beyond Amelia's laughter, I was able to tap into sickness.

My lungs and chest began to fill up with fluid. I began to start choking. I literally felt like I was drowning on the inside. I could feel that she was very confused and so frightened. She could hardly breathe. The breaths were very shallow, few, and far between. I felt like I was slowly drowning. The fluid was overtaking me. Breathing became more and more difficult. I was fighting for each breath. It was getting too hard. I was weakening. The fight was literally being sucked right out of me. I took a few last breaths and then I was out of the body. This strongly indicated to me that Amelia had died of tuberculosis or pneumonia.

The problem was that Amelia was still confused and not completely aware that she has passed.

This precocious little girl pulled at my heartstrings. My healer-guardian-protector side couldn't help but want to just grab this poor child in my arms and take away all of her pain. I had to leave this room. Her emotions were strongly intermingling with my own. I needed to stay focused. I took my deep pranic breaths to center myself. I collected and reorganized myself. I left the room and my little friend, who I was sure we would be seeing more of that night.

I entered into another room. This room was larger in size, but very acute in emotions. I sensed that there once had been a twin bed, which a servant couple had shared. I could pick up that they were a married couple, but there was very little intimacy. Sexual relations were very scarce. For this couple, sex was not really for pleasure, but for procreation. They especially hoped for strong males who could help work in the field to bring in extra money. The couple was very stoic. Their relationship is not the "love of your life" where your heart goes boom type. Far from it! Most likely, the marriage was arranged by the farm's owners, in order to fill the fields with more male workers. To each his or her own, but I find this not to be living, more like just existing. There is no creativity, no spark. Zip. Zilch. Nada. No thank you. I got outta this room pronto.

The crew followed me up the stairs to the second floor. This floor had a really nice cheerful vibe. The energy felt so much better. We first entered a fun double bedroom. I felt waves of passion, love, sex and lots of laughing. I saw and felt the spirit of a twenty seven-year-old male. I knew him quite well. As a matter of fact, I had known him very well in life. This was Elle's brother Steven. Steven had always been ignited. He was a burst of life, who would light up a room with his hilariously upbeat presence. He had always had a crowd of friends around him. Unfortunately, some of the brightest sparks of light who burn so brightly are extinguished well before the rest of us would like them to be.

Steven had had a truly brilliant, inquisitive mind. He had always been interested in understanding how things worked. Now he was checking out the film equipment and the various devices being used to help measure paranormal activity. He was very amused that the shoot was taking place in his own house. He was very happy that I was a part of the investigation. My clever friend was also a big-time prankster who loved to get a rise out of people. I could see Steven as clear as day. His laughter was contagious and I started laughing right along with him. He still hadn't lost his sense of humor, not one bit. He just loved messing with me. He showed me that the vibe in this room was the total opposite of the frigid couple's downstairs. This room was all about passion, love, lust, laughter and a lot of really good sex. My body was filled with all sorts of yummy feelings. Even the crew was feeling the groove.

Steven kept showing me lots of former sexual escapades that had happened in this room. Spirits just love to mess with me like that. It doesn't matter who the person I am reading for is. It can be the spirit of an 85-year-old lady and I can still be flooded with images of past sexual intimacy. In my personal life, I like to keep those things to myself. But I am always forced to see, feel, hear, taste, smell it and then have to tell to whomever I am reading for about it. In this case I was reading for The Hill for an audience, who would watch this investigation when it aired on television.

As a rule, I will not edit what messages and impressions are being shown to me in a reading. Sometimes, the message is the very last thing I would like to discuss with someone. When it comes down to it, though, this work and the messages usually have absolutely nothing to do with me. I, like everybody else, am a sexual person by nature. But most of my friends, and especially my husband, Michael will tell you, that my sex life is one of last subjects that I choose to talk about. This is a complete mystery for some people, who see me as someone wild and uninhibited. Well, news flash! There are some things that everybody needs to keep private in their life. When I was younger, I used to dress quite a bit out there. I guess you could call me a Victorian exhibitionist. No matter what it is about me, I can never be fit squarely in any box.

I bid Steven farewell and promised to give Elle his message to her in private. Far away from the cameras or anybody else for that matter.

Suddenly, both of the camera batteries were completely drained, even though we had only been filming for ten minutes. Mind you, both batteries had been fully charged just before we started the taping. We took the batteries outside the house and put them back into the chargers. The meter instantly showed that the batteries were now once again fully charged. More of good ole Steven's pranks! I just loved it. He hadn't changed a bit.

We are all electrical beings. Our bodies are essentially made up of carbon-based matter, which lowers the electrical vibrations. When we leave the body, our souls are raised back to the higher electrical vibrations. This is why sometimes you may feel a cold chill throughout your body, when you are in close proximity of a ghost, spirit, angel etc. There are times when I will feel the exact opposite. On occasions, I feel intense heat, instead of a chill. I was feeling this heat that night in different rooms of the house, during the investigation.

In the next few rooms, I didn't encounter any spirits, just place memories. In one room I was drawn to look at the window. I saw plants and colorful flowers. I picked up that it was a very creative room. I could see lots of drawings and paintings. Apparently, Elle had picked up that same vibe, too. She had the room setup as a mini drawing studio. The desk was angled to optimize the window's vantage point.

As I walked up the stairs to the top floor, I could feel the heaviness of what we were approaching. I was immediately drawn to the room at the top of the stairs. The one that was renamed The H Room, the very room I had first stayed in on my very first visit to The Hill. I opened myself up to allow the room, as well as any spirits who wanted to make an appearance, to communicate with me. I was quickly filled with the impression of Amelia and her two little girlfriends. The girls were excited that the crew was there and they began to play their tricks. The temperature began to spike. The little girls giggled profusely. They began tugging at my leg to get my attention.

It's okay sweethearts, I can hear you loud and clear.

They start tugging on the pants of one of the crew. He had to keep pulling his pants up. They were amused. As I continued to tap into the room's energy, I was able to feel a hot spot, where the temperature was ten degrees higher than in the rest of the room. Then the girls started to play hide and seek.

I left this room and was drawn to the room directly next to it. The energy was extremely heavy. It felt very thick. It was a bit uncomfortable for me to breathe in this room. My head started spinning. When this occurs, you need to center yourself quickly. As per my previous instructions, I took several deep pranic breaths—inhaling through the nose, down to the diaphragm, and slowly out through the mouth.

After reorganizing myself, I could then tap into the room's energy. I picked up deep emotional imbalances. The emotional pain was coupled with the physical pain. I started to experience what felt like daggers or needle pricks, up and down my spine. Everything started to feel a bit hallucinogenic. Whenever I experience this feeling, it is an indication that intoxicating substances have been heavily used. I sensed this was from a long time ago, somewhere around 1910 – 1918. I could see a man working in the fields. He was stumbling and his leg was slashed deeply by a rusty tool used for shearing the grounds. There was a lot of blood. It was very painful. An infection set into the leg, which caused rivers of painful waves. The feeling of pins and needles up and down my spine magnified considerably. My leg started giving me difficulty. I couldn't stand on my left leg. I had to stand on my tippy toes. My right leg was feeling rather heavy from having to carry all the weight. I felt a constant, throbbing pain. This man had needed to numb the increasing pain. He started by drinking large amounts of alcohol, and then he began taking drugs in the hopes of alleviating it.

The continuous intoxication and pain lead him into a deep depression. The depression grew. It forced him to face his problems. With a gimp leg, he didn't feel like a full-fledged man anymore. He literally hit the brink of despair. If only he could have faced his problems and addressed the issues he needed to work on, it would have been a transformative ordeal. Unfortunately, this was something that this poor soul never got a chance to do. He died from the infection combined with a drug and alcohol overdose. Because his death occurred while he was still intoxicated, his spirit was, in a sense, still intoxicated. He was still in a hazy fog, unaware that he had died so many years ago.

Next I felt the presence of another troubled spirit. I picked up a younger female, middle teens, fourteen to sixteen years of age. She is not married and feels barren and unwanted. In her time, by that age, many girls had already been married and had started families. It may sound a little surprising to us. But at one time, if a girl was not married by her middle teens, she was already beginning to be considered over the hill. This spirit felt that nobody loved her. The emotionally depressive residue of the previous man had affected the energy of this room, exacerbating her insecurities and perpetuated her feelings of worthlessness. She began having suicidal thoughts. She too was drawn toward drugs. The power of The Hill had forced her to confront her painful issues. Why did she feel so hopeless and why did she want to die?

It may not have been the most pleasant of things, but if she had finally confronted her broken spirit, it would have allowed her to begin the process of healing. I did not sense that she had died here, but she had passed long ago. However, her distress and turmoil had remained.

Both of this room's former occupants had left this residence long ago. But the depth of the emotional pain of each of these tortured souls had become imbedded in the very walls of the room. They were both going around in circles in their turmoil. Neither could even see me. I asked the Archangel Michael to lift all that could be lifted and heal all that could be healed. We left this room and headed back downstairs to the kitchen.

The kitchen is very big and has a homey feeling to it. It was the center and heart of the house. This was the room where everyone congregated. Before the filming, it had been agreed that there would be no filming in the kitchen. Nevertheless, despite the restriction, while the crew and I had been upstairs filming, the kitchen had had its own paranormal activity. A crewmember had been silently sitting in the den, next to the kitchen. My husband Michael and our furry child Precious had been sitting on the side porch, next to the kitchen. Both Michael and the crewmember had heard a female's voice calling out. Later, Elle and I also, separately, heard the same female voice faintly calling out our names to us.

The camera crew prepared to setup in The H Room for a séance. I was feeling reluctant about conducting the séance at this particular time. Something was telling me, that this séance would not be like any of my prior séances. Granted, this would be the first time it was filmed. But there was something else that was just a bit off. The film shoot was going well, but it was also a little bit different than what

I was accustomed to. That was not the problem. The whole crew were really good people and the experience was well worth it. However, I normally conduct a séance with another intuitive or medium with whom I have previously worked. That would not be the case this time.

The director had previously told me he was a little bit psychic. Being a little psychic is like being just a little bit pregnant. He asked me if I would be interested in using a Ouija board. I politely answered, No Thank You.

The director respected my refusal to participate with the Ouija. As a matter of fact, I didn't even feel comfortable having it in the house while I was there. The director agreed to postpone filming that sequence until after I had concluded all of my work for the evening. I would not be present in the house, when the other psychic on this film shoot used the Ouija.

In many situations in life, if you feel strongly against something, do not allow anybody to manipulate or force you to go against your feelings. I found the director and film crew to be extremely understanding and very respectful of my wishes. I have been in other situations where there was a Ouija board and the other people couldn't have cared less how I felt about it. I had addressed my objections and I had been told that if I didn't like it, I was welcome to leave. So of course, I was gone like the wind.

When I am working, I always carry an essential oil mixture usually of sage, clary sage, lavender, rosemary, rue, sandalwood, frankincense, myrrh and good old-fashioned Wray and Nephew overproof Jamaican rum with the green and yellow label. At times, I buy a gallon of this white Jamaican rum at a shot. The liquor store thinks I am having a party. Yeah... an exorcism party.

My late healing intuitive partner, the amazing Rev. Sylvaine Wong was an extremely powerful fourth generation medium, psychic, shaman and healer. She had a heart of gold. Syl as I affectionately called her, was easily one of the most knowledgeable people I have ever had the pleasure of knowing. She taught me how to clear myself, as well as an entire house and property. She once explained that the spirits attached to Wray and Nephew are powerful and will assist in spiritually cleaning everything in its path.

If Sylvaine told you something, she was usually always on the money. She was, and still is, a spiritual powerhouse!

Before I do any spirit work, I anoint the space and myself with this powerful mixture. At the same time, I also chant, for the highest of good, all in the path of Light. I like to purify the space and myself by burning sage. However many people do not welcome its thick smoke, which can linger for quite awhile. As a compromise, I use the pure essential oil of sage in my mixture. It has the same effect, just no smoke. My clients have never had a problem with it either.

When somebody refuses to have any part of my oils, sage smudging, sound healing or any form of purification, that instantly tells me that this person is holding onto their pain and problems like a vice grip. He or she will not be open to have any healing take place. My practice is not called H Is For Healing for nothing. The nature of my practice is to assist in bringing forth the optimal conditions, which will allow a person, living, or deceased, to have a healing take place. A doctor or healer can only lead a patient to water. The patients themselves have to be willing to drink. Dark energies are always repelled by the Light. All the tools I use in my practice are there to assist in the transformation to the Light.

There are many people who are drawn to me like moths to the streetlight. However, many of the same people are too attached to their blocks to even step through my doorway. I have had a few would-be clients who literally just couldn't step foot into my apartment. They were just not ready to start the healing process. But there is always hope. In time, we all will be healed and once again be part of the Light. And the darkness will be banished permanently.

Let's return to the séance at The Hill.

We began the séance in The H Room. The participants were Elle, the Director, Julia, another psychic named Jason and myself. I anointed the room, as well as everyone in it. We sat around a table and held hands. I surrounded and sealed the circle with ultraviolet light. I welcomed in the four Archangels (Michael, Gabriel, Raphael and Uriel), Jesus—The Big J, and all higher beings of the Light.

All those who come to us in the path of Spirit are welcome. All others gently and respectfully please leave.

I said prayers and we began. For a while, there was absolutely nothing. The crew's meters didn't detect even the slightest disturbance. I did not sense any activity whatsoever. This was not unusual. Not every séance attracts activity. This seemed to be the case this night. We were getting ready to call the séance to an end, when the other psychic, Jason, anxiously called upon and conjured up his guide Arachneia. He started trying to anger the spirits in order to coax them into doing something. It is a technique that some have used, when no activity is present. To be honest, that just isn't my style. Children shouldn't play with fire. People should not welcome in inter-dimensional dark beings and then piss them off.

Without provocation, Jason continued to antagonize and anger this dark being. All of a sudden the temperature spiked. I could feel and smell a horrible entity. Jason was channeling, yelling, and screaming. I wasn't sure if he just didn't have enough experience doing séances or if he was being theatrical for the cameras. His feelings seemed genuine, so I gave him the benefit of a doubt.

Jason continued to raise hell both figuratively and literally. I could now feel Amelia. The dark being was scaring her. I was not pleased. All of a sudden, the director started choking. He was under attack by the dark being. It was trying to take him over. He was in danger.

I wasn't going to tolerate any more of this! I asked everyone to immediately send him the highest form of light and love. I called upon the Archangel Michael to help remove whatever was trying to take over the director. Sensing that this could quickly start to get out of hand, I called upon The Big J and all four Archangels to jointly kick this dark entity's evil ass!

I performed an immediate exorcism, banishing all the darkness out of the room and back to its own world. Poor little Amelia was so frightened. But I was hoping that we might be able to help her transcend up to the Light. The Big J was there to help bring this scared child back to the Light once and for all. Everybody in the room was praying and sending Amelia Light and love. She began to accept. She slowly moved toward the Light. I wished my little friend Light, love and laughter. I told her it was okay that she needed to go to the Light. With our assistance she moved to the Light. She waved goodbye and was immediately transcended up to the Light. She had made her journey back home. I cleansed the space once again and ended the séance.

Weeks after the shoot, Elle reported a significant change in the feelings of the upstairs rooms. Whereas before, she would attend to the beds and quickly exit, now the feeling of barging in on someone was completely gone. Elle said that every time she would come to the house, the door on one room would be closed, preventing the sun from entering the hallway. Since the filming of that night, the door remains open. We eagerly awaited the results from the shoot.

Over a month later, the director spoke with Elle. All the footage had lines and a noise going through it, so nothing had recorded properly. As a result, he wasn't able to use any of the film we had shot. This result is fairly common when filming or taping paranormal activities. The Hill had had the final say.

SECTION 5

TRAVELING BACK TO THE PAST

GREECE

In September of 1998, I went on an amazing adventure to Greece with one of my best girlfriends. Athena and I had instantly clicked with each other from the first moment we met in college and we always knew one day we would travel to Europe together. In 1998 we decided that the time was right.

We both knew that we had shared past lives in Greece together. For us, it was sort of a pilgrimage. From the moment we stepped off the plane, it felt like we had come home. With the very first intake of the Greek air, my whole being began tingling. A myriad of images and memories overloaded my senses. It was as if time was crashing in on me like waves on the ocean. I had always had a strong pull toward Greece and Egypt. Arriving confirmed all my hunches. Now I was 100% sure that I had spent several lifetimes in ancient Greece.

I can only imagine how brightly Athena and I must have been glowing. The native Greeks greeted us with such intense warmth that we felt like long lost family who had finally made their way back home. For some uncanny reason, the native Greeks just seemed to immediately know I was able to see and talk to Spirits. I might as well have had a neon sign over my head flashing PSYCHIC MEDIUM HEALER, because several times I was approached for advice. People never hesitated to come and ask me questions about their lives and their loved ones who had already passed on.

I was at an outdoor café in Athens, eating a delightfully delicious Greek yogurt, when a young woman just walked right up to me.

"Excuse me, I know you're a mystic who can speak to spirits. Can you help me?"

I helped her resolve some lingering issues with her recently departed mother. She was very grateful.

"Sometime long ago we all could communicate with Spirits. But somewhere along the way, many of us lost our way and forgot how to use this ability." She lamented, "It's a blessing that you still have it."

As Athena and I explored the ruins of many famous ancient Greek monuments, we both felt like we had taken a step back into ancient times. We both caught flashing glimpses of the ancient sites in pristine condition, as they had looked in the glorious luster of their heyday.

Athens' Acropolis had a very powerful effect on us both. I could smell the burning incense and oils. I could faintly hear the music that had been playing in the temples still lingering from several thousand years ago. As we walked around the grounds, I became inundated with spirits. I felt rushes of energy going through me. Overwhelming love and bliss oozed through every pore of my being. It was a wonderful feeling! It brought back so much.

A vision of one of my Greek lifetimes quickly flashed through my mind. I was a priestess at one of the temples for Athena, at the Acropolis. I could feel my flowing dress and could hear ancient Greek and Latin being spoken. For the moment, I could even understand it. I knew I was definitely a priestess at the Acropolis and that I had achieved an elevated position in the hierarchy. The regal vibrations surrounding me, as well as the superb quality and nature of my clothing made me very aware of the prominent position I must have occupied.

One day, we traveled to see the temple of the ancient mystical Oracle at Delphi, subsequently known as the temple of Apollo. WOW!! It felt like I had just returned to my old workplace. I had always known I had been one of the countless mystics who had served as a priestess at the Oracle at Delphi. Now it was suddenly all coming back to me. Although the name suggests a singular persona, in actuality there were many priestesses in residence at the temple at any given time. I could remember my daily routines from distant millenniums. I would burn oils and enter into a meditative trance, seated upon a triangular shaped chair. In this trance, I would communicate with Spirit and be given messages for my patrons.

Amazing rushes of energy pulsed up and down my body as we explored the ancient temple. The name Pythia kept repeating in my head, but I didn't understand why. It was only when I researched the word at home that I discovered it's meaning and major significance. Pythia was the name that referred to the priestesses who comprised the order of the Oracle at Delphi.

I re-experienced a very distinctive and specific interaction that I had had with a patron seeking assistance from the Oracle at the time of my service. A man named Arcko had made the long trek to Delphi. He had been a wealthy businessman and landowner. However, by the time Arcko had come to see me, his life was in shambles. His previously successful business had suddenly fallen into major trouble. A terrible fire had destroyed his property and killed both of his sons. He had come in search of knowledge. Most importantly, he wanted answers. Who had done this to him, and for what reason? Why? Why had all this tragedy befallen him?

I could see the face of the man who wanted to destroy him. He was a trusted family member who was extremely jealous of Arcko's achievements. He believed that Arcko had somehow caused all the struggles and failures in his own life, and the fact that nothing ever worked out for him.

I taught Arcko how to perform a small ritual, which would cleanse and rejuvenate him. It would also help him reflect back all the destructive energy to whence it came. In doing this, he could expect his business and family to blossom once again. I told him, his sons would return to him. This time they would come together.

Arcko journeyed back home and followed my instructions for the ritual. As I had predicted, his business flourished. But most wonderfully of all, Archo's wife eventually gave birth to twin boys. His life was restored to its original abundance.

Karma caught up with the man who was responsible for all that had befallen Arcko. As he was walking in the woods, a large tree branch had broken off and fallen upon him, crushing his skull. Hungry wild animals then devoured his body.

As I had explained to Arcko, vengeance is never necessary. The best thing to do whenever anyone is directing negative thoughts and energy toward you is to envision yourself surrounded by a shield of white light, which reflects all negativity back towards its sender. If a person is bombarded with the negative energy that they themselves have sent out, it's only a matter of time until they reap what they have sown.

Athena and I went to another of the famous monuments at Delphi, where I spontaneously attuned her to reiki and gave her the mastership symbols. I initiated Athena into the wonderful world of the healing arts of reiki at a spot where miraculous healings had taken place thousands of years ago. This was, and has been, the most powerful reiki attunement that I have ever performed on anyone. After this attunement, the spiritual activity around us magnified enormously throughout the rest of the trip.

An ancient spirit of a tiny woman kept hovering around me. After much interference on her part, I decided to intuitively talk to her, to see what was troubling this poor, lost soul. She had an elongated face with a prominent nose. She asked me where her son Ziam was. He had gone off to war during one of the many Athenian campaigns and had never returned. She had been waiting for him and had promised not to leave until he returned. I opened up and asked Spirit for assistance.

This poor soul Adria had been waiting for her son Ziam to come back from war for at least 2,400 years. I called upon her guardians for assistance. I also called for her lost son Ziam. Shortly thereafter I felt the faint vibrations of a young male. I welcomed this male spirit, who had come to me in the path of Spirit. I opened up further, allowing his presence to come through much clearer and closer to me. He was dressed in ancient military garb. His aura was shining ever so brightly. He was here to assist. Ziam had finally come home to assist in bringing his long-suffering mother back to The One.

Ziam showed me how, at seventeen, he had gone off to battle in the Athenian army. His troop was resting in a shady patch of trees after an eighteenth hour unsuccessful siege. There were many casualties and they were forced to retreat. One of his fellow soldiers heard a noise and spontaneously stood up to see its origin. A whistling sound pierced through the air and the soldier fell down dead with spears and arrows through his chest. The enemy appeared from out of the woods in a great circle. They were surrounded. They were ambushed and fell quickly. Ziam hardly had time to react before the spears and arrows had pierced his heart, thrusting him out of his body. Ziam now had come back for his mother.

He appears to her as the seventeen year-old boy she had last seen leaving for battle. With the help of her guardian angels, she is finally able to open up and see Ziam. With a twinkle and a tear from her eyes, she and her son are reunited and transcend to the light together.

I love family reunions. It doesn't matter, living or deceased. Who doesn't want to be reunited with their loved ones? This always moves me.

As part of my pilgrimage to my ancient homelands, traveling to Greece was extraordinary. It opened up so many aspects of my being and helped me to integrate them cohesively. While I was walking down the street with Athena in Athens, a blonde woman, whom I will call Gitta, came out of her shop and directly walked up to me. Gitta was originally from Germany, but had moved to Athens and was now the owner of a very successful travel agency. She had seen me passing in the street and literally ran out of her shop to talk to me. Gitta also has the gift and recognized mine instantly. She called out, "Son ... Son" as she chased me down. As I was speaking to her, the spirit of a strong, dominant older female came around. She was very forceful, and insisted that I mention she was there. I asked Gitta if she knew this fairly tall, thick-built, older woman with heavy hands and a birthmark behind her left ear. Gitta instantly knew whom I was seeing.

"Mama, why can't you let me see you?" Gitta cried.

Gitta and her mom had locked horns from the pregnancy onward. Her mother had had a very difficult pregnancy with Gitta, as well as a prolonged labor and birth. Her mother resented her for everything she had had to go through. And to top it off, her mother had wanted a son, which she repeatedly told Gitta throughout her life. She never would have gone through the pregnancy, if she had known she was having a girl. She was very heavy handed with Gitta throughout her whole childhood. Gitta had been forced out of the house when she was barely seventeen.

Gitta met and married a neighborhood boy barely eighteen himself. They both had come from harsh childhoods and had struggled for every dollar they had. Gitta had always had the travel bug and eventually vacationed with her husband in Greece. She fell in love with this wonderful country and she knew she had found her calling. She had an epiphany: she had to move to Greece and open up a travel business. Her husband reluctantly agreed. They moved lock, stock and barrel and set up shop in Athens. Her intuitive instincts quickly paid off. She began working in the travel business and learning the ropes. Eventually she owned her own agency. She became Mama to all her clients and in a short period of time, her business flourished. She made numerous attempts to reconcile with her Mother, who was very stoic and as cold as the Berlin wall. Her mother's bitterness hadn't lessened with time. If anything, she had grown harder. When her mother grew ill, Gitta went to visit. Her mother ranted about how Gitta had been her life's biggest disappointment and that she wished they both had died in childhood. Even on her deathbed she still shunned Gitta. She ordered her out of the room, saying that she just wanted to die in peace. Gitta had made every attempt to break through, but her mother would have no part of it. In spite of everything, Gitta still loved her mother. She tearfully left and within six days her mother had died.

Gitta had been trying to communicate with her spirit ever since, with no success. That's where I came in. Her mother now wanted to make amends and show her daughter the love that she had so longed for throughout her life. She had never once even given her daughter a hug. Now she was ready to help repair the emotional damage that she had caused. When I relayed her mother's message, Gitta started shouting out, "Mama ... Mama ... Let me feel you ... touch me."

After assuring her mother it was all right, her spirit finally came around Gitta and put her arms around her. Tears started flowing down Gitta's face. She could now feel and see her mother's spirit. I was able to assist in opening up the channel of communication between them and they were both very grateful.

I later noticed an Egyptian tourism poster in Gitta's office. She asked me if I had ever been to Egypt. I had not. Athena knew that I had always wanted to go there, but that I just needed an extra push. She gave me that push with pleasure.

Athena told Gitta, "Yes, book him a trip to Egypt NOW!"

These two women knew that I was a little gun shy and they simply took the decision away from me. Within an hour, I had full reservations for my trip to Egypt. I would be fulfilling the travel dream of my life by going to the land of the pharaohs. Athena needed to return to New York. So within a few days, I would be heading to Egypt by myself. If I hadn't gotten that extra kick from Athena and Gitta, I might never have gone. At least, not at that time. Every once in a while we all need a good push to keep us moving in the right direction.

When it was time to leave Greece, Athena and I accidentally went to the wrong airport. I didn't have much time before my flight was scheduled to depart. We had to make a mad dash to the international airport. We arrived with only moments to spare. A phone call was made to have them hold the plane. I said good-bye to Athena and made plans to meet her back in New York City. I was quickly whisked away on a motorcar, surrounded by soldiers with machine guns, and escorted onto the plane. Within minutes we were taking off.

Cairo, here I come.

EGYPT

As I stepped off of the plane in Cairo and took my first breath of the Egyptian air, tears of joy began to flow. In every fiber of my being I felt that I had finally and truly come home. In relation to my past lives, I feel connections to many places in the world. But no other connection feels as strong as my connection to Egypt. I have always been well aware that I have had numerous incarnations in ancient Egypt. In the majority of those lives, I have served in the role of a Priest/Priestess, magic man/healer. As a respected spiritual advisor, many people, even those who lived in the palaces of the Pharaohs, had sought after me.

My mother reminded me about the time she had taken me to see the King Tut exhibit in NYC when I was a child. I had lingered for hours, describing details about each and every artifact to her. It was back then that I swore to myself that one day I would return to Egypt. And now I had.

The native Egyptians sensed the strong vibrations surrounding me. I wasn't sure if it was at a conscious or subconscious level that they recognized my energy, but I was definitely causing a bit of a stir. Figures! I never could blend into a crowd, even if I tried.

I wanted to stay in Giza, just to be close to the Sphinx. Even as a little boy, I had always had a fascination with the Sphinx. My mother once showed me some of my early drawings. Wouldn't you know it? Many of them bore a resemblance to the Sphinx. I have always felt an enormous connection to this wondrous creature and have affectionately referred to it as my little boo boo. I couldn't wait to finally see it. Filled with anticipation, I quickly dropped off my things at the hotel and went off to explore the Giza markets.

Walking down the streets, I couldn't help but notice how everybody had a pleasant smile on their face and was very friendly. Even the armed soldiers, who stood on virtually every corner, were jovial and very helpful. As I walked past an outdoor Café, I was invited in for a beverage. In Egyptian culture, it is customary, bordering upon obligatory, to accept an invitation to sit and chat for a while. To do otherwise would be considered an insult. That was the last thing I wanted to do.

I sat down with the owner who had an infectious smile. I explained to him that I thought of my journey to Egypt as a pilgrimage, a return to my ancient homeland. The owner said that my features could easily pass for those of a native. In fact, I could even be one of his sons. He showed me the family picture and I could see how we shared similar bone structures, high cheekbones, and large prominent eyes. He advised me that if I didn't open my mouth, I would certainly be taken for a native. He invited me to an afternoon get together with his sons. He wouldn't take no for an answer. I graciously accepted.

I quickly bonded with his oldest son Ali, who was close to my age. Later that day we met up with an American friend of his who was originally from Washington

State, but now lived in Giza. She was an enchantingly beautiful woman, with a very old mystical aura around her. She was fabulous! There was an immediate mutual recognition of our spirits. We had traveled together several times in the past. She introduced herself as Cleopatra and it suited her very well. Cleopatra also was an intuitive healer. When I introduced myself as H, she replied, H as in Healer.

She gave me an impromptu reading. Many things that she told me, I had already known, this was another confirmation with details. She said I was a healer, who was very involved in the mysticism of the ancient Egyptian temples. I had definitely been a high priest several lifespans. At times, I was involved advising those in the pharaohs palaces. We had worked together performing many of the sacred rituals. She specifically mentioned that we had performed rituals together at the temple of the great Sphinx. We had also conducted some of the major ceremonies in Thebes at the temple of Karnak. She reminded me that I had performed many wedding ceremonies and had proceeded over an even greater number of funeral rituals. With my very own distinct way of mixing herbs, oils, crystals, and magical incantations (spells), I had been a well sought after healer.

Cleopatra was a fascinating woman in her own right. She was an archeologist. She had been born and raised in Seattle, Washington, but she had always felt Egypt calling her home. So she relocated to Giza and never looked back. Cleopatra was no ordinary anything. She was an American woman living in an Islamic nation, yet she was treated with the same level of respect given to men. She owned her own small home, and, most magical of all, she actually owned her own camel. In some walks of life, owning a camel is the equivalent of owning a Porsche. It was practically unheard of for a female to own her own property, let alone a camel. But Cleopatra most certainly did.

My new friend Ali rented camels for us and we joined Cleo on a camelback excursion in the desert. During our excursion, Cleo jumped off her camel to show me some tricks. She had taught her camel to dance, stand on two legs, and give kisses. She had even taught her camel to help her with her work. When she was searching for artifacts from a particular period in history, the camel would trot along like a bloodhound. When he had found the right spot, he would stop and bury his head in the sand and then lift it back up with an artifact in his mouth. Remarkably, it was usually from the period that Cleo was studying at the time. The camel did this twice during our trot. This was pretty amazing.

It had only been a few hours since I had stepped off the plane in Egypt, and here I was, riding camelback at sunset. It was a new moon and I was in viewing distance of the Great Pyramids and the Sphinx. It also happened to have been the opening night of AIDA at the Giza plateau. So a spectacular fireworks display was about to take place. What a wonderful welcome home!

The next morning, Gitta had arranged for me to have a private tour of all the familiar treasured sites of Cairo and Giza. My guide was a docile Egyptologist. I felt so much anticipation as we began to tour the Egyptian Museum in Cairo. I knew the museum was going to be intense. I was familiar with many of the ancient artifacts. I recognized them from books and past life memories. The King Tut exhibit at the Cairo museum is truly spectacular to behold. The pictures do not do it any justice. There, right in front of my eyes, were many of the treasures my mother had taken me to see as a child. King Tut's famous death mask especially caught my attention. It totally brought me back to the time in New York, when I had seen it with my mother. I wanted to thank her all over again. If you can, you really should try to go see it for yourself. And to think, he was considered to be just a minor Pharaoh. Yet he was buried with such breathtaking treasure. We can only imagine what amazing sacred splendors must have been buried along with Ramses the Great!

The Pharaohs' Royal Mummy room had made my hair stand on end. I could feel a prominent presence in this room. As I viewed the mummies, certain ones really struck a chord with me. On viewing SETI I, I could innately feel his presence, images of how he looked in life flashed through my mind.

But it was Ramses II who really set off the alarms in my entire being. I could easily see his face right down to his hooknose. I was aware of his imposing stature. I had flashbacks of performing rituals for him and about him. After a couple of deep cleansing breaths, I began to feel his presence. All of a sudden, I felt a hand pressing against my shoulder. Here was one of history's most enigmatic figures and he still was making his presence known. I intuitively remembered that he had had back issues, which caused him to be a little hunched over in the later part of his life. I silently began sending reiki energy to the great Ramses II. Now that was a first for me. I had never even seen the mummy of a great Pharaoh up close before. Yet I had been able to connect to their spirits and had visions of exactly how they had appeared in their ancient lives. The whole experience was incredible.

Next, we returned to Giza to see my little boo-boo. The Giza plateau is the site of the Great Pyramids and the Sphinx. As we approached, powerful vibrations surged through my body, almost like spasms. My tour guide asked me if I was feeling ok. I had never felt better in my life! The largest of the pyramids was closed for maintenance, so I went inside the second largest instead. For whatever reason, there were hardly any tourists around. My tour guide even commented on how strange it was. She hadn't seen so few visitors in many, many years.

Excellent. All the better for me I thought, as I went off alone into one of the great pyramids.

Upon entering the pyramid, one had to kneel down and practically crawl up the inner stairs. The temperature inside was brutally hot. While I walked down the corridor, vibrations pulsated through my body. I took three deep breaths and collected myself. I began to hear faint voices reciting an ancient incantation. When I looked around, there was nobody near. Then I approached the room that was considered to be the Pharaoh's burial chamber. Luck must have been on my side, because as I entered the room, everyone else that had been in it exited. I now had the privilege to enjoy the Pharaoh's burial chamber all to myself. Here I was, alone in one of the most powerful places in both the ancient and modern world.

I almost couldn't believe it! I had been lucky enough to score a private audience. Taking full advantage of the situation, I decided to meditate and I immediately entered into a trance. When I finished, I quietly collected myself and exited the chamber. I looked at my watch and was shocked to discover that I had spent almost ten minutes alone in the chamber. Phenomenal!

Then I heard someone call out my name as I walked down the corridor away from the chamber. It sounded like it was coming from a passageway, which had been blocked off by a steel gate. I peered through. I could see an Ultra-Violet mist appear. As the mist dissipated, I was clearly able to see Anubis (the god with a man's body and the head of a jackal). He materialized before me in full flesh for almost ten seconds. Those ten seconds felt like a lifetime. I could feel Anubis course through my core being. The ancient Egyptian Gods were so much more than just mythical figures. I had just had an encounter with Anubis, the protector of the dead, the afterlife and the Pharaoh. He had just manifested right in front of my eyes.

When I emerged from the pyramid, my guide noticed the expression on my face. "You saw something!" she insisted, "Please tell me about it."

"It was nothing." I politely replied.

I was still taking it all in and I didn't want to disconnect from the experience.

Next we stood in front of the Sphinx. By far, the Sphinx is the most incredible figure that I have ever been blessed to encounter first hand. Majestic and prominent, my little boo-boo was absolutely breathtaking. The Sphinx was even more spectacular in person, than in pictures. As I gazed upon this extraordinary creature, I silently began to open and send it reiki energy. The Sphinx has given so much to so many millions of people. It was time somebody gave something back. I could hear the purrs of this regal cosmic being. The Sphinx liked the reiki. The more energy I sent, the louder I could hear the Sphinx purr. I could feel and visualize some form of a temple inside or underneath. (A couple of years later, archeologists discovered a secret temple located directly under one of the paws of the Sphinx.) After spending some time sending reiki, it was time to move on.

With my guide, I explored the ruins of an outdoor temple, which was located by the entranceway of the creature. I could smell the oils, perfumes, and amber burning. I knew I had walked the steps of this set of ruins before. I automatically started reciting something. My guide later explained that I had been reciting an ancient purification prayer. Only high-level priests and healers were permitted to recite this prayer. My guide kept looking at me with a most perplexed look on her face. I just smiled and continued on.

My final stop in Giza was at an essential oils and perfume factory. The owner was named Omar. I was ushered into a private room, where Omar had requested that I wait for him. An older male entered the room. He had an incredible aura and presence. He looked at me and asked my guide to leave. He wanted to have a private visit.

"I am Omar," he said as he greeted me, "I see you are a reikimaster my friend, H born Harvey Lewis. You have studied under my tutelage before and have returned to study with me again. You have a special gift. That is why THEY have brought you here to me. So I can assist in elevating you to the next level."

This completely caught me off guard. I was speechless, which for me is highly unusual. My tour guide knew nothing about reiki. She didn't even know what my first name was. So there was no chance that she had told Omar anything about me.

Omar was absolutely the real deal. I could feel his eyes penetrate right down into my soul. This was one of the most powerful human beings I had ever met. He told me, he had been waiting for my arrival for some time. He had summoned me and had known that it would be just a matter of time before I appeared before him in the flesh. He asked permission to speak freely. Was he kidding me? I had traveled halfway across the world and I now had the privilege of a private audience with this very enlightened man.

"Do not hold back," I told Omar. "Please tell me everything."

"I can see that you have become reacquainted with Anubis and the Sphinx," Omar began. "When you lived here before, you worked with Anubis many times. (Representing the human embodiment of this high being.) With his assistance you channeled the expertise of higher beings and performed what you would call psychic surgery. You have studied with me in prior lifetimes and it is now time for me to elevate you to the next energy level. As we converse, I am energetically raising your abilities, which will allow you to reclaim more of your healing connection. This will also restore you to the energy level you had attained back in our previous time together. You are not here by accident. Our world is in dire need now of healers and enlightened ones. We must assist in raising the levels of consciousness on our planet. Over time, you will reflect back on this conversation. I will be able to assist you with your work and serve as one of your guides, who just so happen to still be in human form. As you work with the reikimasters in spirit, you will now work with me."

Omar proceeded to tell me about detailed, pivotal events that had changed my life. He spoke very non-chalantly about things. I knew his words were true.

"H, why do you equate love with pain?" he asked me. "Love is supposed to ignite, to heal. It is not supposed to cause further pain and discomfort. Love and sex should be pleasurable, not painful. There is a part of you that feels that if you allow yourself to love, you will automatically be hurt. Your sexuality is a part of you. Why do you deny and push away this aspect of yourself? This time around, you happen to be homosexual. This aspect is as much a part of you as your left hand. Why would you want to chop off your left hand? Why would you want to cut off your sexual nature? Allow yourself to open to love. Remember, love is bliss. It should not be a burden."

"You never commit yourself to anyone." he continued. "You try not to allow anyone to get close enough to that side of love. You are going to meet your partner in this life. Let go of your fears of commitment. Let down your walls and allow your passion to flow. You are here in this world, in this time period to work. One of countless many healers to assist in helping heal the planet and raise its energy level to the next plateau. That is why I have called for you. I will continue to raise your connections and your abilities. They need your commitment now."

Wow! You could have knocked me over with a feather. I couldn't have agreed more. What is H for? H is For Healing! After my meeting with Omar, I felt like a thousand pounds had been lifted off my shoulders. My soul was recharged. Everything was clarified for me.

I would like to explain to you exactly how liberating this entire experience was for me. Have you ever had a pain in your neck and throat, or shoulders, for so long that you have grown accustomed to it? Then you finally go to a chiropractor or massage therapist or some other kind of healer. They crack and twist and pull you until everything realigns correctly, and all of a sudden the pain is gone. It was that euphoric feeling of finally being liberated from longstanding pain that I experienced, thanks to Omar's words.

Later in my trip, I traveled to the Philae Temple, also known as the Temple of Isis. The original location of the Philae Temple was actually located on Philae Island, just 550 meters away from where it was now. However, due to the flooding caused by the building of the High Dam, the temple had been dismantled and reassembled on Agilika Island, its current home. As I waited for the small ferry that takes you over to the Island temple, I encountered a petite, blond American female, whom I will call Beth. I was able to detect that her energy had been fractured and could use a series of my healing sessions. We began talking instantly and formed an immediate connection. We discovered that we were both from the Northeastern part of the United States and that each of us was traveling alone in Egypt.

I heard Omar's gentle voice in the back of my head telling me to give Beth one of my business cards. "Talk to her about reiki," he whispered."Spirit has brought you together for you to help heal her."

As we explored the temple together, we talked about reiki. Beth was fascinated by the origins and practice of reiki. So I gave her my card. If she was ever in NYC, she should give me a call and we could set up a few sessions. She took my card and smiled. About six months later, she unexpectedly found herself moving to NYC. Beth called me up and we began healing and intuitive sessions, which continued for the next year and a half.

Beth was an incredibly sweet, caring soul who was a successful businesswoman. She had control in the office, but no organization or control in her personal life. Throughout her life, she had had a subconscious tendency to play the role of the helpless damsel in distress. Beth always wound up looking like Bambi caught in the headlights. Whenever her life would spin out of control, she would revert back to being a little girl, who wanted some authoritative, parental like figure to just make everything all better. Her subconscious would go on autopilot and she had virtually no idea that she was acting this way. This wreaked havoc on her relationships. Part of Beth was severely fractured and needed to be repaired.

Beth wanted desperately to become a mother, and I knew she would be an excellent mother someday, but something was blocking her from conceiving. Her health was in excellent order, so that was not a factor. Her soul needed to be healed. And that is exactly what we did.

After a few sessions, I was able to get to the core of Beth's issues. There was a part of Beth that was afraid to bring a child into this world. She found our world to be very unsettling, and, at times, a very dark, scary place. Mind you, she had traveled solo to many areas of the globe that most people would never even entertain the idea of visiting. She had been to numerous third world nations without the slightest fear. At times, this woman could be a dynamo and a true force to be reckoned with. She was very caring, and that was her problem. At times, she was a little too caring, particularly with some people, who didn't put her best interests first. That never troubled her.

Beth was so sensitive that just thinking about all the pain and suffering in the world would literally make her physically sick. This part of her didn't want her child to have to be subjected to the hardships that our troubled times had brought. This is why she unconsciously blocked herself from conceiving.

I took her back to some of her past lives where her child had died of disease and despair. Part of her was afraid this might happen again. "Just because it happened before, doesn't mean it will happen again." I explained. "There were lessons that you and your child had to learn and experience in that hardship, which allowed your souls to evolve. This won't happen again in this lifetime."

I worked with her on these issues and I was eventually able to break through. Beth came to accept that although nothing in life is guaranteed, she shouldn't have to deny herself the joy of motherhood because of the what ifs. I knew something inside of her thankfully had shifted. Her fractured state had finally been healed. Now she knew that conceiving a child would be possible for her.

Before you can be the All to somebody else, you need to first be the All to yourself.

Spirit made no coincidence of our meeting. Our first encounter was halfway across the world, significantly, by the temple of Isis. Isis was the Egyptian goddess considered to be the eternal mother and patron of nature, magic and healing. In the ancient world, it was also believed all beginnings arose from the goddess Isis. I knew this was a crystal clear signal of how my practice, as well as my person, had been transformed in just the short time I had spent with Omar. I could definitely feel the higher energies exuding from me. For the duration of my Egyptian pilgrimage, I could feel Omar's subtle presence with me. It was very comforting.

At times, I could hear his voice very clearly, almost as if he were standing next to me. As I visited the various grand temples, Omar would send me visions of what actually used to take place there. Out of respect, I always dressed in my ministerial garb at each of these incredibly sacred ancient sites. The temple guards would take me to passageways and other sections of the temples, reserved mostly for the ancient priests.

I found the Egyptian people to be absolutely wonderful and very hospitable. I noticed that I was walking around the streets amongst people who had only a fraction of the luxuries that could be found back home. However, all I ever saw were smiling, happy faces everywhere.

I purposefully did not go to the breathtaking Abu Simbel Temple, also known as the Temple of Ramses the Great. I would save that for my next trip to Egypt. Since I want to see that temple really badly, I knew for sure that I would have to go back. As a matter of fact, I never took a single photograph of myself in Egypt. There would be plenty of time for that on my next visit. This was truly a spiritual pilgrimage that has affected every aspect of my being, all for the absolute highest of good. Fabulous!!

I will say this. While visiting the Valley of the Kings in Luxor, I had the overwhelming sensation that there are many more tombs with spectacular caches of precious treasures that still lay untouched and have yet to be rediscovered. My experience at the Giza plateau in the Pyramids, in addition to the time I spent with Omar, surely convinced me that we only understand a fraction of the true intensity and brilliance of the ancient Egyptians. There is much yet to be deciphered. In time, many more of these treasures and secrets will reveal themselves to us once again.

FROM HEALER TO A HEALER'S HEALER

AGELA AND SYLVAINE

My travels to Greece and Egypt opened up an ancient treasure chest of experiences for me. Upon my arrival back in New York, I was soon to find out those incredible manifestations were not finished.

While Athena and I had been on the Greek island of Rhodes, we both had felt a strong urge to visit the Acropolis of Lindos. Lindos was an ancient city located on the eastern coast of Rhodes and its acropolis was considered to be the summer home of the Goddess Athena. The view was just spectacular. The Acropolis Temple at Lindos buzzed with activity. Although I was viewing the temple in its current state, once again images of how it looked in its glory days were flashing before my eyes. The area was saturated with spirits who came in, around, through, and near me. At one point, the feelings were so strong that I pulled out my camcorder to try to capture some of this activity on video. At the same time, Athena had also felt compelled to take pictures with our regular camera we had affectionately named Baklava.

When I got back to New York, I developed the film. As I looked through the photos from the twenty-five roles of film that we had taken, I came across the pictures from that day at The Temple of Lindos. My hands starting shaking. I thumbed through the stack and then came across the one picture that has had an enormous influence on my life and practice ever since. There was a photo of myself on the steps to the temple. I was holding my camcorder and right next to me there was an image in a rainbow. As I looked more closely, the rainbow in the photo started to appear brighter. As I continued to look, the image of a woman began to appear within the rainbow. She was looking at me. As I kept looking, the woman's image became increasingly brighter. I was now totally shaking with excitement. I could actually make out clearly the spirit form of a woman looking at me in the photo. I had a booking that day, so I took my photo with me.

Before going on the trip, I had decided that the last person to leave a message on my answering machine would be the first person I would call back upon my return. That particular message happened to be from Joanne, a fellow medium whose psychic fairs I had worked from time to time. Joanne had a client whose house had a lot of strange things happening and wanted to know what was going on. Joanne was gathering around twenty of us to investigate the numerous activities at her client's house.

Upon arriving, my eyes immediately connected with those of this incredible soul, my dear friend and fellow healer Rev. Sylvaine Wong. She was a strong multi-cultural woman with the presence of a powerhouse. Without missing a beat, Syl called me over.

"It's about time " she exclaimed. "I thought it would take forever for us to meet up again in this lifetime."

I was overjoyed to be re-united with my soul sister. I recognized her spiritual presence instantly as someone I have been familiar with for several lifetimes. We talked for a bit and took a walk around the house. We had had many similarities in our practices. Syl was a fourth generation psychic, medium, and trans-healer with a heart of gold. Like Omar, I knew she had entered my life to assist in taking me to the next level in my work.

After investigating, we both concluded that satanic cult rituals had taken place in this house. Through these rituals, a portal to the darker side had been opened. This was causing all the hardships that affected anyone who lived there. Great! All it needed was a Ouija board and my girl Linda Blair spitting up some pea soup. Yuck!!

Syl and I sat on the couch and I showed her my picture from Lindos, the one with the female image in a rainbow next to me. As soon as we held the photo together, the image of the woman started getting brighter. The woman's image continued to grow brighter, more detailed and larger in size. Syl and I began to psychically brainstorm. The spirit started speaking to us. Her name was Agela. She had been a priestess at the Temple of Athena at Lindos. She had lived somewhere around 200-270 B.C. Agela was a very beautiful woman with a very maternal vibration. Her lover had been a man named Stavio. He was from a higher social class than she was. Due to their vast difference in societal hierarchy, they had to be secretive about their relationship. They had both wanted children. Eventually they threw caution to the wind and secretly married. She soon became pregnant. Sadly, a serious complication quickly brought upon a severe and fatal illness. Unfortunately, Agela died without ever carrying her child to life or publicly bringing forth her marriage to Stavio.

Agela told us that she is around to help us with our work. She recognized Syl and myself as mystical healers from our ancient Greek lifetimes. Agela had enjoyed the spotlight in her lifetime. Imagine how difficult it must have been for her, having to keep her marriage secret. She wanted to shout it from the temple stairs. But her duties forbade her. She could relate to my struggles as a gay man. I too, had previously had to hide parts of my life from a harsh society's eye.

Agela has not lost her maternal instinct. She enjoys mothering those of us who are still here in this realm. Syl and I promised her that she would always be given her due credit. Her picture is a remarkable example of a Spirit of a person who has long since past, but her essence still exists.

When I began showing her photo, I noticed a very stark contrast. People who are spiritually evolved and open to life's experiences are able to see her image in the photo very clearly. On the flip side, those who are spiritually and emotionally blocked can't see anything. As a matter of fact, I had some friends at the time say it was nothing more than a smudge on the lens.

Well, to counter that, a photographed smudge on the lens doesn't increase and decrease in brightness on a printed photo. There have been times when Agela's image is as bright as a Christmas tree and takes up a great deal of the picture. Other times, her image is very faint and quite small in size. I once showed Agela's picture to my Mom and Grandma. They both were astonished and silent. When I left the room, I could hear them discussing how crystal clear they could see an image of a woman in the photo.

Agela's photo comes with me to every session and on every trip I take. She has become a part of my family. Many people have commented how they can feel her presence when they see the photo in my home. She loves attention and when I publish her photo, she will get plenty of it.

Shown exclusively on my website is the photo of Agela. Please take a look at it with an open mind and let me know what you see. Sometimes, Stavio will even appear with Agela.

SYLVAINE: MY FRIEND, MY TEACHER AND HEALING TEAMMATE

Sylvaine, like myself, had a presence that was larger than life. She never just entered a room. She strutted in large and in-charge, like she was walking down the red carpet. Syl was fierce. She was an absolute phenomenon.

We always used to joke about how many of our friends considered us to be the rock stars of psychic communication. From the first day we met at a haunted house investigation, we became constant companions. Our instant soul connection was very apparent and we embraced it wholeheartedly. Omar had told me a very powerful woman was going to enter my life and help fine-tune my healing abilities. She would be another soul sister for me.

Syl, a dynamic woman from a multi-ethnic and multi-cultural background had family roots thick with knowledge and wisdom. She was wise well beyond her years. She was a very spiritual person who actively worked with virtually all the realms of the energetic world. In addition to being a reikimaster, she had expertise in the area of spirits, herbs, candles, oils, tarot, psychometry, and so much more.

I had already been ordained as an interfaith minister, but had never attended a thorough training in seminary. My talent was still raw in this area of my practice. With Syl's encouragement, I enrolled in the New Seminary of New York's two-year interfaith ministry program. The New Seminary is the oldest established certified interfaith seminary program in this country, possibly even the world. Their program was truly a life changing experience. Thank you, Rabbi Roger Ross and Rev. Deborah Steen-Ross, Rev. Diane Berke and Rev. Joyce Leichenstein.

Sylvaine's vast experience as a fourth generation spiritual medium and shamanic healer made her a wonderful person to work with. Syl and I joined forces and she became my practice partner. I knew how to communicate with spirits, but had never had formalized training before Lille O'Brien. Syl practically wrote the book on spiritual communication. Her brother also shared these abilities and became another major influence in helping to sharpen my abilities. According to Sylvaine's description, I was a diamond in the rough and they were going to polish this diamond to a level of exceptional clarity and frequency.

My collaborations with Syl were nothing short of explosive. My Grandma's incredible love and guidance had helped me to build my spiritual foundation. I had been blessed with Lille, who had helped to put me on solid healer's legs and build a sturdy healer's home. Then it was Syl who had intensely polished my healer's chops and helped me to turn my home into intuitive spiritual healer's palace.

Syl and I both enjoyed a flair for flamboyant fabulousness. Together we could exorcise a person, spirit, house, building or whatever you could think of. We could banish the darkest energies and transform the densest frequencies to a brilliance of light and love. We found that by adding a humorous theatrical flare, it would lessen the severity of the work we were doing. If our client were pleasantly distracted, he or she would be more at ease. Defensiveness would disappear. This would allow us to do our deep intensive work more effectively and with fewer obstacles.

An analogy would be: a child going to the doctor to get a shot. A good doctor will joke and amuse the child. The child will be consciously occupied by the humorous distraction. This will allow the doctor to administer the shot with minimal discomfort to the child. If a child is frightened and his defenses are all the way up, the last thing you want to do is to come at the child like a set of bricks. The same applies to psychic healing. The results many times are even more effective. You can be extremely serious and humorous at the same time. Your work will be more accessible and more effective.

Sylvaine and I both interacted with the spirit world with a keen sense of humor. Just because the person may no longer be in a human body, doesn't mean that he or she have lost his or her sense of humor. Many aspects of one's personality are carried through from lifetime to lifetime. I have had many encounters with spirits who are just funny, like nobody's business. As a matter of fact, my godmother, Grandma's baby sister, Aunt Ronnie was, and still is, a real pistol. She had a terrific sense of humor and was a true delight to have around. If you ever asked Aunt Ronnie at a party how she was doing, her response was always the same. She playfully would answer, "Ronnie Frank always has a good time!" When she passed, her spirit came to me shortly afterwards. She was as zestful as ever. I asked her how she was doing. Of course, she laughed with her infectious laughter. "Remember bubbala, Ronnie Frank will always have a good time." Her occasional visits are simply delicious.

Syl was an absolute master in creating oil and herbal mixtures. Her recipes were passed down from generation to generation. Different oils had specifically different energetic and magical properties to them. The properties of one oil mixture would relieve migraine headaches. Another oil mixture was an elixir for easing mental anguish that had resulted from deep-seated trauma. When we were going to perform an exorcism, we would charge up a certain oil mixture to a very powerful vibrational light energy. We would use that particular mixture to assist us in breaking up any blockages or darkness that might be present. The properties of certain oil mixtures could banish dark negative energies and confuse evil spirits. Each mixture is energetically charged to vibrate at a different specific vibrational level.

A female client I will call Jill, came to us for a major healing. Jill was in the middle of a destructive storm that had almost destroyed everything sacred in her life. Jill had a jealous neighbor who just had it out for her. Jill was a hard working, driven woman who was a very successful real estate broker. She was married to a devoted, gorgeous, loving husband who adored her and she had a special little boy. Her family life was picture perfect.

Jill's neighbor I will call Eva, was a bad seed. There had been bad blood between Jill and Eva since the first day that Eva had moved next door to Jill. Eva's car had been blocking Jill's driveway and Jill had needed to pull her car out. Jill had politely asked Eva to please move her car. Eva turned and gave Jill an evil look and just walked into her house. A month later, Jill woke up to find her car had been key-marked from front to back.

Jill enjoyed her precious flower garden. It was her pride and joy. She had poured many hours of love and patience into cultivating her beautiful garden. When Jill's family went on vacation one time, they returned to discover that somebody had put lye into her flowerbed, destroying her entire garden.

She had begun to experience horrible migraine headaches. It would feel like somebody putting a dagger through her head. From out of nowhere, her adoring husband had started pushing her away. He couldn't explain why, but he had started to become repulsed by Jill. She didn't understand the sudden change in her husband. He was acting like he was under someone's influence or someone's spell. Her son had started having nightmares every night and would always wake up screaming. Jill's life was quickly spiraling out of control. She felt like she had been punched in her gut and that the wind had been taken out of her sails.

Jill's best friend had come to Syl for a few sessions. She advised Jill to make an appointment immediately. Jill was frantic when she called. Within a few minutes of the phone conversation, Syl could sense the real problem. Jill's neighbor had put some serious roots, a.k.a. a spell, on her and her family. Jill was unprotected and extremely vulnerable to further attacks by Ms. Eva. Syl knew Jill needed an exorcism and she needed it fast. She called me up for my insight. I quickly came to the same diagnosis. Jill needed an exorcism by Syl and myself ASAP. Jill called back very upset. She now had found blood in her urine. She was petrified and hysterical. She wanted us to come and exorcise her whole family and house. The sooner the better!

Syl and I were both excellent medical intuitives. We could tap into someone's energy field to scan the person and find out what was going on. By doing long distance scanning intuitively, we were shown any problems and energy blockages that might exist in that person's life. One of the most innovative medical intuitives is Caroline Myss. Her work is exceptional. I strongly recommend reading her books for a detailed explanation of medical intuitive science.

Syl and I energetically tapped into Jill, her husband, her son and their house. All of her problems were manifesting from a destructive energy cloud looming over her. Upon further exploration of this dark cloud, we discovered that somebody had indeed put some roots on Jill's family. Syl and I tracked the roots cloud directly to a female who had long dark hair, a thick build, dark eyes and a very dark soul. This description fit none other than the neighbor, Ms. Eva. She was responsible for the destruction to Jill's property, as well as for turning her life completely upside down.

Jill was afraid of her. This fear gave Ms. Eva her power and strength. The more power you give to dark forces, the more of a hold they will have over you.

We scheduled an exorcism and complete cleansing for Jill and her family within three days of her first phone call. Syl and I got together to plan the cleansing. We knew the neighbor was using lesser, darker energies to attack Jill. She had sunk her teeth into her and was not going to let go so easily. That was okay. She didn't intimidate us.

Syl and I only work with the light. Dark energies and spirits are pathetically weak and tired. Light always prevails over the dark. The only thing darkness has to use against you is fear, but fear can be extremely powerful. Winston Churchill wasn't kidding when he said, "The only thing we have to fear is fear itself." When somebody puts roots on you and you allow it, it does exactly what it sounds like. The darkness energetically roots itself onto your life force and like an evil vacuum, sucks the very life out of you.

Well Jill was in the right hands. Syl and I had lots of experience kicking some serious dark energies ass! Light is always right and will kick the dark's ass every time. Syl had taught me how to destroy roots and all other energy work that was not based in the light. She had guided me through the shamanic realms until I could find my way myself.

In preparation, Syl and I performed long distance reiki healing treatments on Jill's family and house. We even sent her nasty neighbor, Ms. Eva, some loving reiki energy. The best way to get back at your enemies is to send them some wonderfully positive loving energy. Next, we prepared a potent essential oil mixture, a floor wash, a bath mixture and several candles. We could tell that Ms. Eva's roots were not going to loosen their grip that easily. We were prepared for a fight.

When we arrived at Jill's house, Ms. Eva was standing on her porch trying to intimidate us. Oh, Please! This evil troll certainly couldn't do anything to me. I am of the light and was not afraid of any of her garbage. She started chanting something at us. We immediately started splashing holy water and our exorcism oil combination nearby. We started loudly chanting psalm 23. Ms. Eva was not at all happy. She knew we were there for some serious business. We both looked directly at her and just laughed at how lame her darkness really was. Ms. Eva could feel the light exuding from and around us. As well as our spirit guides.

Syl spoke to Ms. Eva in Patois. She didn't pull any punches.

Get your dark-energy, roots-throwing self out of here or we will do it for you! We are of the light. Your ugly stuff isn't going to work here anymore. This family is of the light. They are ours. You can't have them. Only those that come in the path of the light, those that come in the light of Christ, Yahweh and Spirit are allowed to stay. By the love of the holy Christ, the God/Goddess, Light, all darkness be gone!!

Then Syl started chanting a Sanskrit purification prayer over and over. I kept channeling reiki, the four Archangels and the Christ light.

The nasty Ms. Eva began to cough. The light had started to penetrate her subtle energy bodies. She still tried to spout evil, but she could hardly get the words out. The light of Christ would not allow her. She ran into her house. I was sure she was up to no good. But it didn't matter. The light had already started blocking her darkness. The light had started breaking apart each of her evil building blocks. One by one, transforming them to the light. We could actually hear Ms. Eva screaming like a sick animal in pain. There is, and will be, no sympathy for the evil forces in this and all other worlds. Syl was working full force. She walked onto the evil one's porch while still chanting. Syl and I now both began to splash our exorcism mixture, sending energy of the light to breakup this darkness and transform it all back to the light.

Ms. Eva opened a window and attempted to throw a bucket of pigeon's blood on Sylvaine. The bucket broke and spilled all the blood on her instead. The light will always protect you against all that snake charming nonsense. I channeled Guru Muktananda and Syl channeled St. Germaine for further assistance. Now that many of the heavy spiritual guns had been called in to help breakup this darkness, Ms. Eva finally relented. She opened her window and dropped out a bag of personal possessions belonging to Jill's family. With her source gone, Ms. Eva was now utterly powerless.

She called to Syl in Patois, "Okay, no more. I let go. She is yours."

Sylvaine demanded that she leave the area immediately. Her front door opened and Ms. Eva bolted for her car. She shouted, "No more. I go."

With the source of Jill's attacks destroyed, the hardest part was over. We entered Jill's home and prayed with the family. We blessed every speck of the house and grounds. Then we anointed Jill, her family, and the house with our oils. We gave Jill the floor wash and instructed her how to use it. She did so immediately. Next all three them had to take a bath with our bath mixture. When it was all done, you could literally feel the light and love emanating from the house and Jill's family once again. Score another one for the Light! We came back two more times and repeated the cleansing for Jill and her family.

Within two months, Jill's life was back on track and bright as ever. Jill's neighbor Ms. Eva never did return to her house. One month after the final exorcism, a moving truck pulled up and moved all of her stuff away. The house lay vacant for almost a year before another person moved in. Jill met her new neighbor and was ecstatic. He was kind, peaceful and a Rabbi. Perfecto!

Syl was just amazing to watch and to work with. She was a wonderful ambassador of the light. She was also an extremely accomplished painter. Her artwork was a prayer, a blessing channeled and painted on canvas. She was a devoted mother to her three children and one grandchild. She was a loving sister to her wonderful brothers. Syl had been solely responsible for my entrance into the New Seminary of New York.

When I first met Michael, I knew within minutes that he was the One. When I got back home, I spoke with Sylvaine. She did not miss a beat. She told me that Michael was going to be my husband. That it was a match made in the stars. About one year after our wedding, Syl was supposed to come to our house for a visit. She couldn't make it, so we said we would reschedule very soon. That was mid-August 2005. One month later I received a letter from Syl's brother. I was a little confused when I saw the envelope. I opened it. Upon reading the letter, I let out a heart-wrenching scream.

The letter was an invitation to celebrate the life of the late Rev. Sylvaine Wong. As I am writing this chapter, I can literally feel Sylvaine's hands on my shoulders. It still stings as much now as it did then. We still work together, but Syl is just in another place now.

On the fourth anniversary of September 11th, 9/11/05, there was an electrical fire in Syl's house. The fire had spread very rapidly. Syl had made sure that all three of her children and her one grandchild had made it safely out of the house. Syl was overcome with the smoke and the exit was blocked. Her only chance was out the window. She either jumped or fell from the only available window to exit. She fractured her neck upon impact and died instantly. In the blink of an eye, one of the best soul friends I have ever had was gone. Her sudden, tragic death absolutely destroyed me. It was just inconceivable. I had just spoken with her less than a month before and now she was in Spirit.

It was hard enough to lose Syl, but that it occurred on the anniversary of 9/11 just made the impact all the worse. I constantly think about her. Like clockwork, she still works with me in sessions, but now as one of my spiritual guides. On the day of her memorial service, I was fully prepared to attend. I was all dressed and then I just broke down. My body went numb and I couldn't gather up enough strength to leave the house. I remained shell-shocked for the next few weeks.

I love you Syl, and I will still carry out our work together.

THE THREE MONKEYS: MY HEALING TRIO AND OUR POST-9/11 WORK

Spirituality has always been a huge part of who I am. I was born into the Jewish heritage. Though I consider Judaism as my ethnicity, I do not prescribe to any one particular religious practice or tradition. I am open to most of the forms through which Spirit is expressed in our world. So for me, the role of an interfaith minister was a very natural fit.

Upon my friend Sylvaine's insistence, I enrolled in the New York Interfaith Seminary's two-year minister program. The program is outstanding and I highly recommend it to all who want to explore their spiritual journey on another intensive level.

During my seminary experience, I made friends with many wonderful people. Most importantly, this is where I first met Lynn and Kim. From the very first conversation I had with each of these dynamic women, there was an immediate soul-mate bond. When the three of us collaborated on something as a group, there was true magic in the air. We all quickly realized we had worked together as healers in several previous past lives. As a trio, our individual abilities as spiritual healers were magnified exponentially.

Let me quickly explain exorcisms. You don't always need a dark demon to require an exorcism. An exorcism simply brings light where darkness and despair exist. You can exorcise and transform to light many illnesses and energy patterns that are becoming destructive in your life.

As a class ritual, we performed an exorcism. Afterwards, when we were together, we could not help but notice abnormalities in the energy patterns in other people's auras. We would do impromptu cleansings and energetically rip the disturbances out of their energy fields. During lunch break at Seminary, we regularly performed mini healings for our fellow classmates. Many times these would take place right in the restaurant where most of the class would dine.

To some people's objections, we continued to perform our services for our fellow classmates. Eventually, the Seminary asked us to curtail our work to outside of class time. Out of respect and total understanding, we agreed. That is when our work blossomed outside of the confines of the seminary. Many came back to us later, thanking us for the healings they had experienced as a result of our work.

After being ordained, we continued to practice our work. Together, Rev. Lynn, Rev. Kim, and myself formed a healing group called The Three Monkeys. Each one of us is an excellent healer in our own right. But as The Three Monkeys, we were a very effective energetic healing trio. We were sometimes called in by the medical, religious, spiritual or psychological communities, when traditional conventional medicine and psychological treatments had not been effective. We have received referrals from many religious institutions for our work with exorcisms.

One of the things we did together every month was to perform a full moon ritual. Once, a couple of days before these rituals, the impression of a young, confidant woman, came upon me very strongly. For privacy reasons, lets call her Pam. Pam was a slender Caucasian woman. She was about twenty-three years old. She had an oval shaped face and reddish brown, hi-lighted hair. She was an office assistant/secretary. It was her first real job. She dreamt about traveling all around the world to the most exotic locations. On many a lunch hour, she would drop by the American Express travel office at the World Financial Center. Nothing warmed Pam up more on a blistering cold, wet winter day than to pick up brochures and dream of her trip to Hawaii, Tahiti, and Bali. She spent hours in the travel section of Border's Books reading about how she could bring her fantasy into reality. She was saving up. Well, at least she was trying to save up. She was just waiting for her dream vacation. She could taste it.

Pam appeared to me psychically wearing a grass skirt, doing a hula dance. As I looked at her closely, I began to notice bruises and a pool of blood dripping on the hula skirt. I was confused. I looked more closely and saw a WTC ID around her neck. I immediately understood. Suddenly, I was looking through Pam's eyes. I had the impression of being in an office behind a desk. I heard a loud explosion. I turned to look out the window, only to see a plane headed straight for the building. I became immobilized. I couldn't move my feet. I couldn't budge them even an inch. I wanted to get the hell out of there right away. But I couldn't. My mind wanted to flee but my body was completely in shock. I was frozen in place like a poor little deer, tragically trapped in the headlights of a speeding truck.

Pam knew right then and there that she was not going to make it out of this one. In her crazier, younger days as she referred to them, she had gotten into some tough scrapes. She always had a reassuring feeling deep inside telling her everything would be okay. But not this time. This time there was a much different feeling and it wasn't good.

"Oh My God!!! I'm not going to make it this time. I'm going to die," was the panicked thought racing in her head.

She instantly immersed herself in prayer. "God, please help me. Don't let me die like this."

The protective love of The Divine immediately enveloped her, filling her with bliss and the highest form of unconditional love. I was shown that her guardian angels had shielded her from experiencing any further pain. When the plane crashed into the building, they had pulled her spiritual life force from her body. Her spirit was catapulted out. Unfortunately, because everything had happened so fast, her spirit was still in shock and she was totally unaware that she had died. She was still emotionally and energetically attached to this world. Poor

Pam was not able to move on to the Divine light. Pam came to me in the hula skirt asking many questions.

When a death is violent, and happens very rapidly, many times the person is not aware that they have perished. They will still continue to act out whatever they were doing in their life. They will continually re-live the events leading up to their death without understanding why they can't get back into their body. They are in a constant state of agitation and confusion.

An array of questions repeats in their heads. Why can't anyone hear or see me? Why can't I feel my body anymore? Why can I put my arm right through my loved ones, when I try to give them a hug? What is going on? Why am I in a dream that I can't seem to wake up from? What is going on?

They honestly just don't understand. They are unable to realize that their life is over.

When they see me and realize that I can actually see and communicate with them, I am then hit with a barrage of questions and impulses. Why can you see and hear me while others can't? This is the hardest part of being clairvoyant. You cannot imagine how difficult it is to have to explain to someone that they have passed on. The very life they think they are still living has actually ended. They're stuck in between the different planes of energetic existence. They need to go to the Light, away from everything and everyone they were familiar with. Their pain is enormous. If there are a lot of attachments that they haven't been willing to let go of, and if they are not ready to process all this information, there is a very good chance they might not be willing to leave to go to the Light of Spirit. Easy work this is not!!

On the morning of the full moon ritual, Pam came to me again. It was two days in a row that she had appeared. She was eager to make her presence known to me, but a bit resistant to any sort of resolution that would help her to move up to the Light.

"Tonight, I am going to my monthly full moon meditation ceremony one of my fellow Ministers regularly holds each month." I told Pam, "You are more than welcome to come to the ceremony if you choose to do so."

As I was getting ready for the full moon ritual, my stomach started erupting, causing me severe pain and discomfort. It took most of my energy to concentrate on this pain. It felt like daggers stabbing me from the inside out. In order to determine the source and cause of the pain, I began to focus on where it hurt. I proceeded with deep diaphragm, pranic breathing. This helped to ease the discomfort and also helped to center me. At least enough to figure out the who, what, where, when, why, and how of the pain. Soon I was able to scan my body internally and externally. I found nothing out of the ordinary. This told me that the pain that I was experiencing was not my own pain, but someone or something else's. I rode the wavelength pattern of the pain to see where it was coming from.

It was then revealed to me that the source was Pam. Pam was no longer occupying a human body. But the painful residue of what she had experienced in the final moments of her life right before she had died was still very much a part of her being. This residue had to be transformed to Light before Pam would be able to transcend back up to The One.

As an empathic person, I am able to directly experience in my own physical body, what people, places, things, beings, etc are feeling. Once I had been able to determine if it was my pain or not, I then knew what procedures and techniques I needed to use to release the pain. Or at least reduce it. In this case, the pain definitely was not mine. It was Pam's. I knew I would be able to move and release the empathic patterns I had been experiencing with a series of deep pranic breaths.

However more often than not, when I am trying to release pain and can actually feel the pain subsiding, some trivial and nonsensical thoughts start to enter my mind. I started thinking about my grocery list. I wondered, "What do I intend to wear to that party?" It seemed like everything was trying to divert my focus and concentration. But I needed to lift, transform, transcend and heal the pain that now felt like an anvil crashing down inside of my body. Occupational hazard! I said to myself. See, we're getting side tracked again.

I concentrated on my breathing: deep diaphragm-solar plexus- pranic breaths. Your breath combined with your intention is an enormously powerful tool. Breath and intention are the true building blocks essential to energetic healing. The breath is like a surgeon's hands. With each breath, you are able to feel the pain. By varying the breath, you increase or decrease the pain's intensity. With each breath, you can discover how large or small the pain is and where it is located. You can allow your breath to become like an elevator to your higher energetic self. Your breath is like your rocketship to the higher realms of the energy kingdom. With the breath, you can scan your human, physical body, as well as your emotional, mental and etheric bodies. You can scan all of your bodies to see if there is anything wrong.

After clearing away the pain transference from Pam, I collected myself as a whole once again and prepared to leave for the full moon ritual at Rev. Kim's. As I walked the one and a half miles to Kim's apartment, I began to feel a lot better. As I walked, I created a circle of ultra violet light all around myself and breathed deeply. I began to channel the UV light inside and through me. I became part of the light. I began to feel the presence of the four Archangels around me. The Four, as I affectionately call them are: Archangels Michael, Gabriel, Raphael and Uriel. I could feel my own set of angel wings beginning to sprout out of my back and these wings were BIG! As I confidently graced down the street, the wings began to flap and my speed increased. In my mind, I felt like I was flying. I could feel Spirit beginning to integrate with me, preparing me, and my body, for whatever the evening would bring.

As I approach Kim's building, I could definitely feel that this would not be an average, run of the mill, full moon ritual/meditation ceremony. Then again, at Kim's, nothing is ever run of the mill. As I arrived, I found that I would be the only male there that evening. Among the guests would be my fellow monkeys, Rev. Kim Leslie and Rev. Lynn, as well as Rev. Jeddah, Rev. Sierra and her friend. Also in attendance were Kim's friends Gwen, Darlene and her daughter Sara. Sara had just gotten back from summer camp and looked fantastic. She had grown and was very quickly becoming the beautiful, young woman she is today.

We gathered in a circle, as we did every full moon ceremony. With her beautiful voice, Kim led the circle with some chants. We started with a powerful OHM and then followed with OM NAMAH SHIVAYA. Both Kim's and Lynn's voices are amazing instruments, which they have both fine-tuned to near perfection. Kim then began to work the Tibetan crystal-singing bowl. She was using my bowl and was fiercely working its great potential. Kim was the person who first introduced me to the beauty of the Tibetan crystal singing bowls. She had used the bowl at one of her recent workshop retreats in the UK at Glastonbury. Glastonbury is the enchantingly mystical place where the whole King Arthur/Merlin consciousness originated. This timeless place exudes history and ancestral energy.

As Kim worked the bowl, you could feel yourself quickly meshing into the higher realms. It is a huge sixteen-inch, frosted quartz crystal bowl. The sounds coming from the bowl were truly uplifting and carried us through an energy portal. This opened the circle up to the higher realms of consciousness. A deep silent trance had been brought on by the journey. It was magnetizing. By just letting go to Spirit, I was experiencing a feeling similar to that which is evoked on the centrifugal force wheel. It spins you around and its force practically holds you glued to the wall.

Jeddah broke the silence. This brought our attention back to the circle. There was the spirit of a woman, standing outside the circle, who was too afraid to come in. Her name was Jane. She was extremely shy and very frail. We encouraged Jeddah to talk to Jane for us. We asked Jane to join us in the circle. But she was too afraid. We sent Jane the highest form of unconditional love to help ease her fears. This would help her feel welcome enough to then enter the circle.

In case you hadn't guessed, Jane was a lost Spirit. Though she was deceased, she still had a major emotional attachment to the mental state of her most recent lifetime. She had not been able to let go of her attachments and had been unable to completely transcend to the Light. As is the case with most lost spirits, letting go was by far the most difficult part for her.

Someone in the circle brought it to our attention this was the last full moon before the first anniversary of 9/11. As soon as those words were spoken, I knew immediately what was in store for us that evening. What was supposed to have been a full moon ritual was quickly turning into a grand séance.

Jeddah informed us that Jane had sat down next to her in the circle. Within moments, as if a floodgate had opened, the room began to fill up with spirits and ghosts. Almost every one of the spirits had been a casualty of 9/11. Each was carrying their pain, panic, terror, and confusion about what had happened. They were all at different levels and intensities of denial. Some were much more severe than others.

I was able to feel the presence of a man we shall call Oliver. He was around 5'6 or 5'7 inches tall. He was of Indian descent and he had a potbelly. As I felt Oliver, I immediately began to smell an egg and cheese sandwich. At first I thought I was imaging this, but I wasn't hungry at all. Then I saw Oliver eating a sandwich. Apparently, he had been in the middle of eating his breakfast when the impact had happened. Oliver had a very vivid sense of humor. He was partially aware of the 9/11 disasters. But he was unaware that he had died. He was able to tell me about the impact of the plane and how the whole building had shook to its core. People in his office had started to panic when the announcement had been made on the loud speaker, telling everyone things were fine and asking them to please go back to their desks. By the time the second plane hit, it was already too late. The stairwells were too smoky and inflamed to get down them. He turned in the direction of Mecca, kneeled down and began to pray. And at that point, his guides had plucked him out of his body moments before the floors had collapsed upon him. Oliver knew both planes had hit the WTC, but he was confused. He didn't know where he was and why nobody was able to see, hear or speak to him except for us.

Like I have said before, this is the hardest part of my job. You can only imagine how hard it is, to be the one who has to tell a spirit they are no longer with the living. Their life as they knew it, is now over. It never gets easy. You just learn how to deal with this type of situation. You send them the highest form of unconditional love and ask assistance from your guardians, Angels, Deva's, Spirit guides, Guru's, Jesus, Buddha, Yahweh, Allah, etc. To bask them in a bath of Divine love, and to please help them to let go and transcend back to the One. LET GO … LET GOD …

At this point, Kim's living room was packed with Spirits. A really thick, heavy, gross odor was intuitively permeating the air. It was a horrific combination of gasoline, melted steel, and burning flesh. Many of the lost souls were there by the grace of Guru Muktananda. The enlightened Yogi, who in spirit had been a major factoring in helping to bring about much of the evening's activity. When Muktananda was alive, he had had his own struggles with the human experience, just like the rest of us. During his life, through discipline and devotion, he had been able to overcome the limitations of what the human mind, body and spirit allows us to see, and what not to see. It is said that Muktananda had spoken with some of his disciples in one part of India and by the evening he had spoken with others on the complete opposite side of the country. Mind you, no cars, planes, trains, nor boats had been taken. Through the journey inside, Muktananda had been able to uncover, discover and understand many of life's mysteries that escape most of us. I shall get into my own personal experiences of working with him in more details another time.

All members of our circle realized what part we were playing in all of this. The lost souls were coming to us through our love of Spirit and we were serving as the ambassadors between the physical plane and The One. Since the souls were still attached to the experience of human emotions and consciousness, we had to help embody these beings back into the human experience, so they could finally process the death experience. This would allow them to let go of their attachments to this world. It would enable them to follow their emissaries of Light, back to The One. Kim became the voice and Light of Guru Muktananda.

During all of this, it dawned upon me that this was the very first time that Sierra's friend had come to one of our full moon circles. On her first visit, she was participating in one of The Three Monkeys' full blown séances and doing a wonderful job holding and sending love and light in our circle.

All of a sudden, the presence of a teenage Asian female immediately came right through me with the velocity of a locomotive. This was not an easy one. She was extremely traumatized and appeared to me still all bloody. As I looked at her more closely, I noticed that this fragile child was missing her arm. In its place was a bloody stump, with veins dripping with blood. There was a thick and pungent, rotting, rancid smell. She was in a heightened hysterical state. When she finally began to speak, she started repeatedly screaming and vehemently cursing.

"Where is my arm? Where is my freakin arm? I want my arm."

Her pain was crushing. As she had tried to escape down the stairwell, the floors had collapsed on top of her, first severing her arm, before taking away her very young life. She was crying and shouting for her severed arm. Her blood curdling screams were absolutely heartbreaking. Shrills began to take over my body, until her spirit finally entered into my body. She was so young, just a little bit of a thing. And this precious little girl had been the victim of one of the worst, incomprehensible horrors that someone could have to bear. She was in absolute total shock and had no idea what she had gone through.

Pam, once again, made her presence known to me. She had gathered with the other disincarnates. Muktananda let us know when it was time to gather all of our guests into the center of the circle. Our guests began to raise questions, as we started to bring the disembodied into the center. They channeled through Rev. Lynn. They asked WHY?

I explained that it was indeed time for them to leave all the pain and all of the emotions attached to it. I told them we were there to help all of them to lift away the huge burden, for which they all had been carrying. Lynn channeled hesitation and more questions. Finally my spirit guides showed me the entire horrific picture. The souls of those who perished during 9/11/01 had been rescued from their bodies only moments before their painful deaths had occurred. They had been saved from having to experience such torturous deaths, but their emotions and energetic consciousness had remained at the scene of the tragedy. So they kept on re-living it over and over. They needed to be assisted in understanding that this particular lifetime had come to a conclusion for them. They now needed to go back to the Light for total healing and rejuvenation. An understanding of what they had experienced in this lifetime, and the purpose of it all. In the Light, they would truly understand. Love will always prevail. Through enlightened molecules of matter, I was able to create an airplane made of light and love in the highest of forms. After several more rounds of explanations, it was time for our guests to board the plane, which would help them transcend to the higher realms of existence. Back to The One.

Right before these beloved brave souls began boarding, I called upon a departed soul, whom we shall call Chris, for help. Chris was a fireman who had perished trying to rescue many other souls on 9/11. Very early on after the tragedy, Chris had come to me in spirit. This blessed soul had made his successful transition to the other side. Chris made regular appearances during many of my private sessions with some of the 9/11 lost souls who were drawn to my own light. He told me he would be coming back to aide many of the souls who were still stuck between the physical world, which they no longer were a part of, and the spiritual realm, which they were to afraid to accept. Chris had repeatedly stated that he, as well as several other beings, was there to help guide and assist us in the delicate work of helping those trapped souls finally find peace, resolution and transcend back to The One. It is unconceivable how beautiful a soul Chris is. His loving presence had been an enormous influence in my own personal recovery from the events of 9/11. He has helped free countless tortured souls from a self-imposed sentence of pain, limbo and nothingness. Chris helped us with the enormous task of boarding these souls onto this plane of ethereal light. Their resistance dissipated. He welcomed each and every one of these poor lost souls aboard. When the plane was ready, and most of the souls had boarded, the plane began to takeoff up into the sky, fading back into the cosmic makeup of eternity.

Not everybody had been willing or ready to leave and you just can't force them. Only when they are ready, will they be able to transcend. Pam, Oliver and the Asian girl were all part of the group who had boarded the plane. However, Jane was not amongst them. But Chris had assured Jane that when she is ready, he will be there to guide her back personally. And with that, the séance and the evening had been brought to a close.

PHOTO ALBUM: PART TWO

THE HEALER'S REALM

I SPENT TIME IN GREECE COMMUNICATING
WITH SPIRITS ON DELOS, AT THE SITE OF
THE TERRACE OF THE LIONS.

ON THE ISLAND OF MYKONOS, I TAPPED
INTO SOME MY ANCIENT PAST LIVES: YOU
NAME IT, I WAS A PRIEST, A PRIESTESS, A
HEALER, AND ONE OF THE MANY PYTHIA
(WHO SERVED AT THE ORACLE AT DELPHI).

PHOTO, TOP: BEING ORDAINED AT ST. JOHN
THE DIVINE AFTER GRADUATING FROM
THE NEW SEMINARY OF NEW YORK.
PHOTO, RIGHT: I FELT INSTANTLY BACK AT
HOME IN GREECE AND EGYPT, EVEN THOUGH
I HAD NEVER BEEN TO EITHER COUNTRY.

THE THREE MONKEYS AT WORK:
ON THE LEFT IS REV. KIM LESLEY, AND ON
THE RIGHT IS REV. ISHWARI LYNN KELLER,
SEEN BEFORE ONE OF OUR SESSIONS
HELPING TO HEAL SOULS THAT HAVE
PASSED.

Celebrating an Inspiring Life

Sylvaine Humes Wong

SYLVAINE AND I HAVE WORKED TOGETHER IN
MANY OF OUR PAST LIVES. THOUGH OUR
TIME TOGETHER WAS SHORT IN THIS
LIFETIME, SHE HELPED PUSH ME TO THE
NEXT LEVEL.

PHOTO, LEFT: WHILE PLAYING MY TIBETAN
CRYSTAL SINGING BOWL, A SPIRIT STARTED
CHATTING WITH ME. PHOTO, ABOVE:
EXPLORING HAUNTED PLACES IS ALWAYS ON
MY LIST OF THINGS TO DO. HERE, I AM IN
EASTERN STATE PENITENTIARY, IN TRANCE-
COMMUNICATION WITH A PISSED-OFF
FORMER INMATE.

SECTION 7

MORE SESSION SECRETS

DELTA DAWN, WHAT'S THAT FLOWER YOU HAVE ON?

Delta Dawn is another friend I met while I was working at various places doing readings and reiki treatments. From the moment we met, I knew she would be a good friend, as well as a client. The two usually do not mix well with me. I must be able to discriminate between my personal and professional lives. Delta is one of those rare, special people for whom I can still receive intuitive messages even though I am close to her. With close friends, it's normally hard for me to distinguish between my own feelings and the true intuitive messages. The closer you are to me, the harder it is for me to maintain my unbiasedness with my intuitive impressions.

Delta happens to be a female blacksmith. "Old School" would be the best way to describe her craft. Her metalwork is true artistry. Done with the skill and expertise of a prosperous blacksmith from the renaissance age. Delta has obviously been honing her craft over several lifetimes. Her work can be seen in various museums, galleries, showplaces, top notch nightclubs, etc.

Delta is most definitely an old soul who would give you the shirt off her back, or the last dollar she had in her pocket. This is not an exaggeration. I have personally witnessed her incredible generosity first hand. Her benevolence is remarkable. Delta is such a good-natured soul. Unfortunately many view kindness as a weakness and an opportunity to scam.

She is a very spiritual person. Delta's spirituality is a mixture of both traditional and non-traditional disciplines. She synthesizes a variety of spiritual practices quite nicely. Delta is the person that helped me to reconnect with some of my prior mystical practices.

She is extremely proficient in working with seals, particularly the seals of the legendary King Solomon. Seals are sacred geometric symbols drawn or placed onto an object. They open up wonderfully powerful portals for healing energy. As they are concentrated forms of prayer, using seals is just another way to access the divine. Mysticism has always played a strong role in all religious and spiritual practices.

Delta and I collaborated on combining the seals of King Solomon with sacred reiki symbols. I channeled the synthesized symbols, bringing them into this time/space reality. Then Delta crafted those symbols onto metal wands. These were extremely powerful tools when used in deep meditative, transcendental healing sessions. They empowered the work immensely.

Delta is one of the many unsung heroes I have encountered during my healing practice. Despite her tremendous talent, Delta had hardly been recognized as a master designer and builder. Instead, someone else had taken the credit for the majority of her work. There were absolutely some deep-seated issues I would be able to help Delta with. When I tapped into Delta's energy field, I could detect that lack of recognition was not her only issue. That was just the superficial problem. As brilliantly talented as Delta was, she had difficulties seeing her own mastery herself.

Others perceived this weakness in her, and repeatedly used it to their advantage.

In particular, there was a interior decorator/designer we'll call Emily. Emily legitimately had an excellent sense of fashion, furniture and design. Her design visions really were remarkable and impeccably laid out. Emily truly was a talented artist herself—if only she had directed her powers toward good instead of dishonesty! Like many smart, creative people, her success had gone to her head. She produced excellent work, but at the same time overcharged her clients and underpaid her laborers including Delta. Emily would string the client along always finding something else needing to be done. She would promise everything under the sun to Delta and others to convince them to finish their work. She always said she would compensate them when the job was completed. This would go on for months and in some cases, years. In the end, she never paid them the full fee that had been agreed upon.

Ms. Emily was definitely a piece of work. She was a true psychic vampire, as were her two closest vampire friends. Together, the three of them would look upon you as if you were a tall drink of water on a hot summer day. I actually had a few sessions with Emily. In one of them, I experienced her trying to feed off of me first-hand. I stopped the session and read her energy-draining self quite fiercely. I proceeded to explain to her what she was doing. But then I thought better. Ms Emily was already well aware of her vampire appetite and saw me as a smorgasbord feeding frenzy. What she hadn't expected was that I am always prepared for energy draining people.

Vampires like Ms. Emily can try to drain me all they like. The only thing they can, and ever will get from me is my excess baggage. Stuff I no longer need. They get my mental anguish. They get nothing but crap from me. I strongly advise you to do the same.

Ms. Emily had royally screwed Delta out of payments for three separate projects. It was about time that Delta was paid. I decided to get personally involved. Ms Emily learned really quickly that payback is a bitch.

I began doing energy sessions with Delta. I continually cleansed her and cleared away all the garbage that had become attached to her. As I removed layers of blockages from Delta's energy field, things started picking up for her. I created an energy-cleansing vacuum around her, which would send all the negative energy back to whence it came.

M
E
D
I
T
A
T
I
O
N

A QUICK REJUVENATING CLEANSING OF NEGATIVITY

Allow yourself to picture a circle of ultra violet light all around you. Ultra violet light is unconditional love in the highest of forms. Allow this Ultra Violet light to surround you, to become a part of you. Inhale through your nose, breathing from the diaphragm. With each deep pranic breath, you are becoming at one with this light. With each exhale through your mouth. You are this ultra violet light.

Allow yourself to imagine there is a circle of garbage cans outside of this circle of ultra violet light. These garbage cans are magnetic. They attract all the negative energies. With each breath, the garbage cans keep filling up. When the garbage cans fill up, they automatically explode into rainbows.

During our period of energy work, Ms. Emily dropped out of sight. Nobody knew where she was. Especially the bill collectors who were owed back pay. I could sense that all the negativity Ms. Emily had spewed was now coming back to her. According to the Wiccan Threefold Law, all the energy you send out be it positive or negative, comes back to you three times as much. Well there is a lot of truth to that. Ms. Emily can tell you that herself, if she ever crawls back out from under the rock where she is hiding.

I eventually did run into her. It wasn't a pretty sight. She looked like death warmed over. She begged me to help her.

I bluntly responded, "You reap what you sow. First you will need to pay back Delta and everybody else who you have scammed. You will have to ask for forgiveness and be genuine about it. Only then will your darkness turn around. You need to start living your own life with your own energy. You must stop trying to leech off other people's life forces."

Ms. Emily sarcastically snapped back at me, "You are a minister and healer. You are supposed to help me. You owe this to me."

Oh, have I heard this countless times. The Brooklyn came out of me, and I didn't attempt to keep it at bay. I told Ms. Emily, "The only thing you are ever guaranteed in this world is life, death and taxes. You are nothing but a psychic vampire, a money-scheming barnacle that feeds upon the energy of anyone trying to lead a positive life."

Ms. Emily deserved everything she got. She had it coming to her. I did offer to pray with her for help to change her darkened ways. She refused. As with everything else, she wanted me to do all the work to help her redeem herself. Well it doesn't work that way. I am able to create the ideal conditions conducive to your healing, but the intentions must come from you. I wished her well and went on my way. That was the last I have seen of Ms. Emily.

Delta was never fully paid, but she was now free from this evil, corrosive force.

The next step was to cleanse and exorcise Delta's space. Her loft building was the remnants of what had once been a large factory during the WWI era. There had been a deadly fire in the factory. There were a large number of causalities. It was a horrific scene. When I first walked into her loft, intuitively I could smell and taste toxic smoke. There were several spirits who had been victims of the tragic fire in Delta's loft. I went to work immediately and burned sage, rosemary and rue. I channeled the four Archangels and the Ultra-Violet light of unconditional love in its highest forms. After several hours, I was able to help some of the lost souls transcend to the Light. Many of them had been poor immigrants without much family when they had tragically died. I knew this would not be a one-shot deal. The energy there was very thick. I had a lot of work to do. Over the next several months, I exorcised as many of the dark energies as possible, but the building was infested with dark lost souls who would not—or just could—not leave.

One time I brought my close friend Karen with me. Upon entering the loft, Karen instantly saw a graveyard spirit. When these beings are present, it is extremely difficult to get rid of them. After seeing one myself, we both quickly started to see a whole nest of them. These darker, thicker energies were constantly trying to attack Delta. I created an energy shield of higher light to protect Delta from these beings. As long as she lived there, she would need to have this higher light flowing through her loft. Dark beings are repulsed by the light and would leave the shielded Delta alone.

As long as she lived there, she would be under attack. As a matter of fact, all the other tenants in the building seemed to have a rather negative vibe to them. Like will attract like. The graveyard spirits fed off of the other tenants' negativity. I taught Delta how to protect herself. She is a very strong person. With spiritual guidance I was able to protect Delta from any further infection from these beings.

With daily cleansing and prayer, Delta began to feel the weight of the world lifting off her shoulders. She was able to find and reclaim her voice and self-confidence the negative energies had tried to destroy. She would now be out in front of her designs, metal work and sculptures. Now, when she entered a room, you could sense her confidence as an extremely talented ingénue.

Delta eventually moved out of the loft and her business has been booming ever since. Her former loft building is still haunted and probably always will be. Sometimes a building is so infested with graveyard spirits, that exorcism can only do so much. The building actually needs to be torn down and the grounds must be blessed. It is just like toxic mold or termites. Once they are imbedded in the building's foundation, it is extremely difficult to get them out. The building will eventually need to be torn down to release these negative sinkholes.

MR. S AND BOBO

Over the years, my practice has had a very diverse clientele. People have to me from all walks of life. Being born and bred in Brooklyn, NY, naturally I was quite familiar with many different types. As with all my clients, their privacy has always been given the utmost respect. Therefore, they always felt comfortable enough with me to let their defenses down and allow me to do my work. One day I got a phone call requesting a session. It was mandatory that I make a house call. The man on the other end of the phone, Mr. S, said that I had come highly recommended. I am not opposed to making house calls. We confirmed the appointment and travel arrangements were made.

On the day of the appointment, a chauffeured car arrived at my door. The driver explained, he was there to take me to and from the session. Then handed me an envelope.

Mr. S thought you might need this for the appointment.

The envelope contained his exact birth information: name, date and location. There was also a scarf. As I held the scarf, my body became immediately charged with electrical energy. I knew that the owner of this scarf was very powerful individual. I pictured a male of average height, with a thin muscular build. I felt an extremely heavy hand. This man's word was the law. An image of the man's face came through as clear as a bell. I knew this face. I was familiar with him.

A short woman, approximately 76-78 years old appeared to me in the car, on the way to our session. She told me that her son had been totally devoted to her. He had treated her like a queen. Regrettably, she had treated him like garbage. She had never even told him that she loved him. Instead, she had told him he was vile. Now she wanted to make amends with her son. I assured her, I would try my best to help reunite her with the child she had alienated. She told me to ask him about BoBo.

The car pulled into an underground garage. I was escorted into a beautiful, prestigious house. I wasn't sure if I had walked into somebody's home or if it was a museum. It was impeccably decorated with a collection of statues, paintings, antiques and other wonderful things. It wasn't over the top. It was just enough. I was led into a fabulous room where my client was anxiously awaiting me.

Like I had sensed, my client had a very powerful presence, but he also had enough charisma and warmth to make me feel totally at ease. He thanked me in advance for the session. He explained that his daughter had come to me for a session and he had come up quite a bit in her reading.

His mother now reappeared. I have to say, she was a pushy little thing.

She kept repeating, "Ask him about BoBo!!" She was a handful. A real pistol.

I told him, "I have an older female here with me. She is definitely not a shy one. She is insisting that I ask you who BoBo is."

His face turned as white as a sheet. "Can you run that by me one more time?"

So I told him once again. He was blown away. I told him, "I keep getting images of Bozo the clown." He laughed. He told me that he understood and he directed me to please continue.

"I believe this older female is your mother. She must have been a heavy smoker because my throat and lungs are feeling very thick and I am feeling heavy coughs. Now my lungs are filling up with fluid. I believe she passed from lung cancer."

Mr. S began to tear up.

"You were always trying to help her," I explained, "However, she constantly cursed at you, taking all of her pain out on you. I am given the image of you trying to wipe her forehead and she keeps pushing your hand away. She even goes as far as to spit at you."

She was giving me confirmation that I was correct. This is definitely your mother. She wants you to know how very remorseful she is. She now knows how she was never a mother to you, her only son. She is sorry she was unable to give you the love that you deserved. She wants me to explain to you that she had a very volatile relationship with your father. She loved the lifestyle that his business provided for her, but she hated the life your father led. When she married him, she thought he was one way. But he turned out to be the complete opposite. He was sweet, passive and honest while they dated. After they married, she quickly saw his darker side and she hated him for it.

Mr. S completely understood what she was talking about. She continued to explain things to me and I continued to relay her messages to him.

When you were born, you looked just like your father and she couldn't help herself. She took out all of her anger towards him on you because she thought you and your father were almost the same. She blames herself for your rocky relationship. She really didn't even let you have one with her. Each time you tried to be a good son, she couldn't separate you from your dad. She was far too bitter and closed-minded to see what a loving boy you were and what a passionate man you grew up to be. She blames herself for pushing you into the family business.

She is so sorry for all those harsh things she said as she lay dying. The love she wasn't able to express to you in life, she can now, and is sending it to you in spirit. You mother is asking for your forgiveness.

Mr. S was composed on the surface, but I could tell that the little boy underneath was finally getting his mother's love. He absolutely forgave her.

"Mama. I love you." He shouted, "Yes. Yes I forgive you. That is all I ever wanted was for you to love me."

Mr. S explained to me that Bobo was the raggedy clown doll his mother had given him when he was a child. In fact, Bobo was the only real gift she ever gave him.

"I feel so much better," he said. "Thank you for Mama. You were very good. We will have to continue this again." He became my regular client over the next several years.

Mr. S was always a very generous man. During another session, I once commented about how I liked a beautiful porcelain doll I had seen in his house. When the session ended, the doll was already wrapped up and in the car waiting for me. Not long after, Mr. S passed away. He came back to visit me. But he was not alone. He appeared with his mother. These two reunited souls were delightfully loving together. He kissed his mother. Then he turned around and thanked me. I still get goose bumps whenever I remember this wonderful visit.

MS. MONA AND MR. BRUNO

I was booked for a session by this pretty, young woman in her twenties. I will call her Mona. It was to be a double session, first her, then her boyfriend. As I was traveling to the sessions, I kept getting the image of a Hispanic female, who was very much alive and a practitioner of Yoruba. When I met Mona, she was very excited. Just like a child about to open her presents on Christmas Eve. She was very outgoing and started talking a mile a minute. I joked with her, "Are we going to do a session or an hour of chit chat?" Without even meeting the boyfriend, I could sense he was completely wrong for her. She was just so wonderfully vivacious and full of life. He was the opposite, full of darkness, gloom and doom.

I was able to see images of her drawings and paintings. I got the strong impression Mona was an artist, actually a designer who loved to sketch clothing as well as rooms. "Yes .. Yes.. Yes!" Mona exclaimed joyfully, as I told her details about herself. I could sense she had a taste for champagne, but lived on a beer budget. I could see she was an extremely creative and visual person. But she was not grounded and did not have both feet standing firmly on the Earth. I quickly saw her taste for the fast life, as well as a taste for fast men. I advised her not to pick out her china patterns just yet.

She has a very energizing aura around her, which attracts many psychic vampires, such as her current boyfriend. She always had the ability to look at the positive side of life, regardless of what the circumstances may be. She is free with her emotions and is not guarded in the slightest bit. Mona was a very giving, trusting person. That is her problem. She was a little too trusting and too giving to the wrong people.

Mona had a tendency to start and stop things in her life. She had difficulty in keeping her concentration on just one thing. Her energy was scattered all over the place. I instructed her on how to put a circle of light around herself for protection against those draining people and spirits that follow her. This will help Mona with her focus issues.

Here is the guided spiritual healing exercise that I conducted with Mona:

HOW TO PROTECT YOURSELF FROM PSYCHIC VAMPIRES (PEOPLE TRYING TO DRAIN YOU)

Begin by closing your eyes. Allow yourself to imagine a circle of white light all around you. This circle of white light is the universal light of Spirit. Only those of the highest of lights, who come to us in the path of Spirit, are allowed to penetrate this circle. Through your nose, begin taking deep breaths, breathing all the way to your diaphragm and slowly exhaling through your mouth. With each breath, you become filled with this white light. With each deep breath, you begin to let go of all the heaviness of the day. Your shoulders start feeling lighter and lighter.

With each exhale, you become of the light. You continue breathing and just letting go. Allow yourself to imagine a circle of mirrors, facing out, all around you. These mirrors are of a high crystal light energy. They are of a very rejuvenating light energy. With each breath, you begin recharging your internal and external batteries. You are now feeling so wonderfully revitalized. Your chi, your energy flow is so much stronger. Every single cell of your being is feeling completely reenergized. These mirrors are very protective.

Now when somebody tries to drain you, they will now be blocked. As they try to drain you of your vital chi energy, the more they will be pushed back. As these psychic vampires continue to try to feed, they will only be able to drain your excess baggage, only on the things that you no longer need. Like the stiffness you feel in the small of your back. The self doubts that block you from achieving your goals. The more they feed, the more of your garbage they will only receive back. Soon, they will stop trying to drain you. They will realize they can no longer be able to feed from you anymore. No matter how hard they try, they will never be able to penetrate you.

After Mona's session, her boyfriend Bruno entered the room where I was doing the reading. I can recognize his type of energy quickly. He was a man with a shady past, present and future. I explain to him how I work. As I begin his reading, I immediately felt the energy of the same Hispanic female I had sensed on my way here. Lets call her Siena. Siena was laughing. She was not here to harm. I asked him if he knew a Hispanic woman, and described what I was seeing. He denied knowing her. I continued with the reading. Siena was watching him and laughing. She showed me flash images of genital warts and a very irritated genital region.

Thank you Siena. I really didn't need to see those visuals. Well, there goes lunch. Anyhow...

I very delicately asked Bruno if he currently or recently had been treated for a rash infection in his private region. He hesitated, squirmed then very uncomfortably answered, "Yeah. What about it?"

I brought up the woman Siena again. I told him that I kept getting very strong messages about her. "There is no confusion," I said, "You absolutely know her. In fact, quite intimately."

Bruno pounded his fist on his lap. "That Bitch! Damn you Siena. My friend, you are good, real good! We will have to pick this up again. Thank You."

Bruno dropped an envelope on the table and left abruptly, visibly quite shaken up. He broke up with Mona not long afterwards. But he called me to set up a few more sessions. All were scheduled for two to three hours, but no session ever lasted longer than fifteen minutes, if that. During our sessions, I would channel whatever Spirit wanted me to communicate to him. When I hit upon what he wanted to know, he would raise up his hand like a stop sign and say, "We're Good." The sessions would end immediately. I never questioned and would forget the messages immediately afterwards.

On the very last session we had, I sensed impending danger. I explained what I saw around him. He acknowledged his awareness of a dark cloud looming over him. He asked me to pray with him. He thanked me for all of my help and respect I showed him. He said this was going to be his last session. I have never seen him since.

9/11: ANOTHER VIEW FROM BEYOND

Many times Spirit will send someone to me without any impetus. Sometimes during a session with a client, another person continues to come in throughout the reading. The more the second person comes through, the stronger their energy will be for me. I will intuitively know that Spirit strongly believes that the second person needs a session with me as well.

This was exactly the situation I encountered with a female client we'll call Sheena. Sheena was young and feisty. I happen to enjoy sessions with the feisty ones. While I advised her about her education, career direction, and personal relationships, I received the strong impression of another feisty young female, whom we shall call Tami.

As Sheena's session progressed, Tami's energy intensified considerably. It finally became very apparent to me that Spirit was working through Sheena in order to get Tami to come see me. I could feel it in my bones that a reading with Tami would not be a regular session. My work had been pre-arranged by Spirit and Tami's guides.

I asked Sheena if she could bring Tami to me. Sheena was completely on board and arranged everything. Two weeks later, Sheena brought Tami for a session.

Tami was a dynamic young woman with a very strong tenacity about her. Like Sheena, she was quite strong willed and had a razor sharp bullshit meter. She could smell bullshit a mile away. She was naturally very bright with an equally bright future ahead of her. The only problem was that she had many thick layers of an icy, pessimistic wall around her. The spirit of Tami's deceased mother had been coming to me since the session with Sheena. Tami's mother, I will call Sue, had the unfortunate distinct energy pattern with which I had become familiar. I had grown to recognize this pattern in dealing with many of the souls who had perished because of 9/11.

Sue was remarkably different from most of the other 9/11 Spirits. She had full knowledge of the entire horrific tragedy and was totally aware of her death. As a matter of fact, Sue's spirit had transcended up to the light almost immediately without needing much assistance.

I had developed a rather close bond with Sue in the next couple of weeks she had been coming to me. She had thanked me for my work with many of 9/11's lost souls. She also confirmed that it was through her intervention, Tami had eventually come to me. Nobody knew her daughter better than she did. Her motherly instincts knew I would be able to break through to her baby.

Tami had many reasons for not wanting to open up to the world. In her young life she had experienced deep, tragic loses. The majority of the people to whom she had grown close in her young life had either abandoned her or died. Her Grandma was her anchor and made her feel safe, protected and unconditionally loved. Tami's friends were all there for her at a moment's notice. But there is nothing that can replace loving parents. Her Grandma was her world. But Grandma was getting up there in age and her health was not what it had once been. She was absolutely petrified that her Grandma would leave her, just like virtually everybody else to whom she had opened her heart.

Tami entered my apartment with her arms folded. I could intuitively see the thick walls around her. Precious, greeted her at the door. Precious liked Tami and remained in the room for the entire session. My furry child Precious is an extremely perceptive, therapy-healing dog. She exudes an overwhelming exuberance of love and comfort and an extra special healing element to my sessions. As I have told you before, Precious is my litmus test with my sessions at home. After she greets them at the door, she instantly can sense the person's energy. If she finds their energy to be of a good nature, she will remain in the room. When she senses someone of a negative energy, she will leave and go into another room. There has never been a session in which Precious has remained in the room with me, that has not gone well. When she occasionally bolts to another room, those sessions have always been brutally difficult.

Precious really took to Tami. Like her daddy, she could sense the frightened, fractured girl hiding behind the emotionless facade of the brave young woman in front of me. She was brilliant and beautiful with a world of opportunity at her feet. There were many people who had tried to get close to her. But her deep emotional pain was shutting the world out. She was full of life, but her pain was allowing her only to exist.

As with all my sessions, I began with a meditation to relax Tami. This also allowed her defensive walls to loosen just enough for our energies to join together. I was able to tap deep into the multi layers of her emotional pain. I began to energetically break up and begin the transformation of many of these long standing blocks that she was holding on to. With each block, I channeled in Ultra-Violet unconditional love energy to transform the darkness by the healing light.

When I sensed the time was right, I channeled in the spirit of her dynamic mother Sue. Tami could now be sure she was feeling her mother's spiritual presence. Sue assisted in the healing of her fractured daughter. There were so many questions she had for her mother and Sue was ready to answer them all.

Sue was one of those rare souls that had a super, dynamic energy about her. She had me explain to Tami that she had not left her willingly. It was part of her karmic destiny. She had known from the time she was born that she would not live to see old age. She always knew in her gut that she would pass at an early age. She didn't know when or how, but she just had always known that she would die a quick and sudden death.

Sue had lived her life to the max. Each day could very easily have been her last and she wanted to live every second with passion. Tami's grandmother was quite the opposite of Sue. Her grandmother was very calm, laid back, and low key. She was also the glue that held her family together.

Sue never believed in hesitation. She acted on her impulses and had no regrets about it. Sue truly lived life to the fullest. She lived more in her short life than many others who have lived well into their eighties. She never obsessed about when her clock would stop. She was too busy trying to fulfill her dreams and desires. She absolutely loved being a mother. She promised to always be there to love and protect her beautiful child. Her untimely passing has not stopped her from keeping her promise to Tami. She had always been and will always be her guardian angel.

Tami had many questions about her mother's passing. Sue was already prepared to answer them. Unlike many of the 9/11 souls that have come to me, Sue had full knowledge of the horrific events that took place. For some reason, I kept getting flashbacks to my own 9/11 experiences and my connection with Cantor Fitzgerald. When I shared my own experience with Tami, everything immediately made sense. Sue had actually worked for Cantor Fitzgerald in the World Trade Center. Sue had worked with many of the lost souls who had already come to me previously.

Sue had the strongest post 9/11 messages I had heard yet. She didn't want her life to only be identified as a 9/11 causality. As she vehemently proclaimed, 9/11 was only a couple of minutes of her life. She had lived a full colorful life and had many attributes to be remembered. She refused to have that horrific label identify her whole existence. She had lived her life with gusto and intended to help Tami do the same.

Tami really did need her mother's exuberant push to jump-start her life. Sue was determined to help her daughter tear down those protective walls that isolated her. Sue reminded Tami how much she loved her. Just because she was no longer in a human body, she had not stopped being her mother. Just as she was her fiercest protector in life, that was not going to change. She would always be around her daughter to give love, affection, and advice whenever her help was needed.

Sue told me of a fashion business Tami was trying to start. She would help motivate and continue to guide her daughter. The only difference now was that Tami would have to open up and trust her feelings. Tami could feel her mother's love during this communication. Now she was familiar with her mother's essence and spiritual presence. It would take some time to master, but Tami could now communicate with her mom.

By the time the session was over, there was a very noticeable change in Tami. She was absolutely engaging and so much more approachable. She knew her mother was still around her and would help with anything and everything. As she exited my apartment, we embraced with a warm hug. She was no longer the unapproachable person who had stepped through my door with tightly folded arms.

Sue told me about what happened to her on 9/11. When she woke up that morning, something just did not feel right. She had momentarily contemplated not going to work that day, but a voice inside her said she had to go. Sue always had listened to her inner voice. She pulled herself together and trudged to her job at Cantor Fitzgerald in the WTC. Once at work, she began looking over her agenda for the day.

All of a sudden, a horrible feeling arose in her stomach. Within mere seconds, a loud explosive sound pierced the air. The building literally shook to its very core. Imagine a magnitude 10 earthquake on the Richter scale. Smoke and fire quickly engulfed the air, making it very hard to breathe. Everything happened so fast, there was no time to react. The smoke and flames blocked the exits and then a second explosive crash rocked the grounds again.

Sue knew right then and there, this was the event that would take her life. She prayed to Spirit, if she was going to die, to please take her right then. The intense heat of the flames was unbearable, but she no longer felt it. By the blessing of Spirit, she was not afraid and not in pain. She looked up to the sky and her guardian angels guided her out of her body. It all happened so fast, but she was aware of everything that had occurred. Throughout it all, from the very first explosion, she just wasn't afraid. Her powerful energy was stronger than some pathetic terrorist asswipes.

After I finished writing this chapter, I had a session with Dr. Deva. As soon as I told Dr. Deva that I had finished writing this chapter, Sue channeled right through me. My whole body was tingling with the exuberance of this truly spectacular soul. Sue was an incredibly old soul and one of the most powerful beings that I was blessed to have channeled. Her sacredness instantly filled the entire room. Dr. Deva and I recognized the true brilliance of her presence. Sue gave us details, she had never revealed in her daughter's session.

Sue's message of 9/11 will hopefully and finally change the world's perception of all souls lost on this fateful day. 9/11 was only a short moment in the lives of these souls. They should all be remembered for the wonderful achievements they each had experienced throughout their lives. The brilliance of the light that these souls had vibrated during their time with us should be remembered. Not just the evil carnage that ended their lives. Help these wonderful souls reclaim their lives' identities that were stolen from them. Sue has absolutely reclaimed hers.

A majority of these departed souls would like nothing more than for their loved ones to move past their grief. They would like the time they had spent on this planet to be remembered for all the beautiful aspects and cherished memories. There were so many wonderful experiences each and every one of these souls had enjoyed. They were full of life and want their life forces to be remembered and embraced. They understand everybody grieves in their own way. However, having an annual funeral and constantly reopening wounds will not let the horror end.

I am a 9/11 survivor. I have been able to transform a good deal of my own pain related to this tragedy with excruciating soul searching, and spiritual and energetic healings. I am grateful to have come so far. I have transformed much of my pain and I am assisting others to transform theirs as well. I try to honor all souls. Everyone is at their own stage in the transformational healing path. There is no set timeframe or formula. Everybody is different and has to heal at his or her own pace. This must happen. Otherwise, the pathetic cowards will have ultimately won.

In communicating with the spirit world, the living plays a very integral part in the healing of those who have passed. The deceased can feel our prayers, love and the thoughts we have for them. By allowing yourself to let go of the pain, you can transform darkness to light. Pain carries very dense energetic residue, which lingers long after an event has taken place. The more a person holds onto their pain, the thicker the negative residue becomes. When you hold onto pain associated with the deceased, you inadvertently anchor that soul to this planet, denying them the opportunity to obtain a full transformation back to the light.

Marilyn Monroe was one of the most beloved of all screen goddesses to have graced the cinema. When she left us so many years too soon, the world mourned her passing. Her vulnerabilities were finally exposed for everybody to see. We want nothing more than for Marilyn to finally be at peace from her life of immense pain. Many of us can relate to her inner struggles and the delicate fragileness of the tortured soul, hidden beneath her platinum blonde mask. Unfortunately, there are many, many people, some who were not even a twinkle in their parents' eyes at the time of Marilyn's highly suspicious death in 1962 who are still emotionally attached to her. They just will not let Marilyn go. This emotional attachment has anchored her spirit here. She has not been able to completely ascend back to the light for a well-needed, healing transformation. By letting her go, she will finally be able to leave. She will always stay in our memories, but her essence will be free to be again.

There is a segment of the population I refer to as pain junkies. This type of person carries their pain as a badge, constantly reliving their anguish in a never-ending loop. A pain junkie will celebrate the agonizing torments, instead of trying to remember joyful memories from their life and eternal love. In almost every conversation, a pain junkie will repeatedly try to commiserate and worship their painful hardships. The inner voice in their head keeps telling them, "As long as I can feel this pain, I am still honoring the deceased's memory. If I let this go, I will forget." Eventually the only thing a pain junkie is capable of talking about is their misery.

Your deceased loved ones want nothing more than for you to let go of the pain. They are in their own process of letting go and want you to do the same. Love never dies. Their love will always stay with you.

The same can be said for all those beautiful souls who were taken from us on 9/11. By letting go of the emotional pain we have attached to them, they too, can be set free to heal. You can still love them, but give yourself permission to release the pain. This will greatly assist in both your healing and theirs.

On each anniversary of 9/11, I prefer to spend that day at an uplifting place, with a positive state of mind. I have had enough of the insincere political photo-ops and their empty bullshit promises. I just feel less talk and more action is needed. Let's rebuild our WTC already.

Celebrate their lives with positive, loving gatherings. This can and will transform the pain, finally lifting the heavy burden we are all carrying from this tragedy. Allow yourself permission to heal. Carrying that pain around 24/7 is not the only way to preserve their memories. They will live in our hearts forever. Embrace their beautiful life forces, not the horrific pain.

I was pleased that on the eighth anniversary of 9/11, it was finally declared the National Day of Service and Remembrance. It's intended to be a day on which we can honor those that were lost and serve the community with volunteerism. I would love to take it a step further. All employers should give their employees the option of going to work that day or volunteering in some community activity. There should be a huge annual festival. We should embrace the unconditional love and care that everybody had for one another. During the days right after 9/11, there was no gender, color, ethnic, religious, spiritual, sexual or social barriers that separated us. Total strangers embraced each other for comfort with brotherly and sisterly love. We looked out for each other with no hidden agenda. We were all connected with one another. This is what we need to refocus our attention upon.

Instead of the gloomy, deafening silence during the reading of the names of those we lost, how about each name being sung in an uplifting cheer. Imagine how much more transformational that difference would feel like. What is wrong in remembering the love instead of the pain?

Everybody across the planet could participate. Just show genuine kindness to your fellow souls. No boundaries... No borders... No bullshit. The theme of the classic Rocky Horror Picture says it all.

Don't dream it... Be it!!

TIME TO THINK OUTSIDE THE BOX

RELIGIOUS NONSENSE

Mother Teresa, one of the most evolved souls this planet has ever seen, was a truly saintly woman who willingly put herself in the midst of horrible pain and suffering. The self-sacrifices she made throughout her life were enormous. She never showed even the slightest desire for self-gain. In her diary, she admitted to having many doubts of faith. Some people are now trying to say that since she doubted her faith, she can't be a real saint. Instead she was nothing but a big sinner. They naively chirp, "She was not supposed to have doubts." If Mother Teresa was not the epitome of a saint, then no one should ever have been canonized as a saint.

HELLO!! As a living breathing human being, it is natural to doubt things. To question things is not sacrilegious. Instead, it reflects a deeply spiritual being who doesn't take things at face value. Keep in mind, Jesus, Buddha, Moses, Abraham, Jacob, Zoroaster all questioned their faiths and beliefs. All the fundamentals of their societies' spiritual and religious practices were pondered and questioned by these great souls.

Jesus always questioned everything in his life. Even though in the core of his soul, he knew that the things he was experiencing were actually happening, he still did not accept things at face value. In the Jewish faith, it is natural for us to explore and debate almost everything. Being a Jew, Jesus always contemplated everything and listened to his higher self for answers. In the Jewish tradition, if something doesn't sit well with you, it can't have absolute faith. You question details that have been accepted as factual. Even the smallest of doubts ignored will leave you less than 100% sure. Your holding back will manifest into something much more visible and perhaps not particularly pleasant, in order for you to gain the necessary understanding.

Countless people go regularly to religious and spiritual services at their churches, temples, synagogues, sanctuaries, etc. They listen to the speakers conduct their sermons, thinking that they are expected to accept their spoon-fed words with complete confidence. The implicit guarantee is that if every syllable is obeyed verbatim, their souls will be saved and their lives will be good. Sometimes going to a place of worship feels like going to see The Wizard of Oz. The almighty powerful, knowledgeable wizard proclaims to have all the answers that are supposed to come from the highest of sources. Some appear to be holier than thou. But when the curtain is pulled away, there is nothing left but a charlatan and the biggest of hypocrites.

I am a very spiritual person, an ordained interfaith minister in fact. I am committed to truly listening and not just hearing. But how many times, when listening to someone's words, does something inside of you just not sit well with what is being conveyed? People around you may be engulfed in the very same words. Some may even be moved to tears. You might start to believe that there must be something wrong with you because you just don't get it. There is nothing wrong with you. What strikes a wonderful chord in some, perhaps even creating an epiphany, may strike a sour note in you. There is nothing wrong with questioning things. We are all truly unique reflections of Spirit. How else will you explore the vast realm of spirituality and the core of your soul? If something is moving you enough to feel strongly about it, it's imperative to dig deeper. For instance, if you have never questioned what happens after death, you are not being completely honest with yourself. Denial is not just a river that flows in Egypt, Blanche!

Religion's original purpose was to unite the people of this planet with the One and create a strong, mutual bond that would join everyone together. It truly mattered at one time. As time has progressed, those in influential positions have tarnished religion. Now it seems more like a historical dogma tool used to pit one group against another group, rather than bring humanity together. How many wars have been waged and lives have been destroyed all in name of religion? God/Spirit would not be happy with people killing one another over the nonsensical my God is bigger and badder than your God stupidity.

I can also say I have a major problem with some of the misogynistic subservient treatment of women by organized religions. There would never have been Christianity if it weren't for Mary Magdalene. The Apostles should have given Mary Magdalene respect as the true Apostle's Apostle. Instead, she was labeled as a whore, squashing any authoritative power women had held in society. It is only in recent times, the church finally removed the prostitute label from her. Still they will not give her the same love and respect Jesus had given her in his own life.

Don't you also find it really funny how boxers and football players thank God for giving them the strength to beat the daylights out of their opponents? I'm amused by those entertainers who thank God for helping them to write a song about tramps, b@%tches, ho's and killing somebody. Something tells me, that's not exactly what Spirit had in mind to bring people together.

How many times have you been stuck on a train with someone claiming to be holier than thou? They have a captive audience who cannot escape. They proselytize their narrow-minded, twisted views to everyone on the train. Behind closed doors many usually have grandiose judgmental egos, gossip, lie and cheat. In an effort to defeat their own inadequacies, they scream loudly, so you will be forced to listen to them. The longer and louder they rant and thump on, the more I have a problem with them. In their closed, distorted minds, they think that what they are doing is in the name of their Lord. Forcibly shoving one's ways down somebody else's throat is just simply wrong. The universal law of Spirit is never to force your beliefs and ways onto someone else. Do you hear that, radical evangelical right-wingers?

When I am on a train, the last thing I want to hear is proselytizing. If I can keep my intuitive impressions to myself, they can certainly keep their opinions to themselves. There are laws against begging. This also needs to be banned. I am all for freedom of speech. But it is not freedom of speech to subject an entire train of passengers to judgmental, evangelistically twisted rhetoric. This is a captive audience unable to escape the rants of a self-righteous nut. It's verbal harassment bordering on psychological torture. Sometimes all I want to do is just to take a train and be left in peace. Why should I, or anyone, have to be Bible-thumped by those who don't even understand what they are speaking about? They are only interested in forcing others to hear their voice. They are appeasing their own egos and trying to tame their own demons.

Not everyone and everything can fit into a nice, neat little box. Many people try to force themselves and force others into those small boxes. In most cases, things will not fit. I have said it before and I will say it again. Religion and spirituality are growing so far apart from each other that they have very little in common anymore. One quote I really like on the subject is:

"Religion is for those who are afraid of Hell. Spirituality is for those who have been there."

The human race will continue to be besieged with non-stop problems until the barbaric discrimination of anybody for his or her gender, race, sexuality, spirituality, religion, appearance and just about anything else is finally no longer practiced. This practice and treatment is just tired and pathetic. We are all creatures of Spirit. Can't we all just get along? We need to—and quick!

By looking down on someone or something as not your equal is denying and disrespecting an aspect of Spirit. That is why this ignorance is finally boldly coming to the surface. In order for our planet and all its inhabitants to survive, we must move past this discrimination. We are all different aspects of the One. But we are still collectively together the One. We now have to do something about it.

As souls, we each have incarnated on this planet numerous times. In our past lives, we have all been men and women. Rich or Poor. White, Black, Asian, Hispanic, Indian and just about every wonderful combination you can think of. A racist in this life could very easily have been a slave in their past life. A homeless person in this life, could just as easily have been extremely wealthy in their past life. When a child is born, they are not prejudiced in the slightest bit. They are a clean slate with no biasness of any form. We, as a society, help formulate these concepts in them.

In basic terms, the body is just an envelope for the soul. This envelope changes with each lifetime we experience. But the soul, the god-like substances within this envelope always remains the same. Our physical world is school for our souls. With each life experience, our souls evolve to eventually the purest state the soul can achieve while contained inside one of these envelopes. Once this is achieved, the soul no longer has to reincarnate. There are also souls and higher beings such as angels that have never had a human life in this physical world.

We are living in very trying times, but extremely encouraging ones. Archangel Raphael is the spirit of the east and the center of freedom from all negative things that hold you down. Now that he is in full force, all falsehoods, dark, misguiding, hypocritical, corrupted lies and dirty secrets are starting to come to the surface, to the light of day. The man or woman who is standing on the platform preaching and pointing fingers at other people has quite a closet full of his or her own ugly skeletons. They had better be ready. All of it will soon come out for all to see.

DEATH

Death is a very touchy subject. Many religions instill guilt and fear. If you don't follow their doctrines to the letter, you are condemned to go to hell. Unless you do what I say, you will not ascend.

There is a general consensus many share about those of us, who happen to be intuitive, psychic, a medium, a healer, etc. We are supposed to have this impenetrable tephlon shield when it comes to the death of our loved ones and those departed souls who happen to communicate with us. It is very understandable to assume this. In fact there are some colleagues in the field who fiercely perpetuate this ideal. Since I do not live in their bodies, I can only go by my own experiences and feelings. But it just disturbs me to hear some of my colleagues claiming to never have had, even the slightest fraction of the fear of death. That might very well be so, and I give major props to them. I am just not there yet. As a human being, it is one of the most natural thoughts to ponder. I have never met anyone who hasn't pondered this question. My spiritual self has no doubts, is 100% crystal clear that life carries on after death. But as a human being, my human emotions, which are experienced only in a human carbon-based body, does question. This is normal. Nobody wants to die. We all want to be with our loved ones forever. If I am nothing, I am honest.

I am able to perceive terminal illnesses and possible impending deaths of total strangers. But this is definitely not always the case with my very own loved ones or even myself. In fact, the most painful frustrations I have experienced are how I am blocked from this vital information about those closest to me.

I confronted this reality with the death of my beloved guardian angel, my Grandma. Along with all the emotional feelings that came up for me during this time and continues to do so. In her final weeks of life, she taught me so much. But her passing made me aware that as a human being, there is going to be to a certain extent, a fear of death. This is a natural part of the human process.

One thing that separates me from many in the new-age community is I am not afraid to admit. There is a part of me that is afraid of dying. I know this may sound contradictory. Especially with my personal experiences and visitations from angelic beings and loved ones. I speak and communicate to my Grandma everyday. I know with every part of my being, this is my Grandma.

However, there is not 100% proof either pro or con, that what I am experiencing is nothing more than just my mind playing tricks on me. I severely doubt that, but there are really no guarantees on what happens once you die, when you actually leave this physical world and your body for good. Yes I am intuitive, but I also am not opposed to also allowing myself to see other points view.

In a trillion years, I would never have seen Grandma being diagnosed with esophagus cancer. When she received the prognosis, I was as equally as blindsided as she was. Though she was in her early 90's, I saw her easily living past 100 years old. I never got even an inkling that she was ill. I never entertained the possibility that Grandma might not survive this deadly battle. After all, Grandma was indestructible. She was one of the very foundations of my life.

It was only during my very last visit with her, at her deathbed, did I finally perceive she was going to pass very soon. She transcended only a few hours later.

My biggest anger questioned why couldn't I have seen this before. How could I have not received any messages that she was going to pass or that she even had cancer? I was just furious, like an erupting volcano.

How about Sylvaine? I spoke to her only a few weeks before she tragically died in that house fire. I never intuitively received any messages that her time was about to come to an end.

I was absolutely furious with Spirit. Why wasn't I given even just a slight message of either of their impending deaths?

I honestly felt I was an utter failure to my gift and to my loved ones. This wracked my brain for several years. It was only later on did I finally come to an understanding. As part of experiencing the human experience, I would not always be able to receive an intuitive heads-up on what may be happening with myself or loved ones. I cannot always be the wise sage and the life saving healer. I have to experience the pain, torment and anguish like everybody else. I have to accept that when it comes to illness and deaths of my loved ones, sometimes I can't even perceive a grain of sand.

During this time, I happened to have seen the truly gifted John Edwards' appearance on William Shatner's cable talk show. I watched the episode and found John to be as real as he always is. At one point in the interview, he talked about the most transformational moment of his life. Without hesitation, he declared it was the death of his mother. He was super close with his mom. Even with his extraordinary gift, he was not able to intuitively perceive she was suffering from cancer.

He never for a minute considered anything but her 100% complete recovery. When she succumbed to this horrible monster, he also was devastated and filled with fury. How could he not have known she was sick and would die from it? He eventually learned the same lesson I did. He cannot be the all mighty powerful healer who can help everybody. It was part of his mother's life path. He finally accepted he couldn't always be everything for everybody. His brutally honest discussion about his feelings and how he overcame it was beautiful. He also confirmed that there was nothing wrong with me. What I was experiencing was normal. This put my ego back in check. There are some things we will never understand until we are back together with the One.

THE FAMOUS WHO HAVE INSPIRED ME

I want to share with you some famous people in our history who have helped motivate and inspire me.

OPRAH WINFREY

Oprah Winfrey is one of the quintessential motivational influences of our modern time. She is a self-made billionaire, who literally started from scratch. She was not born with a silver spoon in her mouth. In fact, if there was a spoon, somebody tried to steal it from her. In her youth, she experienced major-league, unthinkable horrors, accompanied by both friends and family betrayals. Everything looked bleak. But Oprah had a dream in her heart, her body, and her soul.

The dream motivated this brave woman to overcome every form of discrimination that you can think of. Every single door was shut in front of her, but she endured. Her strong spirit broke through each and every one of these doors. Her approachability is what is behind her success. We all view Oprah as one of our family members. She is not afraid to show that she is not a perfect Barbie doll. Nor has she ever wanted to be one. That is what I love about her.

She has made countless contributions to charitable organizations. She has anonymously spearheaded countless programs for those struggling to break through their own doors. She has created programs for up-and-coming starving artists, healers, businesses and just about anything you can think of. Most important, she doesn't have the egotistical need to broadcast her enormous charitable work. She is thankful for what she has attained and hasn't forgot where she came from. Oprah always has and always will be my grrrrrrrrl!! Fabulous!

GEORGE ANDERSON

For many people when I mention the name George Anderson, they are not really sure who he is. George is perhaps the best living intuitive medium we have today. He has written several books, occasionally lecturing and conducting workshops. George is not exactly attracted to the spotlight. If anything, he tries to avoid it wherever possible. His accuracy is incredible and his loving healing gift is nothing short of remarkable. He is very down to earth. His every sentence doesn't start with I or me. Awhile back, the government and Ivy League universities began conducting experiments to explore extra sensory perception. They started testing many of the leading psychic mediums in the field. George Anderson was the top name on the list and still is. He is in tune with his extraordinary gift, but doesn't have the need to constantly pat himself on the back. In his books, he talks about his struggles growing up with the gift. George first started working for a phone company. The more he honed his craft, the sharper his intuitive tools became. Slowly he began opening up about his abilities. Eventually he was led by Spirit to leave the phone company for his private practice full time. As a child, his ability to see spirits was so strong it impeded his interactions with the physical world. It took him many years to finally embrace his extraordinary gift.

The fact that George openly wrote about his early struggles with embracing his fantastic abilities, truly offered me a lot of peace. It helped me understand that I was not the only one who had severe struggles growing up with the gift. I was not some eyesore or incompetent freak who had difficulties getting a grip. George, being a fellow native New Yorker, gave me a sense of kinship with him, even though I have never met him in person. The fact that George once worked at the same phone company that eventually became my corporate employer was the icing on the cake. Of all places to work for, the same corporate America job really has been a great inspiration for me. George broke the grounds and showed me I can do the same.

Thank You George Anderson.

PADRE PIO

Padre Pio is wonderful saintly spirit who I just adore working with. Like St.Francis, Padre Pio, a Franciscan, also had the stigmata. Padre Pio's services were legendary. Countless many who attended his services experienced deep-seated healings and miraculous recoveries. During his services, the stigmata would occur on his hands. Disbelievers, who vigorously tried to debunk his stigmata, constantly tested him. They would make up all sorts of excuses trying to explain why he bled through permanently open wounds on his hands.

The Church and the public had the audacity to try labeling him a heretic. Instead of embracing his miraculous healing gifts, they tried to witch hunt him. Even after his death, the bible-thumping hypocrites tried to defrock him. Eventually divine intervention and Pope John Paul II heralded the acceptance of Padre Pio's brilliance and devotion. Well, long overdue, the Pope finally canonized him with sainthood. I have worked with Saint Padre Pio for many years, as one of my spirit guides. I have asked and have received his assistance in many of my sessions.

POPE JOHN PAUL II (PJPII)

Pope John Paul II was one of those remarkable individuals who transcended all barriers that the human race has used to separate one from each other. He began his life as a poor boy living in war-devastated Poland. He understood all about discrimination. He made Papal history ordained as the first Polish Pope. Unlike many of the Popes that preceded him, he really became everybody's Pope. You didn't have to be Catholic to embrace the unconditional love and overwhelming compassion he exuded.

He made his monumental visit to Israel embracing the Jewish people and asking forgiveness for the Church's anti-Semitic past. Being a Jew, I cannot describe the healing powers of his words. Growing up, I was constantly berated by the ridiculous Jews killed Jesus rhetoric taught in the parochial schools. I was taunted, where are my horns? Unfortunately, anti-Semitism has been a concept a majority of the world has readily embraced. There are still many hate mongers who ignorantly claim the holocaust was nothing but a publicity stunt, in order to get back the land of Israel. The world also stood by as spectators of a sporting event, watching the televised the kidnapping and brutal assassination of the Israelis Olympic team.

Pope John Paul II single-handedly rectified many of the travesties the Jewish people have suffered by the hands of others all in their supposed missions of God. He was a beautiful soul who asked forgiveness for the destructive hateful messages bestowed on history's favorite scapegoats. There were many other hateful concepts that he didn't agree with, but was not allowed to speak up about. When I visited the Vatican, I could feel his love filling up every cell of my body. For a gay Jewish intuitive-medium-healer to feel welcomed and loved in PJPII's home was something I never would have expected.

What I honestly would have expected was somebody to chase me away or try to stone me or something. I'm sure these fears were based from a few past life experiences. But I felt I was so loved by this Angel in white cloth, I was eternally now connected with PJPII. He was an all loving, all forgiving grandfather who had my spiritual back in a remarkable way. In my deepest gut instincts, I never felt any anti-gay resentment from him. I always felt it was church rhetoric he was forced to endure and repeat. My family absolutely adored him. When he came to NYC we got to see him, which was a true joy. Our world is a much better place because of him and we were blessed to have been alive in his papacy's lifetime.

PRINCESS DIANA: THE PEOPLE'S PRINCESS

Princess Lady Diana Spencer was another huge iconic figure that everybody felt was one of the family. Diana's heart was filled with overwhelming love and compassion, it was impossible not to be moved by her. She wore her emotions on her sleeve and spoke her mind about the injustices she witnessed. Yes, she came from a world of privilege, where you were taught expressing one's emotions was for the common folk. Diana might have been born with the golden spoon, but she was really a down-to-earth kind of woman at heart. She abhorred the prehistoric crap that went along with the circle she was born into.

She was an extremely empathic person who truly did feel the world's aches and pains in her being. She wanted to use her privileged position to bring attention to many causes not chic to talk about. She was aware her popularity could help bring about major changes in people's perceptions of some of our world's hardships. Diana totally understood the power that a picture holds. She was easily the world's most photographed person. She knew that a lot of good could come from the same paparazzi photos that also made her life miserable, that a photograph speaks a thousand words and could help to change perceptions.

She was one of the early AIDS activists. Back at that time, people infected with HIV were treated like lepers due to the massive paranoia which surrounded the virus. Diana single-handedly broke through this discriminatory paranoia, when she visited hospitals' AIDS wards. When she was photographed holding an infected child, her compassion was genuine. The photo of the beautiful Diana embracing this infected child in our minds replaced the scarier propaganda images created by the media and the hate mongers. From then on, AIDS patients were shown in a more sympathetic, compassionate and humanistic light. No longer the face of destitute and despair. Diana just totally got it, but was never really given a crumb of credit for it.

The world watched her fairytale wedding with her wedding gown's train that flowed for days. Our hearts were with her. When the fairytale illusion fell apart, Diana openly talked about the difficulties of being a Royal. She never came across as some spoiled snob having herself a grand pity party. Instead, she was your sister, mother, daughter, friend, who had married for love, but only received ridicule from her iceberg of a husband, and especially despicable treatment from her atrocious In-laws. The Royal family absolutely despised how the world unanimously stood behind the heartbroken Diana. Her fragile vulnerabilities showed how she was human just like the rest of us. We all have problems, but ours are not broadcast on a global scale. She discussed her bulimia, her husband's in-your-face infidelities and the difficulties of living your life under a microscope. We all wanted Diana to be happy, but fate would not allow that to be.

I remember exactly where I was, when I heard of Diana's fatal car crash and probable assassination. The entire world collectively mourned our beloved Diana. The British monarchy was almost brought down and disposed of for their disgustingly cold, non-human reactions over the loss of this beautiful soul. It was no mystery why Helen Mirren won the best Oscar for her spot on portrayal of Queen Elizabeth II. We will always love our Lady Diana, the people's princess.

HILLARY RODHAM CLINTON

I have heard a lot of grumblings from the peanut gallery when I mention Hillary Clinton as one of my inspirations. Say what you will about her, but she is a legendary groundbreaker. From her early days, she has always been a staunch civil rights activist. She is completely against discrimination of anyone, for any archaic reason. As a female lawyer starting in the south, she had to fight to be treated equal to her male counterparts. Politics has always been the old boy's network. Woman's role in the political world has been one big uphill battle. The fat cats expected her to shrink away and serve them up mint juleps. If that is what works for somebody, so be it. But that was not sitting right for Hillary. They didn't expect her to be a pitbull of a lawyer with a bigger pair of balls than her male counterparts.

Hillary served as a brilliant, strong, first lady, and essentially as co-president. She has been the constant target of yellow sensationalist journalism for the past sixteen years. Rarely has one person been so unfairly publicly targeted and scrutinized with such heartless criticisms.

With both of her landslide New York Senatorial campaign victories, Hillary showed the world, she was more than just a first lady. As being a New Yorker and 9/11 survivor, I am well aware of her accomplishments as my Senator. Many of the politicians like Gov. Pataki took meaningless photo-ops after 9/11. Hillary actually rolled up her sleeves and really got to work. She steamrolled the government to finally recognize and provide health benefits to all those brave souls medically effected by 9/11. Now our rescue workers and residents are receiving health care benefits to assist in their deteriorating 9/11 health-related illnesses. She also has fought to protect this country from any further terrorist attacks.

She has shown her strengths and vulnerabilities during her presidential bid. She is nobody's puppet or patsy. She would not play the old boy's network politics and was crucified for it. Hillary Clinton is our modern day Eleanor Roosevelt. If she were born a man, she would likely have already been elected president. Instead she has had to break through the stereotypes perpetuated by a male dominated society for as long as time. With everybody in complete agreement including her detractors, Hillary has done an excellent job as our United States Secretary of State.

BEATRICE ARTHUR: RIGHT ON, MAUDE!
When I think of pure confidence, there are very few people that come to mind. Bea Arthur absolutely was one of the people who appeared to bubble over with confidence. While growing up, Bea was hands-down my favorite TV icon. All the roles that she had chosen beamed that bravado. As the controversial Maude Finlay, she was one of the first to deal with so many taboo subjects. Maude addressed abortion, gay rights, repealing the marijuana laws, women's rights, alcoholism, racism, anti-Semitism and just about any fiery subject you could think of. Maude was the only person who could ever put the self-righteous Archie Bunker in his place.

Her sharp wit and razor-edged tongue were in a class by itself. Nobody could deliver a smartass barb like Bea. As Dorothy Spornak, on The Golden Girls, she stole every scene she was in. Who else could deliver a whole page of dialogue without saying a single word? Nobody gave better deadpan facial expressions than the irrepressible Bea. She could flatten anybody with just one look.

Her characters were all very powerful, super confidant women, not to be messed with. In the beginning of my re-invention of myself, I actually tried to emulate many of the strengths of her characters, especially the bawdy, bold and humorous side of Maude.

To my utter surprise, when Beatrice Arthur suddenly passed, her very private secret was finally revealed to the world. On stage, as her Maude-type characters, she was as tough as nails, but in her personal life, off-stage, she was actually very shy and extremely sensitive.

Born Bernice Frankel, a Jewish girl from New York, she was painfully shy. In order to try to fit in, Bea started using her humor to win people over, just like I had done transforming myself from the timid Harvey, to the humorous over-the-top bravado of H. I had never known this about her. This explained why I felt such a kinship with her.

After Bea's passing, fellow Golden Girl, Betty White, talked about an incident that had occurred with Bea when they were out to dinner together one night. Somebody who wanted to praise Bea had approached them. However, instead of compliments, their remarks had been unintentionally very cutting. Bea had laughed it off and casually headed straight to the restroom, where she burst into tears. She had then composed herself and returned with a smile on her face like nothing had happened. Nobody would have guessed she was that sensitive. It was the same for me. Nobody realized the torment that I was going through. I kept up my composure externally, even when internally I was being torn apart. I know this is going to be very shocking to many who knew me growing up. They had no clue what was hiding underneath my exterior.

Thank you Bea for everything. I know many men and women who tried to emulate Bea's confident boldness, during their own transition from their child selves to their adult selves. Just reading all the accolades immediately after her passing backs this up to the utmost degree.

There will never be another Beatrice Arthur. She was an original masterpiece. For all the strength and support her artistic craft helped me to overcome my own anxieties and fears. Bea led by example: nobody can ever laugh at you, if you can laugh at yourself first.

ALLISON DUBOIS and LISA WILLIAMS

Allison Dubois is the intuitive medium, whose life the hit television show "Medium" was based on. Lisa Williams is the renowned medium from England whose grandmother was the intuitive advisor to the royal family. Allison Dubois and Lisa Williams have brought a whole new look and face to the intuitive world. Now the public is able to think of a medium and the associations are now of a brighter encouraging light. Thankfully gone are the days when you immediately associated psychic with Dionne Warwick or Miss Cleo's psychic networks.

Allison Dubois has been tested by many different places for her accuracy. Her work with the Phoenix law enforcement agencies has brought countless evils to justice, as well as saving innocent people from being scape-goated for something they had nothing to do with. I love how the show was not one big Disney whitewash, where everything was just always picture perfect. In her own personal and professional life, Allison Dubois freely discusses her difficulties with her intuitive medium gift. She brings such approachable and intellectual qualities to the field and to the public's own psyche.

Lisa Williams: Life Among The Dead show on Lifetime Cable Network is a breathe of fresh air. I love Lisa's down to earth approach to her practice and her gift. She is nail-point accurate. She is also so approachable and a genuinely lovely person. You don't know if you want to have a reading with her or just sit down and chat for hours over a pot of tea. Lisa Williams' carefree style is similar to my own. I just love how she is able to separate her practice from her private life. When she finishes with her sessions for the day, she puts on her hat and drives home. Putting on her hat is a signal to Spirit that she is not working, and is able to dim the messages from coming in. During a haunted investigation when she senses a room that has an evil vibration to it, Lisa doesn't hesitate to express her disgust and her own personal issues. She tells you how she really doesn't want to go into the room, but will, to help with a healing transformation. She is also a fellow reikimaster. I absolutely adore her brilliance and her inner light.

Both of these brilliant women have done enormous good to countless many people. They both showed the world, that just because you are a psychic, you do not have to fit into a certain cookie cutter mold the media has pigeon-holed us into. They have helped reclaim the words psychic, medium and intuitive to once again be looked at with positive, powerful connotations.

BOY GEORGE, PETE BURNS AND SYLVESTER JAMES

In the wild 1980's, coming to terms with my true sexuality was both liberating and petrifying at the same time. Once I figured out I was gay, I didn't have too many issues accepting it. To be honest, it actually helped make sense with many areas of my life. But my timing could not have been worse. I finally realized who I was and the world was now immersed in the heightened hysteria of the AIDS epidemic.

The media drummed it through your head that being gay could very well equal death. But the blatant, hate-based fear that being homosexual equivocated an almost certain early death, really scared the crap out of me. There were not many positive gay role models I could relate to. But thankfully, along came the colorful emergence of Culture Club's Boy George, Dead or Alive's Pete Burns and the one and only Sylvester James.

Sylvester was an amazing singer/musician who came onto the music scene in the mid 1970's. He never once hid his sexuality and was one of the very first openly gay music stars. His music was incredibly uplifting, soulful, rock-edged dance music, impossible not to put a smile on your face. All my favorite clubs were pumping his fantastic funk. Whenever I was in one of my depressive funks, listening to Sylvester always lifted my spirits. His music is as timely today, as it was recorded almost 30 years ago. I challenge you give a listen to Sylvester's song Happiness and not be filled with uplifting wonderfulness.

When Boy George hit the public spotlight, his androgynous self was a wonderful breath of fresh air. He had an extraordinarily soulful voice that transcended all musical barriers. His delightfully witty, upbeat personality was very inviting and non-threatening. He touched all age groups and helped the entire androgynous 1980's look become much more accepting. His voice was incredible and there was nobody who secretly did not love his music. George still has one of the sharpest tongues and larger than life presences around.

Dead or Alive's lead singer Pete Burns was another androgynous gender-bending rocker. His music and outrageous appearance always put me in a great mood. Whenever I felt depressed, listening to a Pete Burns song always changed my outlook for the better. Pete had and still does have one of the best voices, too. You could not go anywhere without hearing "You Spin Me Round" playing somewhere. Like Boy George and Sylvester, I really enjoyed listening to his music and watching his playful videos. Pete never gave a pluck what others thought of his own style. He is always just listening to his own drummer. I began emulating that same bravado. My exuding confidence grew, as did my own very theatrical appearance.

During that period of time, I was exploring many different sides of self-expression. There were larger-than-life personalities everywhere. Finally I had some famous people I could actually relate to. In a way, it gave me permission to have a lot of fun playing around with my own appearance without taking it too seriously. Their music had so much life and helped me through quite many rough patches. As I pranced my way through the rough streets of New York City, I would crank their music in my Walkman. With my dark sunglasses and my Walkman blasting in my ears, I could tune out countless obnoxious looks. Especially the barrage of the horrendously phobic comments venomously spewed towards me. I was in my own world and having a great time. Their music insolated me, allowing no boundaries of my self-expression and self-confidence. I look back at my wild pictures from that time period and it always brings me back to that carefree period of my life. It was just fabulous!

SOULMATES

Originally I had no intention of writing this chapter for my book. In writing a book, you have to be aware that once you have published it, it will be out there forever. There is no way to unpublish your words, thoughts, ideas and experiences. It's the same thing as trying to undo a sneeze. You just can't reverse it once it is out there. So you always have to think before you write and speak.

I have revealed many extremely personal details and secrets in this book. I feel that by discussing many of my own trials and tribulations, I might truly be able to help others who are going through their own crises. But there are certain things that have no relevance to my practice that I choose to keep to myself. I never wanted to share how I met my soulmate, my husband Michael. This was something that I thought needed to remain private. I have learned the importance of privacy from public figures like Jodie Foster and Johnny Mathis. They will discuss their professional careers and reveal a little about their personal lives, but that is it. Neither has ever revealed anything private that they might live to regret. They understand the need to balance their public and private lives.

If you were to ask any of my closest friends, they would all tell you that although I am a very open person, I will never discuss certain intimate details of my private life. I guess you could consider me to be a Victorian exhibitionist: with some things I can be as open and provocative as possible, but when the fine line of privacy is crossed, you will see me clam up instantly. I keep my public very public and my private very private.

I have to give a shout out to my fab girlfriend Bliss. At one point, when I thought I had finished the book, my girlfriend Bliss convinced me to include this chapter about soulmates.

"H, not just yet," she told me. "Why didn't you write about soulmates? Most people are very interested in reading about soulmates. There are those who have already met their soulmates. But more importantly, you should give guidance and assistance to those who haven't."

Honestly, I felt the subject had already been written about so many times. What more could I say that hadn't previously been said?

"Cut the crap and just write it!" Bliss bluntly said. "Who wouldn't want to read how you, of all people, met your soulmate Michael? How about the steps you took to help manifest and bring about meeting your soulmate? It will absolutely give hope to so many who are still on their soulmate quests. I was there and remember when everything happened and I still want to read about it. Besides, you know Sylvaine would absolutely insist that you included it in your book. I'm just saving her a little astral visit."

Okay okay. I held up my proverbial white flag. I can see when Spirit is trying to send me a message.

Spirit works in so many wonderfully mysterious ways. In our human life, we will come to many crossroads. Spirit will put people, situations, and suggestions in our paths to help lead us in the right direction at each crossroad.

When there is something that you want in your life, you will have to co-create with Spirit for it to manifest into your reality. Pure intention for the highest good is the absolute key in attracting what you truly what.

First, you have to clean up your house before you bring anything new into it. For instance, let's say that you come across the most gorgeous sofa you have ever seen, the sofa of your ultimate of dreams, something you have always wanted. But your house is cluttered with all kinds of garbage, piled up everywhere. Would you bring this amazing sofa into your messy home? Your house just isn't ready for anything new. First you have to clean up and get rid of some of the old stuff that isn't working for you anymore. You need to let go of the many antiquated things that no longer have a place or purpose in your life. Outdated crap just takes up valuable energy and space. Holding onto crap drastically drains vitality from your life. To put it bluntly, crap stinks.

The changes which need to be made encompass a whole gamut of things: people, ideas, outdated concepts, old patterns and emotions, anything that no longer resonates with who you are today or with the person that you want to become. What may have worked for you in the past, may not serve you in the next chapter of your life.

Sometimes, it's just time to let go. Letting go helps to revitalize your resilience and replenish your energy, which will be needed for the transformation of yourself and your life. Indeed, letting go can be very scary. Everything you are releasing is familiar and comforting, yet is an anchor to further development. Consider the fear to be a sort of growing pain. No pain, no gain. No one said growth would always be easy, but it is always worth it.

After releasing everything that needs to be released, you will be ready to attract and manifest new things into your life, be it a soulmate, a new relationship with a loved one, a new career, a new condo or anything else you might desire.

Here are the instructions for a special kind of meditation that I used to attract and manifest my very own soulmate in my life. You can use it to attract your soulmate as well. In addition, you can simply change what you intend to attract and manifest, and use it to attract and manifest any of your dreams.

I like to use a candle for extra gusto in manifesting. Candles are excellent conductors of energy and have been used for thousands of years in petitioning the universal powers and attracting aide and guidance into our lives. I recommend purchasing a candle in glass that can last for several days. Make an opening between the wax and the glass that will be big enough for you to stuff in a small piece of paper. You will also need a blank piece of paper, a pen, and your favorite essential oil with which to anoint your candle. Put on some relaxing music and you are ready.

HOW TO ATTRACT A SOULMATE (OR ANYTHING ELSE) INTO YOUR LIFE

To begin, you will need to clear your mind of everything. Hold the unlit candle in your hands during the meditation in order to charge it up. Start taking deep breaths, inhaling through your nose, breathing all the way down to your diaphragm, and then slowly exhaling through your mouth. Continue to take deep breaths. Concentrate on your breathing, slowly inhaling, and then slowly exhaling. This will keep your mind from wandering and help you to stay focused. You will eventually no longer be aware that you are holding your candle. With each deep inhalation, imagine yourself bringing in wonderful, Divine, white light. With each exhalation, you are becoming this white light. Now imagine you are able to send a beam of this white light from your diaphragm all the way up to the sky. This white light will travel all the way to the divine higher realms. Now allow yourself to feel this divine connection sending a beam of white light from the higher realms back to you.

Now is the time to picture whatever it is you want to come into your life. In this case, we will use a soulmate. Imagine you and this soulmate are together. Try to imagine all the details of what you are looking for in a soulmate. How do they feel physically, emotionally, mentally and spiritually? What are their positive attributes? Just allow yourself to feel all this. Don't worry. Your higher self and spirit are on board with you. It feels absolutely divine! Tell Spirit how you are now ready to meet your soulmate. Stay with this for several minutes. Just stay in this blissfulness for as long as you can. Then go the extra step and stay there even longer. You know you can do this. You have done this before, just in a different form. When you are ready, it is time to come back down to your body. Slowly begin the deep breaths once again. This time, each deep breath is going to ground you. With each breath, you are starting to feel yourself again. You are starting to feel your skin once again. When you are ready, open you eyes.

Now write down all the positive qualities that you want in your soulmate on your paper, every positive aspect. Write down all of the wonderful blissfulness that you just experienced with your soulmate. Be as specific as you can. Write about what you are looking for in a soulmate. Now on the opposite side of the paper, write everything that you do not want in this soulmate. All the negative qualities that you want to stay away from you. Be as specific as possible. Write every aspect that you want to block, everything you do not wish to attract. When you are finished, fold the paper. Stuff the paper into the space you made inside the candle.

Next you will anoint the candle with the essential oil. Now light the candle. Let this candle burn and allow it to continue your manifesting. The candle has absorbed the divine connective energy that you just experienced. By lighting this candle, you are continually sending this wonderfully blissful energy.

Since this candle will take several days to burn down, only burn the candle when you are awake and present to watch it. (For safety precautions, never leave an unattended candle burning when you go out or go to sleep.) Now you are done. Just allow yourself to be and time will manifest the dreams you have co-created with Spirit.

I continually have used this meditation and have experienced much success. I want to share with you my success story of how, with Spirit's intervention, I met my soulmate, my husband Michael.

As a tradition, every New Year's Day, I perform the manifesting-attracting-removal ritual meditation that I just told you about. On New Years, it's usually just a little bit more intense. On January 1, 2003, I decided to do a soul-mate candle.

In my meditation, I said to Spirit, "If I am going to be with my soul-mate in a romantic permanent relationship, then send him at once. If I am supposed to be with somebody put him in my path already! If it is my destiny in this life to be alone, just let me know. So this way I can heal my sorrow and refocus my attentions elsewhere."

I was in the process of recovering from the posttraumatic stress that 9/11 had caused me. I just wanted to get on with my life already.

I imagined all the qualities that I was looking for in a spouse, not just the superficial ones, but also the deep, intense matters. I also envisioned everything I did not want to attract.

After my meditation, I wrote all the qualities I was seeking on one side of the paper. I flipped the paper over and wrote a detailed list of everything that I didn't want in a partner. I then stuffed the folded paper into the side of the candle, anointed it with oil, and I proceeded to light the candle. I then left it up to Spirit and went on with my business.

In June, I went to Miami with a couple of friends. While I was in Miami, Lilith called me to have a heart-to-heart. She said that it was about time that I thought about settling down with someone. I told Lilith about the conversation I had had with Spirit concerning the whole soulmate issue, and that if I was meant to meet someone I wanted it to happen soon, and if I wasn't supposed to be with anyone, I wanted to know that I was meant to go solo.

Later that same day, one of the friends that had come to Florida with me, whom we shall call SB, decided to call one of his friends to gloat about being in Miami. By coincidence, SB's friend was also in Florida at the same time, visiting a friend in Fort Lauderdale. For whatever reason, SB decided to set us up on a blind date. I personally hated blind dates. I had had the worst experiences on them. They usually turned out to be a nightmare of horror stories. SB's friend felt the exactly same way as I did. But we reluctantly agreed to meet the next day.

Of course SB and I got lost on the way to the meeting and were late. I couldn't help thinking that it wouldn't exactly be a great first impression. When we finally arrived, I was a bit nervous. I said to Spirit, "Okay lets see what you have in store for me."

I got out of the car and saw SB's friend. When our eyes met, the most incredibly indescribable feeling of love instantly overwhelmed me. I knew within two minutes that I had just met my soulmate. He introduced himself as Michael Timbers.

We went inside his best friend Richard's condo for cocktails. As I was talking to Michael, I began sensing a female Spirit that wanted to talk to me. She was an absolutely adorable, petite, grandmother who had passed in the late 1980's. She particularly loved the color purple.

I calmly asked Michael if he knew her. He was blown away. She was his grandmother. He adored her. She had passed away in the late 80's. (SB had told Michael that I was a psychic, but he hadn't expected to get a sample.) I had just received his grandmother's approval. That confirmed it. I knew this was the one.

A few months later, back in New York City, I brought Michael and Precious, our furry child, to meet my family. I had never introduced any of my boyfriends to my friends, let alone my family. So when I told my family that I was bringing someone for dinner that I wanted them to meet, they knew it was a big deal. And it just happened to have been Yom Kippur, the holiest day of the Jewish year no less, so it was a very big deal.

Everything went wonderfully. Grandma took one look at Michael and immediately knew he was my soulmate as instantly as I had. She gave me that knowing look that we always shared. Following Grandma's lead, my family warmly welcomed him into their home. I was given the same warm welcome upon meeting Michael's family.

That November of 2003, on Michael's birthday, I proposed marriage. We were at Richard's condo, the very same place that we had had our first date. The following year, on October 30, 2004, we married in Boston, Massachusetts.

Both sets of my grandparents were married for over 50 years. My parents, as well as Michael's parents, have also been married for over 50 years. We all share the same belief: we expect to walk down the aisle only once. So we really need to know before saying our vows. In my family, divorces are few and far between. When we say, Till death do us part, we mean it.

MOM AND DAD

The story of how my parents met is fascinating. Dad went to New Utrecht

High school in Brooklyn. One day at school, he was hit in the eye with a baseball. He was taken to a doctor's office but the waiting room was crowded and it would be a very long time before the doctor would be able to see him.

As destiny and fate would have it, my Grandma Sallee and Papa Charlie were also there to see the same doctor. My Grandma happened to be the next patient in line. After one look at my injured, teenage Dad, her compassion prompted her to speak to the nurse. She insisted that the nice young man (my Dad) see the doctor before her. Dad and his parents were very grateful for Grandma's kindness.

Grandma never forgot that nice young man she had met in the doctor's office. Dad never forgot that very nice woman either. Of all the doctors available in NYC... to be at the same doctor's office, at the exact same time... Spirit works in wonderfully intricate ways, doesn't it??

Three years later, on a rainy weekend, my Mom and her girlfriends decided to go to a local dance. My Mother never had attended any of these dances before, or even wanted to, but for some reason, she decided to go to this dance on this particular night. They went despite the rain.

My Mom quickly caught the eye of an admirer. This was my Dad. He immediately walked up to her and asked her to dance. Sparks were ignited that night and they soon began dating.

When Mom eventually invited Dad over to meet her parents, he and Grandma recognized each other instantly. Who would have ever thought that my Dad was meeting his future in-laws that day at the doctor's? Now if that was not Divine intervention, nothing is.

My Dad reminded me that on their wedding day it was also pouring rain, just like it was on the night that they met at the dance. More than 50 years later, they are still married and going strong.

MOM AND DAD TIMBERS

When it comes to family, I have been blessed. I had wonderfully caring parents, phenomenal grandparents, and excellent siblings. Now I also have amazing in-laws. I can proudly and openly call Michael's parents my second Mom and Dad. They are loving people and I couldn't have asked for a better family to marry into. Michael also feels the same way about my parents. This is a gift from Spirit.

Just like my parents, Michael's parents also have an inspiring and uplifting soulmate story about how they met. One day, one of my mother-in-law's relatives brought a fine young man to her family's home. She knew quickly that he was a very caring, kind-hearted soul. When he happened to glance at Mom Timbers, their eyes met and they began a lengthy conversation. Dad Timbers knew, from the moment he had laid eyes upon her, that she was his soulmate. She felt the same way. Sparks were ignited.

He came back the following day for Thanksgiving dinner. The sparks were impossible to ignore. Their bond took root. For the next three years, Dad Timbers did not come back around. He did, however, begin his courtship with beautiful letters. He wrote to her constantly for the next three years.

Three years later, Dad Timbers returned to ask permission to date Mom Timbers. Very shortly afterwards, they knew this was a divinely arranged soulmate connection. They quickly decided to get married.

These soulmates have also celebrated their 50th wedding anniversary and are the proud parents of four loving children. They had met around Thanksgiving and it was also on Thanksgiving that Mom Timbers gave birth to my soulmate Michael. Thank God for Divine Intervention.

ATHENA AND GARY

One of my best girlfriends, Athena, who I had traveled to Greece with, was approaching a point in her life where she was finally ready to settle down and start a family. Everybody knew Athena would be a fabulous mother. The only problem was she had not yet met her soulmate.

One day Athena came by to ask me what I thought of this guy whom we had both known. What did I think? Was he the one? Athena knew her other friends would just go with the flow and agree with whatever she said. She knew I was not cut from the same cloth. I am very opinionated and couldn't lie to save my life. She knew if she asked my opinion, I would always give her an honest answer.

I didn't want to burst her bubble, but I told her that he was definitely not the One. I told her that she was one of the most genuinely remarkable people I knew. She was really a good soul and she needed to elevate her aspirations for a soulmate. She wanted to find somebody who was a really kind soul, somebody who was now also ready to settle down and start a family. Although she was disappointed, she thanked me for my honesty.

Athena had her own chat with Spirit, asking that her soulmate be sent to her.

One day Athena and I met with our girlfriend Karen. Neither of us had seen her in a while. Karen was one of the friends I was with when I encountered Archangel Michael in the cemetery in Brooklyn. Karen also has the intuitive gift, but prefers to keep it private. Athena and I met up with her and had a good time. During that afternoon, Karen told Athena that within twelve months she would be married and have a baby. Athena and I looked at each other and knocked down a shot of tequila. Hey, you never know.

A few months later Athena went on a blind date. On the way to the date, she bumped into a friend of hers who told her that the Allman Brothers would be playing uptown at the Beacon Theater that night. The Allman Brothers are one of Athena's favorite bands.

Within a few, minutes on the blind date, she knew it was not going to work out. She decided to not waste either of their time. She ended the date and headed for the subway. In a spontaneous act, she decided to leave it up to Spirit: if the uptown train came first, she would head uptown to see the Allman Brothers, if the downtown train came first, she would head home to chill. As destiny and fate would have it, the uptown train rolled into the station, so it was off to the Beacon Theater to see the Allman Brothers.

Outside the theater, someone handed her an extra ticket that he had for free. It was in row Y. Upon arriving in her seat, she immediately began a conversation with a guy in row X, right ahead of her. As they talked, they realized they had a lot in common. They had the same musical tastes. They both had the same carefree attitude. And both worked in the theater, as stage crew. The conversation flowed. Gary offered to drive her home and she accepted the ride. They made plans for a date.

One month later, they were practically attached at the hip. Athena showed us a picture of the two of them together. She was trying to figure out what their children would look like if they ever had children together. A few months later Athena came to see me again.

She asked me if I would be legally ordained to marry couples in May 2001. My ordination from the New Seminary of New York was to take place on 6/24/2001. I looked at her and I just knew. We both laughed and I immediately congratulated her.

She asked me, "Gary is the ONE, right?"

I told her, "Gary absolutely is the one for you. You are both kind and lovingly wonderful together."

They married in May 2001. They are the proud parents of two of our beautiful godchildren.

All these couples, myself included, trusted in Spirit and hit the cosmic soulmate jackpot. Trust in Spirit and maybe my next soulmate story will be yours!

PSYCHIC HOTLINES – UUUGGGHHH!

Once upon a time, I actually worked for the psychic network for a short period. I was in between jobs and psychic lines were all the rage. An ambitious line operator who knew I was the real deal recruited me to work for the network.

This is how the operation worked back then. A reader didn't work for just one psychic line, but many at the same time. The calls from most of the psychic hotlines went directly to a computer company based in Florida. I would log directly into the computer and would then be open and available for calls. When someone called one of the hotlines, the computer would route the call to one of its open operators. We were instructed to always answer the phone by saying, "Welcome to the network," reason being, we were never really sure which psychic hotline the caller actually had dialed. So when it came right down to it, we were actually working for a computer company that routed the calls. Each hotline hired their own operators to log onto the network. To be quite honest, I hated every minute of it. I actually dreaded my line ringing.

I can't say that all the hotline operators were the same, but I found that many of the so-called psychics were not psychics at all. Many were just hard-working people, often times actors looking for some extra income. One day a club friend of mine told me he was working for a hotline. I had given him a fierce tarot card reading in the clubs, so he figured it couldn't be that hard. When he tried to read cards for a hotline himself, he quickly realized that tarot was more than just pretty printed cards. He found himself reading from several prepared scripts in order to give callers readings. I found this to be the most offensive, disgusting practice that tarnished the whole New Age, Paranormal field.

Not all of the hotlines had script readers. The company that hired me was legit and scripts were not allowed. She only hired real intuitives. The employment interview consisted of three separate cold readings. If you were the real deal, you were hired. If you were not, she thanked you and sent you on your way. Many of the other companies would hire anybody. They didn't really care if you were legit or not. If you weren't an intuitive, they gave you several scripts to read from. There was pretty much a 50% chance of getting a real psychic or a script reader like my club friend. For the short time I worked the hotlines, I lined up many repeat callers. At least I knew they were getting a real reading. I felt horrible about others who just got an actor. This is why I didn't stay very long.

Those misleading practices were eventually exposed and it caused the fall of many of the hotlines. Nowadays the practice has changed. Well, at least I hope it has. I have not had any exposure to them since I disconnected my hotline connection.

OUIJA WARNING

When participating in a séance, a large degree of mindfulness is in order. One can't be careless or haphazard about what takes place. It is very delicate work and can lead to disastrous results if one is not careful.

Children shouldn't play with matches or Ouija! The Ouija board is a very scary instrument. Unfortunately, just about anyone can pick one up and start playing with it. Most people don't take it seriously. They fail to recognize the true reality of it and accidentally open energetic vortexes about which they know ABSOLUTELY NOTHING about.

A rule for the wise, if the only way a spirit can contact you is through a Ouija board, then you definitely don't want that spirit around you. Only dark and weak entities need to communicate through a Ouija board. Those who come in the path of Light and the Love of God/Spirit can make contact in many other ways. They don't require a so-called game by Parker Brothers in order to do so. Late Aunt Betty doesn't need a Ouija board to check-in, letting you know that she still loves you and that everything is okay. As a soul of Light and Love, she can communicate in a multitude of ways. Usually only the weak, earthbound negative spirits come through the Ouija because it is one of the only doorways they have.

It takes a lot of energy and a strong will for a spirit to make contact or to visit you. Late Aunt Betty may attempt to communicate in a variety of ways. If you have a dream in which you are talking with her, you probably are. She might just pop into your thoughts very strongly, from out of nowhere. At times you might almost feel her around you or you might detect a faint scent of Jean Nate gently permeating the air. Have you ever felt an adamant urge to walk down a particular block, even though you usually walk down a different one? Then you passed by that woman who so much reminded you of Aunt Betty? Did you ever see someone out of the corner of your eye, you look back and nobody was there? What about those times when you thought about Aunt Betty, then all of a sudden felt a cold chill down your spine?

Most people usually keep such feelings to themselves. They fear being laughed at and want to avoid being thought of as a crazy. TRUST ME ON THIS! If you do experience such events, you are not losing your mind. Your brain is not playing tricks on you. They are not optical illusions. More than likely, you experienced a visitation or at least a communication from the other side. These things happen so often. They are everyday occurrences. Suspend your disbelief. Allow yourself to feel and experience the wonderful little ways in which your loved ones make contact.

Throughout this book, I would like to guide you with meditations and visualizations that will help you clear your mind and open up to these experiences. Let's consider the body as an envelope for the soul. The human body is a molecularly dense, carbon-based container. It can only expand so far. Meditation and energy work can help you to expand and to feel your existence well beyond the limits of your body. It can help you travel outside the energy field of your body to the higher, less molecularly dense plains of existence. As long as you remember YOU ARE A BEACON OF LIGHT AND LIGHT IS ALWAYS VASTLY MORE POWERFUL THAN DARKNESS, you never have to be afraid. Anytime you work with the other realms, it is always advised and highly recommended to protect yourself before proceeding. But for starters, Psalm 23 works wonders (see page XX).

I once inherited an old fashioned original Ouija board from a recently departed cousin of mine. I put it in the trunk of my car and forgot about it. Within less than a week, my car was stolen and later found burnt to a crisp. So trust me on this, if somebody wants to play Ouija, ABSOLUTELY SAY NO. Children shouldn't play with fire. And people shouldn't open a portal for weak, dark beings to enter and then welcome them in. The results will never be fun.

PHOTO ALBUM: PART THREE
THE FAMILY

MY HUSBAND, AND SOULMATE, MICHAEL AND
I HAVING A GRAND OL' TIME IN ONE OF OUR
FAVORITE CITIES, NEW ORLEANS.

BOTH MICHAEL'S AND MY PARENTS HAVE BEEN
MARRIED OVER 50 YEARS.
PHOTO, ABOVE, RENEÉ AND MEL SCHAEFFER AT
THEIR 50TH WEDDING ANIVERSARY PARTY.
PHOTO, LEFT:
MICHAEL AND I TIE THE KNOT,
OCTOBER 30, 2004, MASSACHUSETTS

You're My Hero

PHOTO, TOP, MY GRANDMOTHER CHERISHED
THIS PHOTO OF US TOGETHER. PHOTO,
BOTTOM, MY MOTHER WITH HER MOTHER ON
GRANDMA'S 75TH BIRTHDAY.

MY GRANDMOTHER AT OUR WEDDING,
91 YEARS OLD. EVERYONE WISHES THEY
COULD HAVE SOMEONE IN THEIR LIFE THAT
WAS AS SUPPORTING, LOVING,
INSPRIATIONAL, AND TOTALLY HIP, AS MY
GRANDMOTHER WAS.

BABY PRECIOUS, MY BEAUTIFUL, LOVING,
FURRY DAUGHTER, WORKED WITH ME IN MY
SESSIONS. IF SHE LIKED A PERSON, SHE
WOULD STAY, IF SHE LEFT THE ROOM, I
KNEW I WAS IN FOR A DOOZY.

GRAND CANYON, 2009

MICHAEL AND I LOVE TO TRAVEL AND FEEL
THE VIBRATIONS OF DIFFERENT PLACES.

MINDFUL MEDITATIONS

THE NEW SEMINARY OF NEW YORK EXORCISM RITUAL

The New Seminary is an amazing program, committed to the wholeness of the individual and the individual's own spiritual search. They honor all paths leading toward a deepening of one's relationship with the Eternal Spirit, Divine, God, Goddess, The One, and all other paths that lead to a positive, rewarding, spiritual life.

During my time at The New Seminary of New York, I was able to create numerous meditations and healing services while attending an intensive inter-faith ministerial program.

As I mentioned already, you don't always need a dark demon to require an exorcism. An exorcism simply brings light where darkness and despair exist. You can exorcise many illnesses and energy patterns that are becoming destructive in your life. Fellow members of the seminary Rev. Kim, Rev. Lynn, and myself, demonstrated and performed an exorcism during one of our classes. Rev. Katie participated as the subject. Everybody in the room took an active part in the healing which became extremely powerful, as was the synthesis of our healing trio of Kim, Lynn and myself: The Three Monkeys.

After the service, many had asked if somebody had walked around the room placing their healing hands upon their shoulders. Many said they felt extremely comforting vibrations and could feel the healing energies flowing from these healing hands through their bodies. To their surprise, there was nobody walking around at all.

At the program's end a few months later, we were all ordained at the extraordinary gothic cathedral, St John the Divine. A couple of days afterwards, I went to the NYC's clerk's desk to register as a licensed minister. Who did I run into but Rev Katie. She ecstatically let me in on a wonderful secret. A couple of weeks before our exorcism service, Rev. Katie's doctor had given her grim news. All the tests taken showed signs of cancer. For whatever reason, a couple of weeks after the exorcism the doctor had Rev. Katie retake the tests. This time the results were flabbergasting. The results now showed absolutely no signs or traces of cancer any longer. Even the high level of calcium deposits in the blood had completely disappeared. He asked her if there was anything she had done because he had no explanation for her remarkable recovery. She proudly told him of our exorcism service and her ordination as an interfaith minister.

Rev. Katie was so happy to tell me of her fantastic healing. She said the doctor told her that she didn't even need a follow up visit, for there was now absolutely nothing wrong. This was the first time he ever had the pleasure of releasing a patient this way. I couldn't have been more delighted.

Here is the actual exorcism service that we performed, in all its parts: creating a sacred space, the prayer, song, a meditation, sermon, and bendiction.

A HEALING EXORCISM

Requirements:
- One Sage smudge stick, candles
- One spray bottled essential oil mixture of: Sage, Cleary Sage, Rue, Rosemary, Basil, Marjoram, Lavender, Frankincense, Myrrh, Rose, Cyprus, Juniper, Vanilla, Sandalwood, Cedar, and White Jamaican Over proof Rum
  - Iodized sea salt (or regular sea-salt) water in bowl
  - Rose Quartz and clear Quartz crystals
  - Roses or other flowers in bloom
  - Music: Tibet - A World of Music cd, selection: Tamdrim Yangsa Shagpa (confession and purification of secret Hayagriva)

Smudge a circle and sprinkle sea salt water counter-clockwise around the room, to purify your space. As the congregation enters the room, spray them with the mixture.

Prayer: Psalm 23 - Stephan Mitchell version
    The Lord is my shepherd:
    I have everything that I need.
    He makes me lie down in green pastures,
    He leads me besides the still waters.
    He refreshes my soul.
    He guides me on the paths of righteousness,
    So that I may serve him with Love.
    Though I walk through the darkest valley
    Or stand in the shadow of death,
    I am not afraid. For I know you are always with me.
    You spread a full table before me,
    Even in times of great pain,
    You feast me with your abundance
    And honor me like a king,
    Anointing my head with sweet oil, filling my cup to the brim.
    Surely goodness and mercy will follow me
    All the days of my life,
    And I will live in God's radiance Forever and ever.

Reading of the passage from "Angel Courage" by Terry Lynn Taylor and Mary Beth Crain:
    The angel warrior is the embodiment of integrity. His or her mission is to reveal and uphold the truth, not as an act of virtue but as a way of life. It's often

uncomfortable to confront the Truth, let alone uphold it, which is why angel warriors are rare beings. The reason most of us have not yet become angel warriors is because we fear rejection or confrontation or just plain loss. Sometimes upholding the truth can cost us a lot, in terms of relationships, jobs, even our freedom. It seems so much easier not to make waves, to stifle our integrity in favor of maintaining the comfortable status quo.

But in reality, when we are not true to ourselves we become a prison of our fear. Any of us can become an angel warrior, if we're willing to let go of our fear of what will happen if we stick up for our principles and our true feelings. The angels are always ready to give us the courage to know ourselves and even more important, to love ourselves, no matter what mistakes we might have made. Angel warriors are not perfect. They are just honest. They know that true strength comes from love and true power from the willingness to accept one's true self and to reveal that self to the world without fear.

Next Rev. Lynn performs her song Faith followed by Rev. Kim playing the crystal bowl. Suggested Music for meditation: Peter Gabriel, Last Temptation of Christ soundtrack, Passion.

MEETING THE FOUR ARCHANGELS MEDITATION:
Close your eyes and Imagine that you are in a circle of Ultra-Violet light, the light of transformation, of the Divine's Unconditional Love, the Christ light, the Light of St. Germaine. As you inhale through your nose, you become this light. As you exhale, you are the Ultra-Violet light.

There is a space a little above your belly button, your solar plexus. The solar plexus is the energetic center of your soul. Imagine you can breathe from here. As you inhale, breathe in the Ultra-Violet light through your solar plexus. There is an orange star all the way up in the sky. Send a line of energy to this star and allow yourself to receive the light back.

This star is a group of enlightened beings. Some who have already completed their paths of enlightenment. Some like ourselves who are on their path and others who have never inhabited a body ever before. You are now part of this group and can always join this group by simply sending a line of energy to this orange star and receiving it back.

There is a crystal light all the way up in the sky. Allow this crystal light to slowly pull you up to this light, like a tractor beam. You are now at the foot of The Crystal pyramid. This is where the four reside, here in the Atman kingdom. You are now at the top, inside the crystal pyramid.

I call upon the Archangel Michael, the Spirit of the South. Lift all that can be lifted, Help us to release all that can be released and let go to the light. Empower us with the strength we need to stand strong in face of adversity. Help resolve our personal negativities, the ability to find strength when we feel all alone.

I call upon the Archangel Gabriel, the Spirit of the West, the center of Truth. Help us to express our truth openly and honestly, respect and honor our Individuality. Help us to listen to our own intuition and inner voice.

I call upon the Archangel Uriel, the Spirit of the North, the Akashic Records, the answers to everything and nothing at all. Help us to acknowledge the Light within all of everything. Guide us to find knowledge to help and to heal, interpret and decode our inner voice.

I call upon the Archangel Raphael, the Spirit of the East, and Unconditional Freedom from everything that binds you down from achieving all that you can be. Help us to seek the gift of healing in nature and universal energy.

It is your job now, to just relax and breathe. This is the place to truly Let Go And Let God. As you inhale, you and the Divine are one. Your connection with them is magnified. As you exhale, the obstacles dissipate and are lifted and removed.

[Stay here for fifteen minutes. The four will directly communicate with you here.]

Now it is time to go. Imagine you are slowly traveling back down, through time and space, to a place six to twelve inches above your body. With three breaths, you re-enter your body. Enjoy the beauty of the Divine and all it's incredible abundance. Reflect for a moment on all that is abundant in your life. Thank the Divine for the abundance that flows through your bodies. You can wake up and open your eyes.

SERMON:

Respect your fear. For if you denigrate or dishonor or fear it, you are not truly understanding and appreciating what lessons your higher self, the Divine is trying to teach you. Our fears are our challenges, which we are here to see through and work out for ourselves. Consider them as friends and embrace them. Loving friends are here to give you advice and pointers in life. They are wonderful enough to help steer us in the right direction in our lives. You can respect and understand their guidance and what lessons they are trying to teach us.

But the bottom line is that it is only advice. And it is up to you to decipher and decide what is right for you and what just doesn't feel right, no matter how many ways you try to look at it. We are here to learn many lessons of Unconditional Love in it's highest of forms. You will never be able to leave, or let go of anything or anyone in your life, if you are filled with a hatred, anger, despair or fear towards it. It is almost a guaranteed boomerang return—until you are ready, willing and able to let go of what or whoever it is, and send it up to the light. We need to be able to embrace it with Love and truly LET GO AND LET GOD!

And yes, I said embrace it with Love. Show love and gratitude for the lessons that you have and are going to learn from this experience.

LET GO AND LET GOD! Easier said then done. I wish it could be as easy as the Classic TV shows *Bewitched* and *I Dream of Jeannie*, where we could erase or easily move past our scariest, darkest fears with just a twitch of the Nose. How about that. With just one twitch...poof ...No more fear of intimacy.... No more low self esteem...poof...a broken heart repaired with just a blink of the eye. No problem.

If this experience that we call life was to be that easy, we would have been born with an instruction book. Instead, while we are here, we are going to have our good times, as well as the unpleasant experiences. However, we have the ability and the power to co-create any aspect of our being. If there is an area in your life, which is a bit too difficult, where you feeling overwhelmed, you can and do have the abilities to change it!

Many times, we forget we are an equal co-creating participant with the Divine in this school called life. Remember, YOU DO NOT NEED TO LEARN THESE LESSONS THIS HARSHLY. We can learn our lessons, easily and comfortably. Part of the very lesson why we go through some pretty horrific times, is to teach us that no matter what happens, certain aspects about ourselves will never change. YOU are a DIVINE SPARK and there is nothing that can or will ever be able to take that from you.

Asking God/Spirit to allow this life's lessons to be learned easily and comfortable, is a big part of the lesson itself. Asking for relief, completely letting go, trusting and asking God/Spirit for a release and then allowing your heavy load to be lifted from yourself is another big part of the overall lesson. Angels, Guides and Deva's are here to help us in every aspect on our path. The world is an illusion and these wonderful Divine beings are capable of helping us change this illusion to any form that we choose, as long as it is for our highest good. But, they cannot help us, unless we ask for help. And the more specific we are with our thoughts, the more exact these Divine beings are then able to help us. Thought is power. Creative power. Thoughts are the highest form of active prayer that we as humans have. The more specific you are with your thoughts, the stronger the intention that you send out, the more specific the energetic outcome will come to you.

In the time it takes to think negatively or hopeless, you can send positive thoughts. The glass is not half-empty it is half-filled. Instead of holding on to your problems like a badge, let it go and bring in the light. You need to clear out what is holding you back and weighing you down, to make room for what is light and right. It is spring-cleaning time. Just like you are cleaning out your closets of all old, outdated junk that you don't need anymore, It is time you cleaned up your energetic closet of all the old thought forms and energy patterns, that no longer serve you in the highest of good. Much of the fears, trials and tribulations that we are holding on, dates all the way back to when we were children. It is much too long to still be going about in life, looking through the eyes of a child. The best thing for us to ask for is nothing.

If you enter a situation with no preconceived notions, in other words nothing, you have everything to gain. If you bring even the slightest baggage into anything, you are now denying yourself 100 %.

REMEMBER, BRING INTO ANY SITUATION NOTHING AND YOU WILL HAVE THE POSSIBILITIES OF EVERYTHING. LIMITATIONS AND CONTROL ARE JUST AN ILLUSION.

LET GO AND LET GOD.

BENEDICTION:

We are blessed and thankful for the abundance that the Divine has blessed us with. Thank you Archangel's Michael, Gabriel, Uriel and Raphael for your presence and blessings. Let God and Let God.

So Blessed it Be ...

TAKE

A

STROLL

THROUGH

MY

MEDITATION GARDEN

I've added all of this book's meditations in one bright place, plus included some from my seminary training. You can adapt them to suit whatever you are striving for, or need to work on. Also, be sure to check my website for guided meditations.

The foundation for most of my meditations include what the wonderful healer Lille O'Brien coined as "spinning," to help cleanse your body's energy fields. Practice doing this before trying any meditations. First, imagine there is a spiral of Ultra-Violet (UV) light around you. With each deep breath, the spiral of UV light begins to enter your body through the left side of your ribcage. This spiral spins counterclockwise, as it continues to travel through your body and slowly exits out from the right side of your ribcage. With each deep breath, the UV light continues to spin from the left side of your body and exiting out through the right side. This counterclockwise spinning is how you can energetically cleanse yourself and just about anybody or anything else of negative disturbances or patterns. The more you continue to spin, your body starts to automatically spin the UV light throughout your body.

Once you cleanse, though, you must also send positive energy back to refill that space. Otherwise, the negative energies will creep back in. So, once your body is automatically spinning counterclockwise the UV light of unconditional love, it is time to spin the UV light clockwise back through the right side to empower yourself. This is exactly what you've just done from the left side, but now are simply reversing it. Your higher self will automatically take over, and continue spinning in both directions.

HOW TO MEET YOUR SPIRIT GUIDE

Close your eyes. Begin by taking three deep breaths. Inhaling from your nose carrying that breath all the way to your solar plexus located just above your belly button. Then slowly exhale through your mouth. Allow yourself to picture a circle of white light all around you. Ask for only those who come in the path of the light/God/Spirit, for the highest of good to be allowed to come to you. All those who are negative, gently and respectfully, please leave. Continue with your breaths from your nose down to your solar plexus and slowly exhaling thru your mouth. With each breath, you begin to become one with the white light.

Now imagine there is a spiral of Ultra-Violet (UV) light, the light of unconditional love at the highest of forms around you. With each deep breath, the spiral of UV light begins to enter your body through the left side of your ribcage. This spiral spins counterclockwise, as it continues to travel through your body and slowly exits out from the right side of your ribcage.

Now, with each breath, imagine the spiral of UV light entering your body spinning clockwise from the right side and exiting out the left side of your ribcage.

With each breath both spirals will continue automatically, and simultaneously. Continue the spinning that clears and then empowers your body. Now your body is automatically spinning out the negative energies from you and replacing that with empowering positive healing energies. You are one with the UV light of unconditional love.

An elevator made of pure crystal appears right in front of you. You slowly step into the crystal elevator. The doors close and you are now engulfed in this wonderful crystal vessel. With each breathe, the elevator travels up through the sky, past the clouds to a rainbow crystal star. As the crystal elevator travels higher, you are getting closer to meeting your spirit guide. With each breathe, the crystal elevator travels higher and higher. You are almost there. You are so close to meeting your spirit guide. You can practically feel them. Your spirit guide has been around you your whole life. The energy feels so familiar, so loving, so safe and so protecting.

This crystal elevator finally stops. The doors open to an exquisite valley of rainbows, incredible flowers and an indescribably beautiful crystal temple. You step out of the elevator and take in this most majestic of sites. You can feel the sacredness of this most divine sanctuary. You see a golden path. As you slowly stroll down the path, prepare yourself to finally meet your spirit guide.

You say to yourself, "I am openly ready with all my sacredness to meet my spirit guide." With each step, you feel yourself being pulled toward the incredible crystal temple. Does it look like a classic ancient Greek or Roman temple with towering columns? Does the temple look like an ancient Egyptian temple from the times of the pharaohs? Allow this temple to take shape to whatever you envision it to be.

You are finally at the opening of this temple. You are feeling so loved, so welcomed. You enter the temple and look all around, taking in how this temple is decorated. You faintly start hearing your spirit guide calling your name. It is time for the two of you to finally meet at last. You look forward to see this crystal gazebo glowing. Your spirit guide is calling you. You can feel them drawing you strongly toward them. You finally approach the gazebo where there is a bench. You step into the gazebo and have a seat on the bench. There is a violet mist which starts to appear in front of you.

Allow the mist to take shape. As the mist dissipates, your spirit guide begins to take shape. Allow the shape to become clear. Do not force it. This will happen naturally and you will perceive it in your own special way.

How does your spirit guide look? Are they in a solid form or an ethereal spirit-like shape? Ask them what their name is or what they would like for you to call them by. Allow your spirit guide to introduce themselves to you. Embrace your spirit guide any way that feels comfortable. Hug, kiss, shake hands, bow, etc. There are no set rules. Give your spirit guide permission to help you in every way. Tell your spirit guide whatever you would like assistance with. Ask whatever questions you may have.

They talk with you about the work together past, present and the future. There is no specific way they will communicate with you. Everybody perceives communication and understands messages in their own way. A part of you is already completely in tuned with what your spirit guide is communicating to you.

Your spirit guide engulfs you in a wonderful healing light. This energy invigorates every essence of you. This connects you to your guide even further. Now you will have a much easier time connecting to your spirit guide anytime you would like. Imagine there a golden cord that now connects you and your spirit guide. This strengthens your bond forever more.

Now it is time to go. Bid your spirit guide farewell. It is time to come back into your body. But you will always have this connection to your guide. You can come back to this majestic place anytime you would like. You leave the crystal gazebo, walking thru the temple and back down the golden path. The crystal elevator doors are now open.

You step inside and the doors close. With each deep breath, the elevator travels back down past the stars and the clouds. The elevator finally stops and the doors open. You step out and back into your body.

First deep breath, you can start to feel your body again. Second deep breath and you can now feel your skin again. The last deep breath and you are now completely back into your body.

Stay with this for as long as you like. When you are ready, open your eyes.

HOW TO PREVENT OR STOP A PANIC ATTACK

When you start to feel a panic attack coming on, the best thing is to try to stop it before it turns into a full blown episode. Panic attacks are electrical, so you need to try and ground yourself. It also uses the "spinning" technique from page 238.

First stand or sit still with your back straight up. Begin by closing your eyes and taking three deep pranic breaths. Inhaling from your nose carrying that breath all the way to your solar plexus located just above your belly button. Then slowly exhale through your mouth. Allow yourself to picture a circle of white light all around you. Ask for only those who come in the path of the light/God/ Spirit, for the highest of good to be allowed to come to you. Continue with your pranic breaths from your nose down to your solar plexus and slowly exhaling thru your mouth. With each breath, you begin to become one with the white light. With each breath, you are becoming more solid and less anxiety filled.

Now imagine there is a spiral of Ultra-Violet (UV) light, the light of unconditional love at the highest of forms, around you. With each deep breath, the spiral of UV light begins to enter your body through the left side of your ribcage. This spiral spins counterclockwise, as it continues to travel through your body and slowly exits out from the right side of your ribcage.

With each breath, imagine the spiral of UV light entering your body spinning clockwise from the right side and exiting out the left side of your ribcage.

With each breath both spirals will continue automatically. Continue the spinning that first clears and then empowers your body. Now your body is automatically spinning out the negative energies from you and replacing that with empowering positive healing energies.

Now imagine there is a beam of UV light that can travel all the way from your solar plexus up to the sky, to a sparking crystal star. This star is a group of enlightened beings always there to assist you. With each breath, this beam of UV light travels all the way up to this crystal star. You are now connected with this enlightened group.

Allow yourself to imagine a beam of UV light traveling from this star back to your solar plexus. This UV light travels from your solar plexus all the way down to the center of the earth to ground you. Allow this beam of light to return from the center of the earth to your solar plexus. So you have now successfully become a channel in between the grounding energies of the center of the earth to the crystal star of enlightened beings. Stay with this as long as you like and then slowly open up your eyes. When you are finished, you will have successfully stopped the panic attack from happening. If you were already in a flown blown panic attack, this will help it to stop.

HOW TO CREATE A CIRCLE OF PROTECTION AGAINST NEGATIVITY

This is the building block I always use to begin any of my meditations, sessions or healing work. And, is the very last thing I personally do before I leave my doorstep everyday. Oh Boy, can I tell when I forget to do this quick and simple meditation in the morning. Yuck!! You owe it to yourself, to take at least two minutes out of your daily life to do this every morning. Eventually this will become as second nature for you as brushing your teeth.

As a beacon of light, all negative diversities have absolutely no power or control over you, unless you allow it. You don't step into a thunderstorm without any protection. You should follow the same precautions and not step outside without energetically putting a circle of positive, loving white around you. This helps to push away the ugliness.

Close your eyes and simply visualize a circle of white light all around you. Ask for only the highest of lights. Only those that come to you in the path of Spirit/God for the highest of good are allowed to come near you. All others, gently but respectfully please leave at once...

A QUICK REJUVENATING CLEANSING OF NEGATIVITY

Allow yourself to picture a circle of Ultra-Violet (UV) light all around you. Ultra-Violet light is unconditional love in the highest of forms. Allow this Ultra-Violet light to surround you, to become a part of you. Inhale through your nose. Breathing from the diaphragm. With each deep breath, you are becoming at one with this light. With each exhale through your mouth. You are this Ultra-Violet light.

Allow yourself to imagine there is a circle of garbage cans outside of this circle of ultra violet light. These garbage cans are magnetic. They attract all the negative energies. With each breath, the garbage cans keep filling up. When the garbage cans fill up, they automatically explode into rainbows.

HOW TO PROTECT YOURSELF FROM PSYCHIC VAMPIRES (PEOPLE TRYING TO DRAIN YOU)

As a beacon of light, all negative diversities have absolutely no power or control over you, unless you allow it. Remember, in the movies Dracula was not able to enter your home or your body unless you invited him in. It is the same thing with those pathetic energy draining human vampires. As long as you know light energy always triumphs over the darker energies, they can never harm or drain you. DO this visualization everyday and those energy draining human vampires will stop even coming near you.

Begin by closing your eyes. Allow yourself to imagine a circle of white light all around you. This circle of white light is the universal light of Spirit. Only those of the highest of lights, who come to us in the path of Spirit, are allowed to penetrate this circle. Through your nose, begin taking deep breaths, breathing all the way to your diaphragm and slowly exhaling through your mouth. With each breath, you become filled with this white light. With each deep breath, you begin to let go of all the heaviness of the day. Your shoulders start feeling lighter and lighter.

With each exhale, you become the light. You continue breathing and just letting go. Allow yourself to imagine a circle of mirrors, facing out, all around you. These mirrors are of a high crystal light energy. They are of a very rejuvenating light energy. With each breath, you begin recharging your internal and external batteries. You are now feeling so wonderfully revitalized. Your chi, your energy flow is so much stronger. Every single cell of your being is feeling completely reenergized. These mirrors are very protective.

Now when somebody tries to drain you, they will now be blocked. As they try to drain you of your vital chi energy, the more they will be pushed back. As these psychic vampires continue to try to feed, they will only be able to drain your excess baggage, only on things that you no longer need. Like the stiffness you feel in the small of your back. The self doubts that block you from achieving your goals. The more they feed, the more of your garbage they will only receive back. Soon, they will stop trying to drain you. They will realize they can no longer be able to feed from you anymore. No matter how hard they try, they will never be able to penetrate you.

A DISTANT HEALING MEDITATION FOR A LOVED ONE

We all know of somebody who is in need of some healing. Here is a distant meditation I created in seminary to assist with a dear one who was going to have surgery. This is a method to send distant healing for someone or something from the present into the infinite future. Many of our prayer group participated in sending this group distant healing energy to our dear one for a very successful and speedy recovery. Take a few minutes out of your day, {insert your loved one's name} and let the healing light flow.

Imagine a circle of Ultra-Violet light around yourself. Take several deep breaths. As you inhale through your nose, breathe in the wonderful, transformational Ultra-Violet light. Ask for only the highest of light beings to be allowed to be around. All those who do not come in the path of the Light, please gently leave.

With each exhale, let go of the weight that is holding you down. Inhale lightens you, exhale you are lighter. Imagine there is an orange star all the way up in the sky. Imagine that you can send a line of energy from you, to the orange star. Allow the star to send a line of energy back to you. You have just made your connection with our enlightened group of beings, who like us, are on their spiritual path, and some who have never inhabited a body at all. This is our enlightened fellow lights that are always there to give you love, support and strength.

Imagine that you can send a line of wonderful light of unconditional love and transformation, from a space six to twelve inches on top of your head, to the space six to twelve inches on top of your loved one's head.

Allow the unconditional loving, healing light to enter their whole body, into the DNA of their cells. Imagine that your loved one sends you back a line of light six to twelve inches from your head. Allow the light to enter your body. Now imagine there is a huge dial above your loved one's head. Turn the dial all the way to the highest setting. The intensity of this loving healing energy now grows brighter and brighter within both your loved one and yourself.

Now imagine there is a calendar hovering over your loved one. You see illuminated buttons for each month: January, February, March ... all the way through December. As you press each illuminated button, you see the Ultra-Violet light pass through the calendar to the space six to twelve inches from their head. The light enters through their body into the DNA of their cells. Next you see an illuminated infinity symbol button. You press this button, sending this healing energy in a constant flow to your loved one forever.

The healing transfer is complete.

HOW TO FREE UP PAST KARMA AND RE-NEGOCIATE YOUR LIFE'S KARMIC LESSONS

Close your eyes and begin by taking three deep breaths. Inhale through the nose all the way to the diaphragm, your solar plexus. Now slowly exhale through your mouth.

Allow yourself to imagine there is a circle of Ultra-Violet light, the energy of unconditional love in the highest of forms. The circle of Ultra-Violet light surrounds you. As you continue to inhale, you begin to breathe in this wonderful light of unconditional love. As you exhale, you begin to become one with this wonderful light of unconditional love in the highest of forms. The more you inhale and exhale, the more you are one with this light. You can no longer feel your body. You now are this light. Imagine that you can float around like a weightless cloud. You can float and arise above your body. You continue to float higher up and then through the clouds. The higher you go, the lighter you feel. You see a glowing rainbow star. You can feel yourself being drawn to this rainbow star. The closer you get to this rainbow star, the more unconditional love you feel. You feel so safe. So comfortable ... so loved.

You are pulled closer until you land on this rainbow star. You can now see a beautiful garden. This garden is the most exquisite you have ever seen. Stop and smell the enchanting fragrances. Don't they smell, just incredible? You see a golden path. You follow this golden path and you are led to a fabulous gazebo. There is a bench and you sit down. There is a violet mist that surrounds you. This violet mist cleanses all the things you are ready to let go of. All the pain and heartache, the troubles, anxieties and worries all gone. You now have never felt lighter.

Isn't this amazing? And the best part is this wonderful loving light beaming from this garden is all you. Our bodies are just envelopes to contain all this vastness about ourselves. We are now in a place beyond time and space, as you know it.

This is a place where you can receive healings of the highest of levels, all for the highest of good. Allow yourself to feel the electric light of Spirit embrace you. It feels amazing, yet so familiar doesn't it?

You are at a place in your life where you are ready to let go of everything that is holding you back from being able to feel this electrical spiritual light all the time.

You have so much love emanating from you. Your love has created this exquisite garden. You can co-create anything and everything you focus your attention to. All for the highest of good. You no longer need those empty relationships. They have well worn out their welcome. You are now so ready to open yourself up to a real relationship based on true love in the highest of forms. You are so beautiful. It is time to finally allow the world to see your majestic loving beauty and allow this to enter your world.

How can someone get to know you, if you don't even know your spiritual self? This loving ecstasy is a very integral part of your higher spiritual self. It is time to take down some of the shields to let your higher self shine through. You have so much love waiting from others to share with you.

I know you are exhausted from repeatedly having to relearn many of your karmic lessons. Once and for all, it is time to rewrite this past. To cleanse and free up your own spirit to pursue the lighter and more loving aspects of life.

The re-emergence of some of these karmic lessons into your life have provoked past feelings and temptations. You are experiencing temptations trying to direct you into the old, but painfully familiar patterns of your past. Remember, this time around you have already agreed with Spirit to finally work on them. To finally understand and end this painful cycle for good.

Now I want you to imagine there is a crystal podium with a book that is emanating the rainbow lights. This is your book of past, present and future. You approach the book, and by thought, it automatically turns to the chapters where your disruptive patterns first began. The pages at the end of this chapter are dark. Now allow yourself to imagine the pages of this chapter starting to lighten in color. Send unconditional love in the highest of forms to this book and each and every chapter. Its is time to renegotiate how you are to learn your life's lessons.

You tell Spirit, I do not need to learn any of my life's lessons so harshly. I am able to learn my soul's journeys gently and easily. I am love. I can to unconditionally accept and receive love. I am able to unconditionally give love.

It starts to glow. You can see the power of love and light transforming this book to wonderful unconditional love and light. These new energies immerse with your soul, beginning this transformation.

All the heartache, the pain, the dark destructive deathness fades away. You are now glowing in this rainbow light. Everything is now so light and love is flowing everywhere. Now picture yourself growing older, happy and healthy.

Now imagine the book closing and sealing itself.

You have just sent major transformation healing energy to change those dark destructive patterns to light in the highest of forms. By freeing up your past patterns, this frees up your present to allow endless wonderful possibilities for your future.

Now it is time to come back. Allow yourself to imagine an elevator made of rainbow light. You enter and the doors close behind you. As the elevator lowers, you can start to feel your body again. The elevator doors finally open. Your gently glide out and back into your body.

Stay with this as long as you like. When you are ready, open your eyes.

HOW TO PERMANANTLY REMOVE SOMEBODY OR SOMETHING FROM YOUR LIFE FOREVER

Close your eyes. Begin by taking three deep breaths. Inhaling from your nose carrying that breath all the way to your solar plexus located just above your belly button. Then slowly exhale through your mouth. Allow yourself to picture a circle of white light all around you. Ask for only those who come in the path of the light/God/Spirit, for the highest of good to be allowed to come to you. All those who are negative gently and respectfully please leave. Continue with your breaths from your nose down to your solar plexus and slowly exhaling through your mouth. With each breath, you begin to become one with the white light.

Now imagine there is a spiral of Ultra-Violet (UV) light, the light of unconditional love at the highest of forms around you. With each deep breath, the spiral of UV light begins to enter your body through the left side of your ribcage. This spiral spins counterclockwise, as it continues to travel through your body and slowly exits out from the right side of your ribcage.

With each breath, imagine the spiral of UV light entering your body spinning clockwise from the right side and exiting out the left side of your ribcage. With each breath both spirals will continue automatically. Continue the spinning which clears and then empowers your body. Now your body is automatically spinning out the negative energies from you and replacing that with empowering positive healing energies. You are one with the UV light of unconditional love.

An elevator made of pure crystal appears right in front of you. The doors open up and your spirit guide is there waiting for you inside. You slowly step into the crystal elevator. The doors close and you are now engulfed in this wonderful crystal vessel. With each breath, the elevator travels down below the ground. With each breath, the crystal elevator continues to travel further down, deeper and deeper until finally reaching the center of the Earth. The elevator stops and the doors open. You and your spirit guide step out of elevator. There is a long corridor in front of you. At the end of this corridor, you will find the person (emotion, an illness, a condition, etc..) you want to sever all connections with once and for all.

As you begin to walk down this long corridor, Your spirit guide is here with you. You feel very safe, protected and so much loved. Prepare yourself to finally let go of this person or condition and the energetic story attached to them. They no longer serve a place in your life and your soul's journey. You no longer have the desire to devote your energy towards this antiquated and painfully draining situation anymore. You are ready to end this bond completely. The closer you get to the end of this corridor, the lighter you are feeling, fearless and all-forgiving. You are ready to let go and let your Spirit take care of it once and for all.

You finally approach the end of the corridor and are face to face with that person. This person is standing there with their own spirit guide as well. Everything is very safe and secure. The golden cord flows from you to them. Look at each other. Say everything that you want to say. As you feel and think it, they will be able to understand. You explain this connection can no longer continue. It is for the highest of good this attachment has to stop now.

Allow them to communicate any messages or insights they may have for you. It is their higher self that is communicating to you. You both agree to say farewell. Imagine there is a golden pair of scissors in front of you. With these golden scissors, you cut this golden cord between the both of you. You pull back the remaining part of the cord back to you. They pull the remaining part of their cord back to themself. Both spirit guides wave their hand over each of your wounds. The wounds are healed perfectly with no trace.

It is time to go. Turn around and proceed to walk back down the corridor with your spirit guide. The corridor is filled with transformational Ultra-Violet light to heal and release this from you permanently. You feel so much lighter. You get to the end of the corridor back to the crystal elevator doors. You step back into the elevator with your spirit guide and the doors close.

The crystal elevator travels back up through the ground. As it continues to travel up, you can start to feel your body again. The elevator's doors open and it is time to go. You thank your spirit guide for their assistance and step out of the elevator and back into your body.

The first deep breath, you begin to start feeling your body. The second deep breath and you can feel your skin. The last deep breath and you are completely back into your body once again. Stay with this for as long as you like and when you are ready, open up your eyes.

HOW TO ATTRACT A SOULMATE (OR ANYTHING ELSE) INTO YOUR LIFE

This is a powerful meditation that you can use to bring things into your life. You just have to substitute the soulmate with whatever you wish to bring into your life. I continually have used this meditation and have experienced much success. I recommend purchasing a candle in glass that can last for several days. Make an opening between the wax and the glass that will be big enough for you to stuff in a small piece of paper. You will also need a blank piece of paper, a pen, and your favorite essential oil with which to anoint your candle. Put on some relaxing music and you are ready.

To begin, you will need to clear your mind of everything. Hold an unlit candle in your hands during the meditation in order to charge it up. Start taking deep breaths, inhaling through your nose, breathing all the way down to your diaphragm, and then slowly exhaling through your mouth. Continue to take deep breaths. Concentrate on your breathing, slowly inhaling, and then slowly exhaling. This will keep your mind from wandering and help you to stay focused. You will eventually no longer be aware that you are holding your candle. With each deep inhalation, imagine yourself bringing in wonderful, Divine, white light. With each exhalation, you are becoming this white light. Now imagine you are able to send a beam of this white light from your diaphragm all the way up to the sky. This white light will travel all the way to the divine higher realms. Now allow yourself to feel this divine connection sending a beam of white light from the higher realms back to you.

Now is the time to picture whatever it is you want to come into your life. In this case, we will use a soulmate. Imagine you and this soulmate are together. Try to imagine all the details of what you are looking for in a soulmate. How do they feel physically, emotionally, mentally and spiritually? What are their positive attributes? Just allow yourself to feel all this. Don't worry. Your higher self and spirit are on board with you. It feels absolutely divine! Tell Spirit how you are now ready to meet your soulmate. Stay with this for several minutes. Just stay in this blissfulness for as long as you can. Then go the extra step and stay there even longer. You know you can do this. You have done this before, just in a different form. When you are ready, it is time to come back down to your body. Slowly begin the deep breaths once again. This time, each deep breath is going to ground you. With each breath, you are starting to feel yourself again. You are starting to feel your skin once again. When you are ready, open you eyes.

Now write down all the positive qualities that you want in your soulmate on your paper, every positive aspect. Write down all of the wonderful blissfulness that you just experienced with your soulmate. Be as specific as you can. Write about what you are looking for in a soulmate.

Now on the opposite side of the paper, write everything that you do not want in this soulmate. All the negative qualities that you want to stay away from you. Be as specific as possible. Write every aspect that you want to block, everything you do not wish to attract. When you are finished, fold the paper. Stuff the paper into the space you made inside the candle. Next you will anoint the candle with the essential oil. Now light the candle. Let this candle burn and allow it to continue your manifesting. The candle has absorbed the divine connective energy that you just experienced. By lighting this candle, you are continually sending this wonderfully blissful energy.

Since this candle will take several days to burn down, only burn the candle when you are awake and present to watch it. (For safety precautions, never leave an unattended candle burning when you go out or go to sleep.) Now you are done. Just allow yourself to be and time will manifest the dreams you have co-created with Spirit.

HOW TO MEET THE FOUR ARCHANGELS

Close your eyes and imagine that you are in a circle of Ultra-Violet light, the light of transformation, of the Divine's Unconditional Love, the Christ light, the Light of St. Germaine. As you inhale through your nose, you become this light. As you exhale, you are the Ultra-Violet light.

There is a space a little above your belly button, your solar plexus. The solar plexus is the energetic center of your soul. Imagine you can breathe from there. As you inhale, breathe in the Ultra-Violet light through your solar plexus. There is an orange star all the way up in the sky. Send a line of energy to this star and allow yourself to receive the light back.

This star is a group of enlightened beings. Some who have already completed their paths of enlightenment. Some like ourselves who are on their path and others who have never inhabited a body ever before. You are now part of this group and can always join this group by simply sending a line of energy to this orange star and receiving it back.

There is a crystal light all the way up in the sky. Allow this crystal light to slowly pull you up to this light, like a tractor beam. You are now at the foot of The Crystal pyramid. This is where the four reside, here in the Atman kingdom. You are now at the top, inside the crystal pyramid.

I call upon the Archangel Michael, the Spirit of the South. Lift all that can be lifted, help us to release all that can be released and let go to the light. Empower us with the strength we need to stand strong in face of adversity. Help resolve our personal negativities, the ability to find strength when we feel all alone.

I call upon the Archangel Gabriel, the Spirit of the West, the center of Truth. Help us to express our truth openly and honestly, respect and honor our individuality. Help us to listen to our own intuition and inner voice.

I call upon the Archangel Uriel, the Spirit of the North, the Akashic Records, the answers to everything and nothing at all. Help us to acknowledge the Light within all of everything. Guide us to find knowledge to help and to heal, interpret and decode our inner voice.

I call upon the Archangel Raphael, the Spirit of the East, and unconditional freedom from everything that binds you down from achieving all that you can be. Help us to seek the gift of healing in nature and universal energy.

It is your job now, to just relax and breathe. This is the place to truly Let Go And Let God. As you inhale, you and the Divine are one. Your connection with them is magnified. As you exhale, the obstacles dissipate and are lifted and removed.

{Stay here for fifteen minutes. The four will directly communicate with you here}

Now it is time to go. Imagine you are slowly traveling back down, through time and space, to a place six to twelve inches above your body. With three breaths, you re-enter your body. Enjoy the beauty of the Divine and all its incredible abundance. Reflect for a moment on all that is abundant in your life. Thank the Divine for the abundance that flows through your body. Wake up and open your eyes.

SEP 16, 2001 LETTER TO SEMINARY
MEDITATION ASSISTING THE LOST 9/11 SOULS TO THE LIGHT

Hello Blessed Ones,

What a week it was that September 2001. On the 12th, the following morning after this horror, I was wakened out of a deep sleep, to find my apartment packed with over a 100 departed souls who were lost. At times, the work is exhausting.

Several of the forms were in partial decay and dismemberment. This is not typical of what I am used to intuitively seeing. The saddest part which is very common, is that a majority of them all were still in shock and weren't completely aware that they had perished.

We all can help them and the unfortunate many others by sending them Unconditional Love and wishing them a safe passage to the light.

Thank You, everyone for the prayers and light and keep it coming.
Light, Love and Laughter,
Rev HL

MEDITATION:

Surround yourself with a circle of ultra-violet light... inhaling through the nose, exhale through the mouth.

Imagine a cloud of grey ash-like smoke slowly traveling up to the sky... as you inhale the ultra-violet light.

The rising grey cloud begins to slowly merge with the uv light...as you exhale, the grey cloud begins to become one with the uv light. Allow the ever-rising grey cloud, to change color to the uv light.

This uv cloud travels up through the clouds, past the stars, up to a divine rainbow bridge. It travels across the bridge and fades away...

SECTION 10

WRAPPING IT UP

SOME LAST THOUGHTS

Life is a sacred path the soul embarks upon through its evolutionary journey back to integration with the One. In each life, we are here to learn many karmic lessons before we can achieve total enlightenment. As we have discovered, some of the lessons are pure enjoyment and bliss. Other lessons are more challenging and require an intensive soul searching deep into the core of your being. The harsher lessons shake you to your very core. But when the shaking stops, much heaviness is permanently lifted from you. With each lesson learned, your soul's energy resonates to a purer vibration. The purer the vibration, the further you assist in promoting the healing of this planet, as we know it.

Throughout this book, I have openly discussed the difficulties I have experienced in learning some of my own personal karmic lessons. As a child, I was blessed with the gift of intuitive and healing abilities. I have always been able to communicate with the spirit world. At times, I found being in the spirit world so much more comfortable then being part of the world of the living. I knew I was here to learn certain lessons I had been working through for several lifetimes. It was an excruciating path I found myself on. But with determination, perseverance and surrounded by unconditional love, I have been able to finally overcome many of them.

Finally, after having enough self-deprecation, I allowed myself to let go and let God/Spirit in. Control is just a figment of the imagination. The only thing that remains constant is change. Once I relinquished control to Spirit, I was guided to different people, places, situations and modalities. As a result, I was able to truly understand many of my life's own mysteries. Along with Spirit, I actively explored many of the various healing arts. My exploration of past life regressions helped to end my ego debilitating stammering stutter. The healing practice of reiki has advanced my energy work exponentially.

By your own willingness to openly explore, you too can also bring an end to many of your own life's obstacles. When you feel your life has tumbled out of control, remember what you learned in reading this book. Your very life is a co-creation between you and Spirit. As in all collaborations, you can always renegotiate to learn your lessons gentler and easier.

Treat your fellow living beings, as you would want to be treated yourself. That same dishelved homeless person you pass by can very easily be an angel in disguise. Many of the higher light beings walk among us everyday. It is just as easy to show kindness, as it is to be a schmuck.

If something just does not sit well with you, listen to your higher self. Try to silence your mind and allow your true, higher self to communicate with you. If you have difficulties trying to achieve this, do not worry. By following one of the book's many meditations, with practice this will become second nature for you.

It has been an honor to share my book with you. H is for what? H is For Healing!

OUR JOURNEY TOGETHER CONTINUES

Visit my website **www.HIsForHealing.com** where you can view my exclusive photo of the ever-ethereal spirit Agela, and share with me your thoughts and experiences reading this book.

Love, Light and Laughter,

H L Schaeffer

EPILOGUE

During the editing process of this book, my life was changed in cataclysmic proportions. My Dad was our family's very own Jack LaLanne, always doing one-arm push-ups and exercising for several hours daily. Dad began having a persistent rash, which would not go away. Overtime he went through a series of doctors to see what this was. He was painfully subjected to every inconceivable test you could think of. Everything came back inconclusive. Unfortunately, he was eventually diagnosed with T-cell lymphoma.

As the horrendous disease progressed, he became a patient at Sloan Kettering Memorial Center for Cancer. Dad fought with every last fiber of his being. He was our Rocky Balboa, who never gave up. It didn't matter what procedure they wanted to do to him. He never resisted and was always the pillar of strength, no matter how uncomfortable or invasive the procedures usually were. He was willing to do anything. He just wanted to stay with his loving family. He fought his way off the respirator four separate times, until his body just couldn't fight any longer. During his courageous battle, he amazed Sloan Kettering with his extraordinary resilience. He carried himself throughout this excruciating ungodly ordeal with his amazing loving dignity and truly the epitome of a superhero. Sadly his doctors held a meeting with us, telling us our time left with Dad was very brief. I cannot express in words the pain to hear these words.

That evening, Michael took our furry child Precious out for her evening walk. Precious was fine. But on her way back upstairs, she became disoriented, bumping into the side of our apartment building. In our apartment, she was extremely disoriented and very upset.

We immediately rushed Precious to a wonderful animal hospital in Park Slope, Brooklyn, NY. During her examination, I collapsed to the floor, just uncontrollably hysterical. We had to leave her overnight. The animal hospital called us back the next day. During the night, Precious had gone blind and was diagnosed with cancer that had spread to her brain. Her doctors told us the only humane, loving thing to do was to put our beautiful, furry daughter to sleep. Less than 72 hours later, my extraordinary Dad lost his battle and crossed over to the other side.

In less than three days, I lost two monumentally loving, powerful foundations in my life. Both my Dad and my furry daughter had died, and were now at rest in Spirit. I am still working through my indescribably painful grief. As I have promised Dad, in time I will eventually write about this in one of my following books.

BIO

HL Schaeffer was born, bred, and currently lives in Brooklyn, NY with his husband Michael Timbers. HL is a Psychology and Film Production graduate from Brooklyn College. He was ordained as an interfaith minister from the New Seminary of New York. HL studied and has been attuned by Lille O'Brien as a reikimaster, as well as certified as a hypnotherapist by George Bein. As an intuitive psychic medium and healer, he has been practicing professionally for almost twenty-five years. As a 9/11 survivor, he continues to counsel both the living and the spirit world for a variety of issues including severe anxiety, panic attacks and post-traumatic stress. HL serves as an intuitive consultant for individuals, groups and corporations with private sessions, lectures and workshops. Additionally, HL is sought after for psychic investigations, medical intuitive consultations, and corporate team building empowerment exercises.